Special care babies and their relationships

Special care babies are at the centre of a complex system of relationships involving both family members and professionals. Prematurity, disability and life-threatening situations create a crisis, which is likely to have a different meaning for each participant. This book focuses on the important relationships which are essential for the survival and development of these infants.

Anne McFadyen looks critically at the system which saves the lives of infants and shows that many factors influence the outcome. She is concerned to make sense of the confusion and ambivalence felt by both parents and professionals whose lives come together and whose needs often conflict in the context of neonatal intensive care. She explodes the myth of the cosy relationship between the hospital and the family, drawing attention to the clash of belief systems which often impedes the infant's progress and the development of relationships. The book explores institutional, cultural and family beliefs about prematurity and infant care, and shows that there are important differences between the beliefs and needs of parents and those of the staff. The author argues that these differences must be acknowledged and resolved, since they are at the heart of the relationship between two crucial systems which have the power to influence the baby's survival and the rest of his or her life.

Anne McFadyen backs up her argument with descriptions of babies, parents and staff as they relate to each other, and with clinical material from her work as a child psychiatrist. *Special Care Babies and their Developing Relationships* will be essential reading for paediatricians, nurses, child psychotherapists, psychiatrists and social workers, as well as for parents of special care babies.

Anne McFadyen is Senior Lecturer in Child and Adolescent Psychiatry at the University of Dundee. She has worked with sick children and their families in a variety of settings and has two children of her own.

Special care babies and their developing relationships

Anne McFadyen

London and New York

First published 1994
by Routledge
11 New Fetter Lane, London EC4P 4EE

Simultaneously published in the USA and Canada
by Routledge
29 West 35th Street, New York, NY 10001

© 1994 Anne McFadyen

Typeset in Times by Michael Mepham, Frome, Somerset
Printed and bound in Great Britain by
Mackays of Chatham PLC, Chatham, Kent

British Library Cataloguing in Publication Data
A catalogue record for this book is available from the British
Library.

Library of Congress Cataloging in Publication Data
McFadyen, Anne, 1957–   .
   Special care babies and their developing
   relationships/Anne McFadyen.
   p.   cm.
   Includes bibliographical references and index.
   1. Neonatal intensive care—Psychological aspects.
   2. Parent and infant.
   3. Infants (Newborn)—Family relationships.
   I. Title.
   RJ253.5. M38 1994
   618.92′01 – dc20   94–8491
                                                                CIP

ISBN   0–415–10613–3 (hbk)
ISBN   0–415–10614–1 (pbk)

For my mother,
and
in memory of my father.

Contents

Acknowledgements

I owe the most enormous debt to my partner, Ian, for all the support and encouragement he has given me while I have laboured in the production of this book. He has been both an inspiration and a nagging thorn in my side. I thank my children too. Stuart and Calum, although not special care babies, have taught me much about early child development. My pregnancies with them fuelled my preoccupation with infancy, and both before and after each of their births, I felt charged with energy to explore the emotional experiences of mothers, fathers and babies themselves around this time.

The initial research for this book was carried out while I was training as a child and adolescent psychiatrist at the Tavistock Clinic in London, and I am indebted to all my supervisors and teachers there, as well as to those who less formally gave me emotional support and encouragement in my roles as both a professional and a mother. During my last two years there I studied for an MSc in Family Therapy, and it was during this time that my ideas about how to begin to think about special care baby units started to take shape. In particular, John Byng-Hall, Emilia Dowling, Caroline Lindsay and Paddy Sweeney helped me to approach the subject in a systemic way. Caroline also gave me considerable personal support, as did Sebastian Kraemer, who has been a source of inspiration to me in many aspects of my life. He has also taken the time to read an earlier draft of the book, and offer some constructive criticism. Anne Alvarez supervised my observation work with special care infants, and functioned admirably in that role, offering containment and providing a sane perspective to temper what were often very distressing, if not simply perplexing, experiences. I also thank Juliet Hopkins, who helped me to learn the value of this method, and Dora Black, who encouraged me in my research endeavours early in my career. The late John Bowlby was also amongst those who offered me the opportunity to discuss my ideas about special care babies and their early relationships, and I remain indebted to him. Many other people have helped me less directly to think about the subject of this book, and rather than try to name them all, I would simply like to thank them.

One of the difficulties I have in acknowledging the help that I have had with thinking about these babies and their relationships is that much of it has come from families, nurses, paediatricians and mental health professionals. Protecting the confidentiality of the infants and their families has felt reasonably easy. However, after much reflection and debate, I have decided that it would also be imprudent to name the professionals working in the units I have been involved with. The dedication of the staff I have talked to has been inspiring. Most struggle day and daily with the emotional issues which surround their task, and in many units this has been formalised too, with regular consultation by mental health professionals. I thank all those involved for their assistance, encouragement and support.

My current colleagues in Dundee have also helped me in different ways. In particular, I would like to thank Kate Harrison, the librarian at the Royal Dundee Liff Hospital, and my secretary, Beth Gow.

Part of Chapter 7 has already been published in an article entitled 'Some thoughts on infant observation and its possible role in child psychiatry training' which appeared in the Newsletter of the Association for Child Psychology and Psychiatry (1991, 15, 10–14). It is reproduced with the kind permission of the ACPP. Part of Chapter 3 has also been published in the *Journal of Family Therapy*, in an article entitled 'Paediatric liaison research: problems at the clinical–research interface' (1992, 14, 389–397). I am grateful to both the journal and to my co-author, Jenny Altschuler, for permission to reproduce it.

Edwina Welham, my commisioning editor, has helped me to have the courage of my convictions and supported the idea of this book from the outset. I am grateful for her encouragement.

A wealth of literature on the subject under discussion is already in print. As will be seen in the References, I have directly referred to much of this work. To those whose writings I have not been able to mention, I apologise.

Finally, I would like to thank my friends for their support and encouragement.

Come at the world creatively, create the world;
it is only what you create that has meaning for you.

Winnicott, 1968: 23

Introduction

The birth of any child occurs in the context of, and acts as a marker for, a particular life-cycle stage of a family (Carter and McGoldrick, 1989). As such it represents a stressor on the family system (Breen, 1975). This stress is felt even more acutely if that child arrives prematurely or is damaged in some way. The admission of a baby to a special care baby unit or to a neonatal intensive care unit has appropriately been referred to as 'the crisis of newborn intensive care' (Affleck *et al.*, 1990).

In this setting, the baby is at the centre of a complex system of relationships involving both family members and professionals. The crisis is likely to have a different meaning for each participant, and the baby's developing relationships will both influence and be influenced by other relationships within the hospital and the family systems. Institutional, cultural and family beliefs about prematurity and infant care inform the actions of parents and staff but may do so in different ways. The development of the key relationship, that of the mother and her child, may be facilitated if these differences are recognised and addressed, or inhibited if left unspoken. The relationship is vulnerable, not only because of the baby's fragility but also because of its position, at the interface between the hospital and the family system.

Of course, no two people ever see the world in exactly the same way. Recognition of this idea, whether at a conscious or unconscious level, is essential in any relationship. The ability to put oneself in someone else's shoes is important for therapists and other professional carers both when working with each other and with families. This is what mothers are expected to do. In the ordinary course of events, mothers do their job well because they are able to empathise with their babies, experience their experiences, help them to sort them out and give them meaning, and then let them get on with having the experiences by themselves too.

In the special care baby unit, staff may quite deliberately try to stop themselves from emotionally stepping into the babies' shoes in order to manage the task of looking after them and helping them to survive. The task of a mother is not so easy. Although her baby may be in a life-threatening situation or may show little sign of being in touch with the outside world, she cannot switch off her feelings or stop tuning in. While coping through distance is a well-recognised way of managing the emotional pain in such a situation, few mothers would ever say that they had got the distance right. Indeed the task of mothering a special care baby is so difficult to think about that professionals have perhaps come to realise that there is no right distance and no right way to do it.

Historically, the last fifty years have seen an incredible shift in Western society's approach to children and childcare. Prior to the Second World War, middle-class parents in particular were strongly influenced by the hygienists (Newson and Newson, 1974). As infant and child mortality rates fell, parents became increasingly receptive to medical advice given in both an authoritative and authoritarian way about how to rear their children. The assumption that *mental* hygiene would be as beneficial as physical hygiene to a child's development was readily accepted, and led to a harsh and inflexible approach. Feeding and sleeping by the clock, and limb-splinting to prevent thumb-sucking and masturbation appear to have been common practice. Although psychoanalysts and educationalists of the time were known to oppose this viewpoint, their influence on childrearing practice was not felt until much later. Even when a more permissive, child-led approach to parenting was adopted, there were always grandparents and others around to temper it. In a climate where gender roles were still fairly rigidly adhered to, it seemed that mothers were often left feeling guilty or criticised. In the 1950s, John Bowlby's seminal work *Child Care and the Growth of Love* was published, and dealt a further blow to mothers. While this book made a significant and outstanding contribution to the understanding of the earliest relationship, its rigid interpretation also led to increased feelings of guilt and responsibility for many women.

In the last twenty years the burgeoning literature and research on infant development and the early parent–child relationship has led to an increasingly sophisticated understanding of the nature of the first months and years of life. This has been paralleled by technological advances in the field of neonatology, which has become the most rapidly developing paediatric subspeciality (Pharoah, 1986). Babies are being born earlier and do survive. Infants of over 23 weeks gestation weighing more than 500 grams are now considered viable (Wolke, 1991). Special care baby units serve not only small and premature babies but also other neonates in difficulty. These latter babies may be suffering from a transient acute illness for which intensive support, including life support, is needed, or may be in a life-threatening situation because of a congenital abnormality or disability, despite having been born at full term. The special care experience will have an impact on each baby in a different way depending on the circumstances surrounding the birth, and the prognosis.

Little has been written specifically about premature babies of very low birth weight (VLBW), that is, weighing less than 1500 grams, from a psychological perspective. These infants account for 10 per cent of all live births and more than one in ten will be left with a major impairment in functioning. Consideration of their experiences has implications for the larger group of babies born prematurely, especially those who survive and are either physically or mentally disabled. Examination of these VLBW babies, who are usually of less than 32 weeks gestation, from a psychological viewpoint presents an opportunity and a dilemma.

Most literature on child development, which tells what 'normal' children do, begins at birth. These babies are younger and presumably less competent than full-termers. Neither their parents nor the professionals yet know what their psychological capabilities are. The uncertainty about what each baby actually experiences, as well as the uncertainty about whether the baby will have a disability or even survive, is perhaps at the root of the debate about the value of supporting the lives of such fragile infants.

For clinicians and parents, the financial cost does not yet inform the decisions made on a day-to-day basis about each infant's care. Yet, questions *are* asked, and justification *is* sought by government for the enormous amount of money being spent on so few individuals. National Health Service reforms in the UK have led to increasing scrutiny and attention to financial detail. In relation to neonatal intensive care, one of the early findings of this audit is that care can be provided more effectively, in terms of survival, and more cost efficiently, at regional rather than local centres (Audit Commission, 1993). This finding has immediate consequences for both staff and parents. The viability of each unit is placed in question, with consequent institutional and personal anxieties. For parents, who often find it hard to spend as much time with their babies as they would wish, the task of getting to know their infant may be made harder by practical difficulties.

Decisions about whether to continue to support the lives of individual babies are difficult to make, and like those at policy level, are often characterised by heated debate and strong feeling. Splits between professionals may be seen as representing different aspects of the baby, and different parts of the family system. Some identify with the infant's tenacity and apparent determination to survive, with optimism and hope, while others see a very damaged baby being subjected to procedure after procedure and identify with the pain and despair. These different perspectives have in some way to be consciously acknowledged and dealt with if staff are to survive the emotional stress of their task, and parents to survive the stress of theirs. For parents, recognition of how their own past experience and beliefs, and present relationships, inform their actions and reactions may help them to care for and make the right decisions for their baby.

Traditional descriptions of babies and their developing relationships have focused on the mother–child relationship, seeing the father in a key role supporting and looking after his partner. With the recognition of the mother's potentially vulnerable state both physically and emotionally has come the awareness that her baby's well-being will depend on hers, and the recognition that her partner or family play a crucial part in this. In the special care situation where infants often remain in hospital for months after their birth, these gender roles are often enacted in quite a concrete way. Choices have to be made, and often the father of the baby will take on the role of breadwinner and become the major carer for siblings, freeing the mother to attend emotionally to their baby. Siblings who, in the ordinary course of events, have to manage the experience of having their parents focus on 'the new arrival', may in this situation feel excluded or abandoned, and thus have more difficulty in resolving their feelings of rivalry.

A mother has to 'hold' or 'contain' her baby well enough to facilitate growth and development. In other words, she has to keep her baby in mind. In order to do this, she too must be kept in mind. In the case of a special care baby, both family *and* hospital will be required to hold the mother–child couple well enough for survival and development to take place. The relationship of staff to mother may be crucial, facilitating or inhibiting her in her task. However, staff will only be able to do their job if they feel contained. They too have to be kept in mind.

The future for even the fittest premature babies is still uncertain. Recent research has indicated that many will run into difficulties shortly after school entry as a result of subtle cognitive problems. The behavioural consequences of these problems may lead to difficulties in relationships at school. Some parents may continue to feel very protective towards children who seem to have survived against the odds. Others may feel that they can never really get close to their children, either for fear of losing them through death or because they feel that they have never really got to know them after a prolonged early separation. Social factors have been closely correlated with outcome, and children born into adverse social circumstances may be at risk of neglect and abuse. Parents' own past experience may be particularly important to consider in this area.

Each child's vulnerability or resilience in the face of adversity is dependent on an enormous number of factors, which include relationships within the family, and later, relationships within a wider social network.

The task of this book is to present some relevant theory about developing relationships, and to illustrate, particularly, the processes involved in the development of the *earliest* relationships. Part I of the book provides a theoretical overview but does not necessarily have to be read first. In fact, I hope that readers will feel free to dip into this book and read it in the order that most suits them. It was not written in the order it is now presented, and seems to make sense just the same. In Chapter 1, theories from psychoanalysis, ethology and developmental psychology are presented, along with a review of Attachment theory. Readers may prefer to read this chapter later if they are unfamiliar with the theories in question. However, this chapter has the potential to serve as an introductory text on developmental psychology and psychoanalytic theory and it is complemented by a short reading list at the end of the book. It is followed by consideration of the special care baby in Chapter 2. Factors potentially influencing the responses of both family members and hospital staff to the crisis of neonatal intensive care are also presented. Chapter 3, which follows, may not be everyone's cup of tea and is not essential to the thesis of the book. In it, I review some recent literature which describes a revolution in the world of the human sciences. In philosophical mode, I consider how we can get hold of, or hold on to, meaning in the face of an increasingly technological approach to medicine and psychology. Psychoanalytic infant observation offers some possibilities, as does narrative.

These methods are discussed in more detail in Part II, the clinical section of the book. In Chapters 4 and 5, this discussion is followed by the presentation of observation material and 'stories' from a special care baby unit. In Chapter 6, I discuss the sense that we might make of these; and in Chapter 7, I present similar material on two older babies.

Outcome and intervention are discussed in Part III of the book. Follow-up studies of special care babies have tended primarily to address neurodevelopmental outcome but some also speculate on the relationship between biological and environmental factors. Consideration of the interplay between the child's well-being and developing relationships has not yet been the subject of rigorous research but is discussed nonetheless in Chapter 8. Some clinical material is used to generate hypotheses about mechanisms of effects and psychological outcome for adolescents and their families. Finally, interventions at every level from the individual through to the family and the institution are discussed.

Part I

Theoretical considerations

Chapter 1

Parent–child relationships from different perspectives

In order to reach some understanding of the developing relationships of special care babies, it is necessary to embark on a journey and visit, or revisit, theories of both child development and the development of relationships in more ordinary contexts. Even full-term babies cannot tell us what they feel, what they actually experience, and we do not really know about how, or indeed whether, infants 'think about' what happens to them. Despite this lack of knowledge about what constitutes the actual psychic experience of babies, there is a wealth of literature about infancy which presents a somewhat confusing picture.

As in other areas of science, each theory represents one perspective, a useful model on which to build ideas and test hypotheses. A number of authors have tried to bring groups of these theories together, and again use a particular model or construction as a framework to help them understand what they see and what they are told about. Their chosen framework allows them to juxtapose different theories in a way that seems to make sense to them. However, their writings do not simply reflect different viewpoints from within one broadly similar way of conceptualising the world but in fact are based on very different epistemologies or ways of knowing.

'Old science' refers to the idea that there is such a thing as objective reality; if we search rigorously enough, we will find out the truth, we will *know* how things really are. Fundamental to this approach to re-search is a belief that the truth is either one thing or another. It is this basic premise which distinguishes 'old science' from 'new science'. New science permits the idea that there could be more than one reality.

With this new way of looking at things in mind, I would like to explore a number of theories which I find useful in trying to understand infants' developing relationships with those around them. It will become apparent that mainstream research has not focused to any great extent on premature babies, and so there is a task in trying to utilise the material about post-term development and about antenatal physical and perceptual development to inform our understanding of the premature neonate's experience. In this chapter, I will review the literature on full-term babies, and in Chapter 2, I will examine the special care situation in more detail.

Psychoanalytic theory, ethology and child development theory and research all contribute to our current understanding of infancy. In two of these fields there has been a shift over time from a focus on the infant in relative isolation to an increasing acknowledgement of the importance of relationships. Of course, psychoanalysts would deny that they had ever (historically) considered children in isolation but I am talking here about a relative shift with time. Ethology, the scientific study of the function and evolution of animal behaviour patterns, by its very nature has always focused on relationships. The shift by others to a focus on relationships has been made to varying extents, and for some, dyads and triads have come to have a life and existence of their own. It is, however, rarely stated explicitly that the whole is qualitatively different from the sum of its parts. This idea comes from systems thinking, and puts into words the recognition that examination of component units of any system will provide some information about it but will not tell the whole story. More fully, 'the whole is qualitatively different from a group of parts, because the properties of the whole derive from the properties of the *relationships* between the parts, interacting with the properties of the parts to mutually define each other' (Gorell-Barnes, 1985: 216). This idea is crucial to the exploration of all relationships, and supported by Belsky and Isabella (1988: 76) who emphasise 'the need to look beyond the characteristics of the parent and infant in order to understand what transpires between them' and advocate a 'contextual view of parent–child relationships'. In a similar way, the information from different theoretical schools may be fitted together, and as a whole represent a greater contribution to our understanding than the parts simply added together.

PSYCHOANALYSIS

Psychoanalysis is a method of investigating the unconscious mind. Understanding is sought through exploration of the individual's inner conflicts and phantasies. It was initially by this route alone that Freud, the first psychoanalyst, formulated his theories on early child development around the turn of the century. Since then others have contributed to theories of personality development by drawing not only on their therapeutic work with adults and self-analysis, which were Freud's main sources, but also on child analysis and observational studies of young children. The 'looking back' through the minds of adults or children to infancy has provided a particular kind of evidence about psychic development. 'States of mind are seen as deriving from the impact of a present situation on a mind already patterned by previous experiences, each of which has had an impact and left some residue' (Gosling, 1968: 1). In psychoanalysis, the examination of the pattern and the residue may contribute to both a therapeutic outcome (for the patient) and an understanding of the nature of development (for the patient and the analyst). Crown (1968) has considered the unique problems of psychoanalysis, in particular in relation to its use as a developmental theory. Its emphasis on the importance for later personality development of the early years, including the pre-verbal period, is central but the methods used to draw particular conclusions are not easy to scrutinise. In some ways, the flourishing of developmental psychology, which has traditionally concentrated more on the observed than the remembered, and the recognition of the value of anthropological research have been useful in helping to support some psychoanalytic theories.

These theories are useful because they help us to make sense of our experience. Each infant in the special care baby unit will stir up a unique mixture of feelings in both staff and parents. Some babies may seem more ready to meet their carers at an emotional level, while others may appear strange and distant, out of reach. An understanding of what this might mean in psychological terms offers possibilities for change. Having an idea about why a particular baby might be hard to reach can help us both to tolerate the experience and to think about how to help.

The contribution of Freud

Freud's early work was characterised by his model of Man as a biological organism governed by drives or instincts, whose aim was pleasure, which was usually only formulated as the subjective registration of the reduction of tension (Symington, 1986). He considered that the organism's drive to reduce tension was through the agency of an object, most often the mother. His later work is seen by some to have begun to acknowledge the importance of the baby's actual relationships, as opposed to the baby's phantasy relationship with someone who existed only to serve the instincts, and by that I mean, for example, to provide food, and thus reduce the tension or displeasure experienced as hunger.

He differentiated between self-preservative drives and sexual drives, and proposed that the infant not only experienced the need to be physiologically supported by food but was also driven to satisfy psychological need through oral experiences. This gave rise to a 'sexual' theory of development. In Stafford-Clark's words:

> The baby's obstinate persistence in sucking gives evidence at an early stage of a need for satisfaction which, though it originates from and is instigated by the taking of nourishment, nevertheless strives to obtain pleasure independently of nourishment and for that reason may and should be termed *sexual*.
>
> (Stafford-Clark, 1967: 90)

He identified different developmental stages, during which the organism's libidinal drive or need to reduce tension was focused on particular parts of the body. Gratification was mediated by different erotogenic zones: thus, the first year was referred to as the oral stage; the second year as the anal stage; and the third and fourth years as the genital or phallic stage. This stage was later called the Oedipal stage, as it was at this time that Freud believed that the young child had as its main developmental focus the task of resolving infantile sexual feelings for the parent of the opposite gender.

In the 1920s, Freud argued that the neonate is born with what is to become id, ego and superego undifferentiated (Mitchell, 1986). He highlighted how helpless and dependent the human infant is compared to other mammals, and postulated that anxiety stemmed from the baby's perception of the principal caretaker, or mother, as separate or missing. By this time he believed that the syndrome of primary anxiety was related to birth itself so, in this context, the mother's absence 'reminds' the baby of the trauma of being born.

The experience of separation for infants in intensive care is, of course, very real. Their separation is not just from their mother's presence but often from their place inside her body. Unlike other babies, their mothers comings and goings are less frequent. In the first days or weeks, they may never experience their mothers as physically close; there will be no warm breast to snuggle in to. Even so, it seems that these babies do come to recognise their mothers. They let them know this by changing their posture or expression or, more dramatically, through their heart rate or breathing patterns.

For Freud, the recreation in phantasy of the absent mother represented the beginning of ego formation. Thus, differentiation of the ego from the id was seen as occurring gradually from birth; the further differentiation of the unconscious and evolution of the superego taking place with the resolution of the Oedipus complex in the third or fourth year. Freud came to see the personality as composed of three parts: the id – ruled by the pleasure principle, and the representation of unaltered drives; the ego – the organised part of the mental structure, ruled by the reality principle, and functioning to bring the organism into harmony with reality; and the superego – the ego's protector and critic, 'constructed on the model not of its parents but of its parents' super-ego' (Freud, quoted in Mitchell, 1986: 15). Freud's critics would say that even later, when, for example, in 1940 (quoted in Bretherton, 1985: 14), he described the child's relationship to the mother as 'unique, without parallel, established unalterably for a whole lifetime as the first and strongest love-object and as the prototype of all later love relations – for both sexes', he had not made the same kind of shift, that is, to a dyadic way of thinking, as that proposed by his followers.

Placing his work in a historical context, Shuttleworth has pointed out that:

There are two distinct, and often contradictory, strands of thought to be found in Freud's work. Over time, Freud's *mechanistic* model of emotional life, derived from modes of thought prevailing in the nineteenth century (for example, that of an organism dealing with different quantities of excitation), became interwoven with, but never wholly superseded by, more *psychological* formulations.

(Shuttleworth, 1989: 23)

Bowlby (1988a) considered that the most widely adopted shift from Freud's early formulations was to focus attention on the child's early relationships with the parents, particularly the mother, and to de-emphasise or discard drive theory. The other major shift from Freud's view is well summarised by Britton (1986: 31) who pointed out that 'as psychoanalysis has developed the period of life on which theory has focussed has become earlier and earlier'.

Object relations

Fairbairn, Balint, Klein and Winnicott were among those who developed and modified Freud's *psychological* formulations. Both Klein and Winnicott worked with children in different contexts, and the latter drew on his direct observations of normally developing infants and their mothers to formulate his particular theories about the influence of early childhood experience on personality development. While differing in some areas, this group's commonality was striking in relation to their focus on early mother–child relationships, and their view of the ego as present from birth. Each has acknowledged, too, the importance of the desire to relate to an object, seeing it as something akin to a drive, by which I mean, of the same intensity as a drive or instinct in Freud's terms. In other words, they stress the importance of the baby's desire to have a relationship with someone, who, in the first instance, is usually the mother. However, this theory (of object relations) does not simply refer to the actual relationships of the subject but also to their perceived relationships with these objects, both internal and external, and thus always implies an unconscious relationship (Kohon, 1986).

Klein

Melanie Klein, while at times fiercely disagreeing with some theoretical assumptions held dear by Freudians, also took forward and added to Freud's original ideas. Her use of terminology similar to that of Freud has at times caused confusion but may have represented her respect for the original 'ownership' of particular theories. She concentrated on an earlier part of life, and in presenting her theories about the infant's inner world, ascribed to the infant a complex yet primitive mental apparatus which functioned from the beginning of life outside the womb. The debate which ensued from this assertion was at its height in the 1940s but still continues (Segal, 1982).

Klein believed that the baby 'exists from the start in a relationship to another person or part of that person (prototypically its mother and her breast)' (Mitchell, 1986: 19). However, she also elaborated clearly a distinction between a relationship to whole objects or persons, and a relationship to part-objects (Symington, 1986). In the absence of the ability to perceptualise 'mother' as a whole initially, the infant relates to each discrete part-object (or aspect of the mother), the most important of which is the breast.

The infant was seen as having to defend against anxieties from both the external and the internal world. Conflicts existed in both arenas: the outside world could be warm and nurturing or cold and empty, and the inner world was characterised by the conflict between innate life and death instincts. The former 'pushes' the infant towards physiological and psychological growth, and more importantly, might be considered to drive the ego from a state of unorganisation to integration. The relationship between the ego and the life instinct is ambifinal, that is, each defines the other; from another angle, then, the ego's natural tendency towards integration might be considered to *be* the life instinct. Disintegration occurs under the influence of the death instinct. In Symington's words:

> Melanie Klein takes as her starting point the fear of annihilation. This fear is of something that destroys from within. This 'something' is the inner workings of the death instinct, but it is experienced phobically. By that I mean that although the feared object is an element within, it is experienced as being outside.
>
> (Symington, 1986: 257)

Special care babies, to a greater extent than others, are in very real life-or-death situations. We don't really know what they are experiencing while doctors and nurses battle to save their lives. Nor do we really know whether their emotional states or their relationships affect their outcome. Staff are often perplexed by the realisation that some babies have survived against the odds, while others have appeared to surrender life more easily. While not necessarily easy to accept, Klein's ideas about the baby's internal struggle may help us to make sense of these observations.

The idea that internal objects, or part-objects, can be experienced as external and vice versa is fundamental to Kleinian theory but difficult to understand without further elaboration. Mitchell (1986) singled out four mechanisms central to the understanding of Klein's work; these are splitting, projection, introjection and projective identification. Splitting refers to the ego's ability to split into good and bad parts, thus preventing the bad from contaminating the good. The ego can fill the object with its split-off parts, that is, particular feelings and experiences, by projection. In introjection, it takes in the perceived feelings of the object. In projective identification, 'the ego projects its feelings into the object which it then identifies with, becoming like the object which it has already imaginatively filled itself with' (Mitchell, 1986: 20). Each of these mechanisms is used as a defence and is the means by which the baby copes with anxieties of both internal and external origin. The most commonly cited example of these mechanisms in action is that of the relationship between the baby and the breast. The mother can be satisfying and comforting to the baby, and when this is the case the baby fills her with its good feelings, she becomes 'the good breast'. At other times, she is seen as bad because she is perceived as either absent or withholding, and on these occasions the baby's own destructive feelings, emanating from the death instinct, which are a source of great anxiety, are projected into her; she then becomes not only a bad but also a persecuting breast. Thus, when the infant is feeling over-whelmed with feelings of rage and destructiveness the breast too is perceived as destructive and felt by the infant to have the power to retaliate or to attack. The 'biting breast' exists because it has been created in the mind of the infant.

In the course of ordinary healthy development the life instinct wins its battle over the death instinct, and this is related not only to the infant's innate way of being but crucially also to the assistance given by the mother or primary caretaker, who is of course the infant's primary object. The way in which this happens contributes to the end result, best described perhaps as personality or character, which is different for each of us.

The infant is seen by Klein as moving through a series of phases or positions. The first is the paranoid–schizoid position, which is characterised by the use of the mechanisms described, and part-object relationships. As the ego becomes more integrated, the infant is seen as being more able to tolerate the existence of good and bad together, that is, developing the ability to relate to whole objects. The consequence of this is that the infant has to somehow deal with rage in a different way, and this change is marked by the advent of feelings of guilt and anxiety about the phantasised damage caused by the destructive feelings. This phase is known as the depressive position. Although Klein placed both these phases in the first six months, moving on from them is never absolute; there is a to-ing and fro-ing from one position to the other with an overall move forward. The defence or coping mechanisms used to aid development at this time remain part of us for the rest of our lives. Klein went on to consider the next phases of development, and in doing so addressed a number of areas that others had neglected, for example, reparation, envy, concern and creativity.

Waddell (1988) and Alvarez (1992) are among those who have drawn attention to Klein's positive approach to development. The former has emphasised the centrality of the notion of development in Kleinian and post-Kleinian thinking about infantile processes – 'It is a description of the nature of an individual's experience whereby he/she may acquire ego strength rather than a way of account-ing for weakness' (Waddell, 1988: 324). Anne Alvarez has emphasised Klein's positive contributions to the understanding of growth in general, and has contrasted this with the Freudian way of looking at character.

> Klein insisted that reparation – the action of restoring a person (or cause or standard or ideal) damaged by one's own ill-treatment or neglect – was not a defence or 'reaction-formation' against guilt, but a creative outcome: that is, an overcoming of guilt and mental pain, a going forward and development. There is, I believe, a huge meta-theoretical leap in this Kleinian theory of reparation, which takes psychoanalytic theory right out of the old see-saw, push-me-pull-you model and, in its place, utilises notions of growth. The forces for change are seen not as mechanisms but processes. Such a relational model implies the type of interactive process between self and object which enables genuinely new elements to emerge.
>
> (Alvarez, 1992: 10)

Winnicott

Donald Winnicott was both a psychoanalyst and a paediatrician and, drawing on his work and experience in both these fields, made an outstanding contribution to the understanding of the early parent–child relationship. He was unique in his ability to convey his thoughts easily to both the professional world and to the public.

He wrote a number of very easy-to-read books for parents, he spoke on the radio about child development, and he also wrote for, and presented theoretical papers to, his colleagues in the world of psychoanalysis. Symington (1986) commented on how difficult it was to summarise Winnicott's thinking and theory, perhaps because he was a truly independent thinker who worked very flexibly.

Winnicott talked a lot about mothers but interestingly always mentioned fathers too, even if it was at times just to acknowledge that he had left them out. He also acknowledged that the function of a mother as the baby's primary caretaker could be taken on by someone else, the father or another man or woman.

While differing from the views of both Freud and Klein, Winnicott also seemed to attempt to act as a conciliator between their respective schools. He used a different language from them, coining his own terms to convey the meaning of his unique perspective. Unlike Freud and Klein, Winnicott began with a belief that newly born infants did not experience the mother or her breast as separate but in fact viewed the breast as part of themselves.

> This scheme of the developing human being allows for the fact that at the beginning the baby has not separated off what is not-ME from what is ME, so that in the special context of early relationships the behaviour of the environment is as much a part of the baby as is the behaviour of the baby's inherited drives towards integration and towards autonomy and object-relating, and towards a satisfactory psychosomatic partnership.
>
> (Winnicott, 1968: 16)

In a paper written in 1960, he went to great lengths to make it clear that his view was in fact the same as Freud's. He drew attention to a footnote in one of Freud's early papers:

> It will rightly be objected that an organisation which was a slave to the pleasure-principle and neglected the reality of the external world could not maintain itself alive for the shortest time, so that it could not have come into existence at all. The employment of a fiction like this is, however, justified when one considers that the infant – provided one includes with it the care it receives from its mother – does almost realise a psychical system of this kind.
>
> (Freud, 1911: 220, quoted in Winnicott 1960, 39)

Winnicott placed great importance on this which he saw as Freud's acknowledgement that the infant and the maternal care together form a unit, and related it to his own statement, 'There is no such thing as an infant'.

As I have said, Winnicott talked a lot about mothers; he talked about 'primary maternal preoccupation', 'the ordinary devoted mother' and 'good-enough mothering'. Unlike many other analysts he was not only interested in infant development as a route to the understanding of later psychopathology, he was also genuinely interested in how ordinary mothers did their job. He thought it was important 'for a mother to have the experience of doing what she feels like doing, which enables her to find the fullness of the motherliness in herself' (Winnicott, 1964: 25). In pregnancy, and after giving birth, mothers become preoccupied with their role as mothers. In this state of primary maternal preoccupation, mothers become able 'to almost lose themselves in an identification with the baby, so they know . . . what the baby needs just at this very moment; at the same time they remain themselves' (Winnicott, 1968: 18). It is clear from this that there was no inherent expectation that mothers would be perfect; rather Winnicott placed great value in the idea of 'good-enough mothering'. The mother is required to 'hold' her baby well enough for development to take place. She not only physically holds but also emotionally holds the infant. As well as providing nurturing and care, she is able to bear the baby's distress, and is not destroyed by the baby's rage and destructiveness. She is in tune with her baby. In the context of being held, the infant can experience states of both unintegration and relative integration, which together contribute to growth.

The concept of good-enough mothering is, I think, very important. There is an inherent paradox in the idea that there could be such a thing as perfect mothering. In order to allow or even facilitate the move from a state of complete dependence to relative independence, a mother has to allow her baby to have the experience of being separate. A mother who anticipates every need, and meets it almost before it has been recognised by the infant, does not allow her baby to experience and learn to manage frustration. She does not allow the baby to grow mentally. Winnicott recognised the importance of reliability and failure of reliability as a communication to the infant.

> Human beings fail and fail; and in the course of ordinary care a mother is all the time mending her failures. These relative failures with immediate remedy undoubtedly add up eventually to a communication, so that the baby comes to know about success. Successful adaptation thus gives a sense of security, a feeling of being loved.
>
> (Winnicott, 1968: 21)

He was careful to distinguish these mended failures from failures not mended in time, deprivation, or failures unmended, privation, which both produce in the baby unthinkable anxiety, experienced as 'going to pieces, falling for ever, complete isolation because of there being no means of communication, and disunion of psyche and soma' (Winnicott, 1968: 21).

Winnicott (1958) considered that the capacity to be alone was one of the most important signs of maturity in emotional development. The capacity to be alone develops as a result of the baby having sufficient experience of being alone in the presence of someone, that is, 'the mother or mother-substitute who is in fact reliably present even if represented for the moment by a cot or a pram or the general atmosphere of the general environment' (1958: 30). This idea has a clear link with the theory of object relations; thus 'the capacity to be alone depends on the existence of a good object in the psychic reality of the individual' (1958: 31). Not only does the baby have the mother 'in mind' but the mother also has the baby 'in mind' even when absent. The difference between Winnicott and Klein perhaps lies in their differing views of where the main threat to the development of a 'healthy' personality originates. Klein places this in the innate death instinct whereas Winnicott places it in the mother's attentiveness and responsiveness to her baby. Winnicott believed that if the mother was not responsive enough then the baby put up a shield to protect its 'true self', and presented a 'false self' to the world. This, of course, is reminiscent of the use of splitting as a defence mechanism.

Winnicott (1968: 24) sums up the baby's communication with the mother in terms of creativeness and compliance – 'in health the creative communication has priority over compliance'. In his own terms:

> These words could represent the communication of the baby with the mother.
> I find you;
> You survive what I do to you as I come to recognise you as not-me;
> I use you;
> But you remember me;
> I keep forgetting you;
> I lose you;
> I am sad.
>
> (Winnicott, 1968: 24)

The contribution of Bion

Bion's idea of containment is similar to Winnicott's idea of holding, and is linked to his concept of maternal reverie (Bion, 1967). The mechanisms described by Klein are used to help the baby to grow. If the mother has the capacity for reverie, she is able to receive her baby's projections, and contain and modify them. In particular, she is able to receive the anxiety associated with the fear and dread which emanate from the death instinct and manage this for her infant. In other words, the mother takes in the infant's emotions, experiences them herself, helps to sort them out and give them meaning, and then, of course, lets the baby get on with having the experience. Her ability to tune in enables her to meet her infant's communications, be they in the form of noises or gestures or simply states of being, with her own and thus she helps the baby to feel comforted, satisfied or safe, and to grow.

Bion very much saw the mind as an apparatus for thinking and learning. He sought to understand the origin of thought, which was recognised as something which happened between impulse and action. He built on the ideas of both Freud and Klein but was probably unique in his preoccupation with thinking, and concern to describe the conditions required for, and the mechanisms involved in the development of the capacity for thought, or perhaps more accurately, the mechanisms by which a thought becomes thinkable. In Meltzer's words:

> Bion's world is one of the questing mind seeking the absolute truth with inadequate equipment. . . . The growth of the mind is not, as in Freud, the natural realisation of innate processes, all going well; nor, like Melanie Klein's, is it a process of complicated unfolding given sufficient nurturing and protection; it is rather seen by Bion as the growth of the capacity for thinking about emotional

experiences which enable the individual to learn by becoming a different person with different capabilities from the person of the past.

(Meltzer, 1978: 116)

Interestingly, Bion differentiated the 'absolute truth' from the truth in any individual's mind, and suggested that some degree of falsification was necessary in order for truth to be contained and allowed to grow – 'the thinker needs to find the truth as an idea which he can make grow in his mind' (Meltzer, 1978: 110). (This idea is not far removed from the ideas of the constructivists.)

Bion was more explicit than some others in his extension and application of the fundamental model of container/contained to other situations. He clearly addressed the links between this original mother–child dynamic and institutional or group processes. A mother will find it difficult to be a container if she herself is not or has not been contained. Similarly, in large groups or institutions, work will be impeded if primitive anxieties are not well enough contained. Bion's ideas both informed and were informed by his own and others' experience of group work and consultation to institutions. The practical application of these theories is well illustrated by Isabel Menzies-Lyth (1959) in her seminal paper which reported on a study of the nursing service of a general teaching hospital. She concluded that the service's social defence system represented the institutionalisation of primitive defence mechanisms. Although the institution functioned to facilitate the evasion of anxiety, it did not reduce it; nor did it improve the efficiency of task performance. The inefficiency of the 'chosen' defence mechanism contributed to problems: for example, high levels of anxiety in nurses had adverse effects on patient recovery rates, and recovery rates directly affected staff morale, further raising anxiety. She considered that the success and viability of any social institution were intimately connected with the techniques it used to contain anxiety. This is especially true of special care baby units, where the emotional tasks of its staff are as important as the physical ones. The institution needs to be like a mother. Staff who do not feel contained or looked after will not be able to look after these babies and their families. They may also experience personal distress or develop stress-related illnesses.

ETHOLOGY

Ethology has influenced thinking about early parent–child relationships. First, a direct comparison has been made between the behaviour of other species and the behaviour of Man. This transposition of theory from one field to the other is unsatisfactory. It is perhaps best exemplified by the use of the notion of 'the sensitive period'. Klaus *et al.* (1972) postulated that human mothers, like some other mammals, were only able to bond to their offspring if exposed to them during a sensitive period, shortly after the birth. This concept has rightly been criticised for its simplicity and inherent sexism (Sluckin *et al.*, 1983), but nonetheless has had an impact on hospital practice. While recent research has supported this criticism, it has also demonstrated the vulnerability to interference of social relations in the neonatal period (Richards, 1983).

Second, inspired by ethologists such as Lorenz and Harlow, John Bowlby created a new theoretical model, using instinct behaviour as described in animals as his starting point. 'The resulting conceptual framework' was

> designed to accommodate all those phenomena to which Freud called attention
> – for example love relations, separation anxiety, mourning, defense, anger, guilt,
> depression, trauma, emotional detachment, sensitive periods in early life – and
> so to offer an alternative to the traditional metapsychology of psychoanalysis
> and to add yet another to the many variants of clinical theory now extant.
>
> (Bowlby, 1988a: 237)

Attachment theory (Bowlby, 1969, 1973, 1980) not only integrated and expanded but also diverged from some key ideas from both psychoanalysis and ethology.

Third, the methods used in ethology 'laid great stress on techniques of observation of animals in their natural habitat' and 'had an immediate appeal for psychologists working with children' (Richards, 1974a: 3).

ATTACHMENT THEORY

John Bowlby was a psychoanalyst and psychiatrist and, latterly, a researcher and theoretician. As I have mentioned, he was inspired by ethologists and sought to apply their models of understanding to human behaviour. In seeking to explain human behaviour, he was not only following in the footsteps of Freud, whom he quoted frequently, but was also taking a stand against the rigidity of the psychoanalytic approach to the construction of theories of development – 'But, although in his search for explanation he [Freud] was in each case led to events of early childhood, he himself only rarely drew for his basic data on direct observation of children' (Bowlby, 1969: 3). Bowlby himself viewed attachment theory as a version of object relations theory (Bowlby, 1988a), but I hope would have agreed that it was improper to include it here merely as a subcategory of psychoanalytic theory. He was careful to draw attention to the similarities as well as the differences in approach:

> Whilst giving systematic attention to the influences of family events on a child's
> socio-emotional development, attachment theory, like all versions of psycho-
> analytic theory, seeks to understand these influences in terms of their effect on
> the child's instinctive urges, feelings and thoughts – his internal world. Distinc-
> tive features of the approach are that it adheres to usual scientific procedures
> and seeks evidence from whatever sources seem to promote understanding.
>
> (Bowlby, 1988a: 231)

Bowlby was impressed by the scientific approach adopted by ethologists to study bonds between individuals, and also by their acknowledgement of the evolutionary context of their findings.

The principal propositions which make up attachment theory have been summarised by Bowlby:

1 Emotionally significant bonds between individuals have basic survival functions and therefore a primary status.
2 They can be understood by postulating cybernetic systems situated within the CNS [central nervous system] of each partner that have the effect of maintaining proximity or ready accessibility of each partner to the other.
3 In order for the systems to operate efficiently, each partner builds in his or her mind working models of self and of other and of the patterns of interaction that have developed between them.
4 Present knowledge requires that a theory of developmental pathways should replace theories that invoke specific phases of development in which it is postulated a person may become fixated and/or to which he or she may regress.
(Bowlby, 1988b: 2)

The idea that the attachment system should be regarded as a behavioural control system with its own distinct motivation was unique. Young children explore the world from a secure base, that is, an attachment figure, and development moves forward under the constant influence of both a desire to be close to the primary caregiver, and a need to find out about, and be stimulated by the world. Bretherton urged a note of caution about the interpretation of this information – 'Although the function of attachment in an evolutionary sense may be homeostasis with regard to the environment, it is experienced by the attached person as a psychological bond to the attachment figure who plays the part of the secure base or haven' (1985: 7). It is also important to note that the attachment system 'does not become organised until sometime during the second half of the first year, although it builds on component systems that are operative earlier' (Bretherton, 1985: 7). Actions that appear to have the function of bringing the infant into closer proximity with its caregiver are apparent at birth but their alleged lack of discrimination prohibits their description as 'attachment behaviours'. This term is also restrictive as it is reserved for the infant's behaviour only.

Research in this area, of which there is a considerable amount, has tended to focus on the measurement of attachment behaviour, particularly in relation to continuities over time. Ainsworth (1967, 1977) investigated the development of the attachment of a baby to its mother, and attempted to disentangle the contributions of each. She noted that early patterns of interaction correlated with attachment behaviour at one year, as measured by the Strange Situation test. This was more true of maternal behaviours than of infant behaviours. Her research, and that of Grossmann et al. (1985), suggests that it may be possible to measure pre-attachment behaviour with some degree of validity.

More recent research has taken Bowlby's idea of internal working models further. Sroufe (1988) has posited that this concept offers a new perspective on the issue of continuity and change. Summarising two alternative perspectives to this model, which he believes are extreme, he stated:

One of these suggests that quality of adaptation is primarily a product of current circumstances; early experience especially is unlikely to exert much lasting influence because its effect will be washed out by later experience. Little continuity from the early years to later childhood is expected. . . . Any apparent continuity is illusory and occurs mainly because the environment was unchanged. . . . The other equally extreme viewpoint would be a rigid critical-period hypothesis. According to this view, one's attachment and basic pattern of adaptation are fixed early in life and determine, in a linear way, later behaviour. Although it is difficult to find anyone who holds this position, it has sometimes been attributed wrongly to attachment researchers, including myself. . . .

(Sroufe, 1988: 22)

In contrast to these, he has put forward his own (and Bowlby's) view:

The idea of *working* models means both that such models are active constructions forged over time and they are subject to change. The inner aspect is meant to imply that the model is not simply formed and reshaped from the outside; rather, new experiences are engaged from within the framework of models already constructed, and change is an active rather than a passive process.

(Sroufe, 1988: 22)

Thus:

Inner working models are constructed over time and are continually elaborated and, at times, fundamentally changed. At the same time, inner working models influence both the child's experiences and how these experiences are processed.

(Sroufe, 1988: 24)

So that, while early attachment patterns do have a predictive validity, they are not permanently fixed. They can both predict behaviour in later social situations, and be modified in the context of development and the environment in which it occurs.

Needless to say, attachment theory has not been without its critics. It is important to consider this criticism but in defence of Bowlby, it is also important to draw attention to the context in which his theories were first presented. The historical context has been summarised by Yelloly:

Throughout the 1940s, evidence was accumulating as to the dramatic adverse affects experienced by children subject to institutionalisation or to separation experiences under certain conditions; of these some of the most distressing (and it would seem often irreversible) effects were to be seen among children in institutions; particularly, marked retardation in physical, mental and emotional development, and sometimes severe depression or psychosis.

(Yelloly, 1980: 76)

Personal context is also important to acknowledge. Bowlby was a psychiatrist, concerned at different times with the treatment of adults and children suffering from emotional or psychiatric disturbance. His early research had focused on the separation experiences of 'forty-four juvenile thieves' (1946), and had attempted to trace the antecedents of 'affectionless psychopathy'.

In presenting his 1951 paper *Maternal Care and Mental Health*, Bowlby not only made a statement about society's attitude to young children but also strove to explain psychiatric disorder. At that point in time, his view of 'maternal deprivation' could have been said to have been too narrow. Not surprisingly, it was rejected in many quarters where the idea that only a mother could provide a satisfactory environment for her child was taken literally and found to be unacceptable. Referring to the concept of 'maternal deprivation' later, Rutter stated that 'no area in psychology has given rise to such widely differing assertions' (1972: 13). Bowlby revised, refined, expanded and developed his initial thesis throughout the rest of his life but his critics, even today, seem almost to have got stuck in a time warp, hanging on to his early ideas, which were of course extremely controversial but also important and influential at the time. His ideas did lead to considerable improvements to the environment surrounding many groups of children; for example, those being cared for in hospital.

Rutter recognised that Bowlby's writings 'were often misinterpreted and wrongly used' (1972: 15) and has pointed out that 'the experiences subsumed under "maternal deprivation" are complex' (1972: 13). He reviewed the topic in great detail, and his book *Maternal Deprivation Reassessed* (1972) is an important text in its own right. In it, he reviewed some of Bowlby's early work and, in particular, attempted to differentiate the effect of a failure to form bonds, as opposed to a disruption of bonds. He speculated that the frequent changes of mother-figures during the time when attachments were usually formed could have resulted in impaired bond formation in Bowlby's 'forty-four juvenile thieves'. More recently, Rutter and Rutter (1992) have reviewed recent research in the field in the context of wider developmental issues.

It is important to recognise that with the passage of time and the recognition of the importance of early relationships in the area of mental health, the term attachment has been used more loosely. As I have mentioned, in Bowlby's terms, and those of his followers, attachment behaviour is a term reserved for the behaviour of infants, while the attachment system encompasses the child and its caretakers. It is, however, common to find accounts in the literature today which include expressions such as 'mother's attachment to the infant'. Theoretically and historically this usage would only be correct if the author was referring to the infant's ability to meet adult attachment needs, most often met by another adult.

Attachment theory's relevance to the study of neonates in the intensive care setting may be considered to be related to two branches of the research that has followed on from Bowlby's original work. The first concerns the idea that pre-attachment behaviour exists, and the second relates to the intergenerational continuity of attachment behaviours, most clearly observed in attachment disorders (Minde and Benoit, 1991). The latter idea is supported by the research of Mary Main and her colleagues (Main and Goldwyn, 1984; Main et al., 1985) who have found that mothers' reports of their own relationships in childhood are related in a predictive way to their style of care and the nature of their relationship with their own children.

Parental factors affecting the developing relationship

Others have described, more anecdotally, the effect of the parents', and particularly the mother's, own childhood experience on adjustment to the pregnancy and the development of relationships following the birth of the child (Brazelton and Cramer, 1991; Kitzinger, 1984).

Pregnancy and childbirth

Introducing their own ideas on 'the prehistory of attachment', Brazelton and Cramer have stated that:

> Each woman's pregnancy reflects her whole life prior to conception. Her experiences with her own mother and father, her subsequent experiences with the oedipal triangle, and the forces that led her to adapt to it more or less successfully and finally to separate from her parents, all influence her adjustment to this new role. Unmet needs from childhood and adolescence are part of the desire to become pregnant and, then, to adapt to the condition of pregnancy.
>
> (Brazelton and Cramer, 1991: 5)

Psychoanalysts have proposed conflicting models in attempts to understand the role of pregnancy for women, one model seeing pregnancy and delivery as part of normal development, and another likening it to a crisis or abnormal state of health (MacFarlane, 1977). Eichenbaum and Orbach (1983) have described the relationship between pregnancy and dependency. Their identification of two styles of adaptation may well fit with the normal/abnormal dichotomy. In the first group, 'the fact of being pregnant brings with it feelings of self-esteem and accomplishment' while the second group 'report feeling more dependent on their partners during pregnancy' and also 'feel a bit more vulnerable and begin to feel the burden of responsibility for this new life inside them' (Eichenbaum and Orbach, 1983: 137). How a woman and her partner view the prospect of having a child may have an impact on the developing parent–child relationship.

This can happen in a number of ways. A pregnancy may have been planned and wanted, or 'accidental', and conception may have been either an easy and straightforward process or a long and difficult one, perhaps assisted by medical or psychological investigation and intervention. A history of miscarriages, stillbirths or planned terminations of pregnancy will have an impact on the parents' attitude to their unborn child, as will the quality of their own relationship. In cases of unplanned pregnancy, the circumstances of the conception will vary greatly, and acceptance by the mother-to-be of her state, and of the baby, are likely to vary accordingly. At one end of the spectrum, for a woman in a stable relationship with a plan to have a child some time in the not-too-distant future, the pregnancy may in fact be a cause for celebration. At the other, a child conceived as a result of rape or in the context of a sexually abusive relationship is likely to be less wanted. A recent example of such a set of circumstances in Ireland received an enormous amount of publicity in the UK. The fact that the young woman in question was not only going against her own personal and religious beliefs to consider terminating her pregnancy but the fact that this was also against the law of the land evoked intense feelings in many people who were not directly involved.

A number of authors have attempted to examine the influence pregnancy and delivery factors have on either mother–infant interaction or the developing relationship. Trowell (1982), for example, examined the effects of caesarian section on the mother–child relationship, comparing mothers who had their babies by emergency section with a group who had a vaginal delivery. She found that early differences in attitudes and interaction were also evident at one year: mothers in the former group had more doubts about their capacity to care for their babies, were more depressed, and felt that their babies were older before they recognised them or became a person in their own right. This finding is in contrast to that of Culp and Osofsky (1989) who found no difference between these groups at three months. Shearer (1989) attributed this difference to study design but also felt that it was important to acknowledge the change in attitude and approach to caesarian delivery, which has become increasingly common, and, perhaps, less traumatic both emotionally and physically.

Other labour and delivery factors have been reported anecdotally to have an impact on developing relationships, at least in the short term. However, this has not been studied systematically in relation to the development of attachment. Studies that have been carried out have tended to focus on interactions rather than relationships; of course, it must be acknowledged that relationships are difficult to measure in any other way. Dunn and Richards (1977), for example, observed mothers and babies in the neonatal period and found that there was a correlation between length of labour and the use of significant amounts of narcotic analgesia and some aspects of interaction.

The experience of being parented

Frodi *et al.* (1989) are among those who have also suggested that mothers' responses to their infant, which affect the developing infant–mother bond, may originate in attitudes existing prior to parenthood. Parenting difficulties, whether transient or enduring, seem to have a complex aetiology. Some can probably be classified as intergenerational. Rutter and Rutter have reviewed some of the possible influences on parenting, which they consider to be 'a quite complex task with several different elements' (1992: 295). Amongst these is the role of a person's own upbringing; experience of abuse and deprivation in childhood has a detrimental effect on social relationships in general, of which parenting is one aspect. Those who have had 'a seriously adverse upbringing' (1992: 296) are likely to experience difficulties in parenting. It has also been recognised that women in this group are likely to have babies at a young age, and often in poor socioeconomic situations, in order to try to deal with their own feelings of insecurity and rejection, and may then neglect or abuse their infants (Zuravin and DiBlasio, 1992). The high risk for relationship difficulties is increased by the higher incidence of premature births and small-for-dates babies in this population.

Mental illness

The mental health of both parents is likely to have some influence on an infant's early environment. This has been studied more frequently and more specifically in relation to maternal depression. The mother's mental health will directly affect her ability to care for, and relate to, her baby, and may consequently affect the baby's development. For example, puerperal depression has been shown to be associated with developmental delay and cognitive difficulties in children (Cogill *et al.*, 1986). The research of Murray and her colleagues has attempted to discern the earlier processes which lead to these later difficulties for children of depressed mothers. She reported (Murray, 1992) that infants of mothers who had suffered from depression after the birth were more likely to have behaviour problems and be classified as insecurely attached at eighteen months. These infants performed less well than control infants on tests of object constancy. This refers to the infant's recognition that an object, a toy, for example, still exists even when out of sight. It is an important developmental signal which marks the time when an infant can be seen to demonstrate clearly that he or she misses someone special. It is a sign that a resolution has finally been reached to the me/not-me dilemma which has been worked on since birth.

Murray *et al.* (1993) addressed the question of whether these adverse effects were mediated by the quality of early communication. The results of this study suggested that the early use of infant-focused speech, or 'motherese', did lead to a better outcome for the infant at nine months. The authors suggested that the impact on speech of a depressive illness may be one of the important pathways by which maternal depression influences development.

DEVELOPMENTAL PSYCHOLOGY

This account of the approach of developmental psychologists to the understanding of infant development must of necessity be seen in a historical context. This, of course, is also true for other theories which I have presented but the move by developmental psychologists towards a broader perspective has been striking in the last ten to fifteen years; this discipline, in particular, appears to have made considerable moves towards a rapprochement with other theoretical schools in recent times. I will discuss this coming together of theories in more detail in Chapter 3.

The main differences in orientation and the reasons for this have been discussed by Urwin (1986). The differences reflect the different purposes and populations under investigation. Traditionally, developmental psychology has sought to be more 'objective', and has drawn its conclusions about causation and outcome from observational studies and experiments with infants themselves. Development has classically been seen as progressing through a series of predictable stages, with recognition that events occurring at one stage may cause or predict a subsequent course of events. On the whole, emotions and feelings have been left on the sidelines, and the research endeavours of this school have, until recently, focused on tasks – perceptual, motor, cognitive. More recently social tasks have been added to this list but again without consideration, in many cases, of the hypothesised accompanying feeling states, internal representations of such behaviours or unconscious processes involved.

Richards (1979) has documented society's change in attitude about the earliest stage of children's lives, from little interest as recently as the 1950s to acceptance of the emphasis on the importance of the neonatal period in the 1970s. He links this to improvements in mortality rates as a result of changing medical practice. Of course, in the period up to the 1950s changes in social conditions had a significant impact on life expectancy. The focus for research then moved towards earlier and earlier periods of a child's life. In his introduction to a collection of papers about mother–infant interaction, Schaffer (1977) noted the increasing number of examinations of the earliest social relationship in a search for the developmental antecedents of particular functions. He considered that the change in the approach of developmental psychologists was distinguished by certain features:

1   *Treatment of social behaviour in dyadic terms.* That infants are capable of organised, spontaneous behaviour from the very beginning of life is now richly documented; the implications for the study of early social behaviour are that a dyadic orientation is essential. . . .
2   *The need to postulate some degree of social preadaptation.* A neonate may be an essentially a-social creature, in the sense of not being capable as yet of truly reciprocal social relationships and of not yet having the concept of a person. However, the nature of his early interactive behaviour is such that it is increasingly difficult to avoid the conclusion that in some sense the infant is already prepared for social intercourse. . . .
3   *Emphasis on temporal relationships in interactive situations.* . . . The nature of the infant's pre-adapted organisation can, in part, be described in terms of temporal parameters. Behaviour is chunked in time, and dyadic interactions are thus based on an elaborate interweaving of the participants' behavioural flow. Techniques of sequential analysis rather than indices based on total amounts of behaviour collated over time accordingly become the principal method of data reduction.
4   *The use of microanalytic techniques.* Experience has shown that the temporal relationships just referred to become most evident at microlevels of analysis. . . . This level of analysis has been found to be a particularly fruitful one for

exploring the manner in which the infant's behaviour meshes with that of his caretakers.

5   *An interest in processes rather than products.* . . . Recent work has concerned itself more with the processes underlying the formation of social relationships, and accordingly questions have been asked as to how these come about rather than when they appear, towards whom they are manifested, or in what way they change across time and situation.

(Schaffer, 1977: 5)

More recently, Greenspan and Lieberman (1989) have suggested that there has been a radical change in the scientific conception of the infant from a conglomeration of isolated reflexes to an organism born with a considerable degree of social pre-adaptation.

The infant

What are newborn babies actually capable of? This question has been the subject of considerable research, which has in recent years also extended to consider the foetus. There is, however, still a dearth of research into the capabilities of newborn premature babies, and in Chapter 2, I will examine in more detail what is actually known or inferred about them on the basis of these *in utero* examinations. In this section, I will attempt to summarise the findings which relate to the ordinary neonate.

Packer and Rosenblatt considered that 'the myth that babies neither see nor hear in the first six weeks has been dispelled by systematic experiments on perception' (1979: 8), and suggested that the infant's readiness to participate in social interaction was dependent on both perceptual abilities and the capacity for sustaining an alert and responsive state.

States of consciousness

There is general agreement amongst professionals about the number and nature of states of consciousness exhibited by the newborn (MacFarlane, 1977; Packer and Rosenblatt, 1979; Brazelton and Cramer, 1991). These states are:

1   Deep sleep, with regular deep breathing, and the absence of movement. In this state the baby may have brief startles but will not rouse, being relatively unreachable to outside stimuli. This state has a restorative function – it 'serves an important purpose, to rest and organise an immature and easily overwhelmed nervous system' (Brazelton and Cramer, 1991: 64).

2   Light or active sleep, with irregular breathing, occasional restlessness and rapid eye movements. Newborn infants go directly into REM sleep and spend proportionately more time in it than older infants (Daws, 1989). It is postulated to be a time of brain growth and differentiation.

3   Drowsy awakeness, with shallower regular breathing and some movement. In

this state the baby will usually be able to be aroused to a more alert responsive state.

4   Alert awakeness, when the baby is quiet and bright-eyed rather than excited. In this alert state, which is relatively short-lived initially, the infant is able to attend to and respond to stimuli.
5   Alert active or fussing awakeness. In this state, babies seem to be distressed but can be soothed back into an alert but quiet state. Stimulation may, however, seem to be too much for the baby, who may begin to cry.
6   Crying. Brazelton and Cramer (1991) have identified at least four types of crying (pain, hunger, boredom, discomfort), which are distinguishable from a very early age, and which all elicit feelings of concern in parents or caretakers.

Recognition of the existence of these states is important for both researchers and carers. For the former, it is important that conclusions about infants' capabilities are made in the context of this state-awareness, and for carers, it is clear that there are certain times when the infant will be much more able and ready to take part in social exchanges, feeding or other caretaking activities, such as bathing and changing, without becoming distressed. MacFarlane (1977) has noted that babies will become more alert if held upright or at an angle.

Perceptual abilities

There is no doubt that full-term babies can see from the moment that they are born. They not only fixate on objects placed a certain distance from them but they also move their heads and eyes to follow these objects as they are moved across their visual field. However, as Daniel Stern has pointed out, 'there is an all-important difference between looking and seeing, as there is between listening and hearing' (1977: 34). In questioning the visual experiences of neonates, he has referred to the experience of adults who had congenital cataracts removed but then found it difficult to make sense of what they saw. He concluded, on the basis of his observations of infants, that they did not have such a difficult experience for a number of reasons. First, they have not had years to develop a scheme of the world in their minds; and second, their focal range is limited, so that they can see objects most clearly at a relatively short distance. Interestingly this distance is reported by various authors as eight inches (Stern, 1977), nine inches (MacFarlane, 1977), and ten to twelve inches (Brazelton and Cramer, 1991). All draw the same conclusion, that is, that it is the distance between the infant's eyes and the mother's eyes in the feeding position in most cases, whether feeding is by breast or bottle. The mother's face therefore acts as an initial focal point for the infant.

'A baby seems to be programmed for learning about human faces from birth' (Brazelton and Cramer, 1991: 54). There has been conflicting evidence about neonates' ability to distinguish faces early on. Packer and Rosenblatt reported that researchers had 'failed to confirm a preference for faces in infants under sixteen weeks' (1979: 10), whereas MacFarlane (1977) has reported that babies from the age of four days look most at a picture of a real face, somewhat less at a scrambled face, and least at a more abstract picture. Brazelton and Cramer (1991) have not only detailed their own experience but also cited the research of others; for example, that of Goren *et al.* (1975), who reported babies fixing on a drawing which resembled a human face and following it through 180°.

The baby's visual competence develops rapidly during the first three months, by which time the infant has a similar focal range to that of an adult. Two steps precede this: at about three weeks, mothers report that infants have begun to recognise their face (Brazelton and Cramer, 1991); and at six weeks, the infant demonstrates reliable visual tracking (Packer and Rosenblatt, 1979), and 'becomes capable of visually fixating his mother's eyes and holding the fixation with eye widening and brightening' – 'a developmental landmark that often catapults the social interaction with mother onto a new level' (Stern, 1977: 37).

MacFarlane (1977) summarised some of the key findings about the infant's perception of sound. Babies respond better to higher frequencies and prefer human to non-human sounds. They will turn more frequently towards a woman's voice than a man's. Early on, they will demonstrate a preference for their mother's voice, and will also sychronise their movements to the rhythm of that voice. Fluid in the ear is absorbed gradually over the first week, and initially serves a useful function, dampening noise.

Sense of smell is also highly developed from an early stage. Neonates are attracted to sweet odours but will turn away from some smells, such as that of vinegar or alcohol. At seven days, babies can distinguish the smell of their own mother's milk and will turn to a breast pad soaked in it as opposed to another mother's; this ability becomes even more marked by ten days (MacFarlane, 1977). Likewise, babies readily demonstrate a preference for different tastes and communicate this in the way they suck. For example, they will resist sucking salty solutions, and suck cow's milk in a different way to the way they take breast milk also given by bottle.

Babies are subjected to different kinds of touch; they are soothed by gentle touch, and with maturity, demonstrate more clearly the pleasure they get from this. They will show reflex responses to particular kinds of touch, and this is perhaps best recognised by parents in relation to the rooting reflex: a baby will turn towards a gentle touch on the cheek, and show searching movements; if the nipple is there it will be mouthed. Swaddling is common to some extent in most cultures, and also appears to calm and comfort babies. Painful stimuli are reacted to but there has been some debate about whether infants, and especially premature infants, actually feel pain. The evidence is that infants withdraw, tense their muscles, and show marked alterations in heart and respiration rates – this would seem to suggest a dislike of the experience, which is similar to the responses of older children who are able to say very clearly that they feel pain.

The wealth of research into infant capability is summed up by Emde and Buchsbaum:

Infants are fundamentally active, socially interactive, and organized. Infants are stimulus-seeking and participate creatively in their own development. Subsequent experience is not superimposed on a formless beginning. For any behavioral development, including emotional development, experience serves to modulate a preexisting state of endogenous organization.

(Emde and Buchsbaum, 1989: 199)

There is no doubt that infants have the competence to contribute actively to their developing relationships, both as initiators of interaction, and in response to the overtures made towards them.

In addition, they will influence their relationships by less 'direct' means. The research of Thomas, Chess and Birch (1968) identifying temperamental differences in infants seems to have stood the test of time, and it is recognised that some children's temperamental characteristics do elicit particular responses from both adults and other children (Rutter and Rutter, 1992). Their physical appearance will also have an influence on how others relate to them, as will the presence of disability. A baby who is developmentally delayed and does not respond readily to invitations to communicate will sometimes leave a parent feeling disheartened and negative. Likewise, a baby who is irritable and seems to require litle sleep may be dealt with impatiently by a tired and overwrought parent, who seems unable to be positive or containing.

More recent research has started to address the way that individual characteristics interact with environmental factors. Recognition of the role of inheritance in behaviour (Plomin, 1990) has led to investigation into within-family processes that lead to differences in the developmental outcome for siblings (Dunn and Plomin, 1991).

The parent–infant relationship

The process by which meaningful interaction between infants and caretakers evolves is related to both the infant's contribution and to the caretaker's, and to each one's interpretation and 'fit' with their partner's actions. The initial emphasis in this dialogue seems to be on the adult's contribution and interpretation of and response to what the infant brings. In Richards' words:

From early in foetal development, an infant's behaviour is patterned in both space and time. Many configurations of behaviour or action patterns not only make units which are functional and are recognisable in form (such as sucking, crying or smiling) but they also occur with highly structured temporal patterns. . . . Adult caretakers recognise these patterns and assume that some of them provide indications of what is occurring inside the infant. They assume that smiling represents a state of contentment or stability and that crying is related to hunger or some other discomfort. By such recognition they confer the status of social action upon these behaviour patterns.

(Richards, 1974b: 87)

Kaye (1982) is probably exceptional in his critique of the mother–infant interaction system. Taking Richards' point further, he has suggested that in the first few months of life 'the temporal structure that eventually becomes a true social system will at first only have been created by the parent' (Kaye, 1982: 53). He rejects the idea that mother or caretaker and infant constitute a system, and is critical of discussion of dyadic processes.

Others, however, have sought to examine dyads as systems, and, as a result, ideas familiar to those working within the psychoanalytic tradition have been supported by child development research. The work of Brazelton et al. (1974, 1975) on the origins of reciprocity, as well as that of Trevarthen (1974) and Stern (1974), is important.

The first two papers describe the microanalysis of mother–child interactions in the laboratory situation leading to the identification of characteristics of the developing relationship. These included the mother's sensitivity to her baby's capacity for attention and non-attention, and her learning how her behaviours were interpreted by her baby, in particular, which of her behaviours set up an expectancy of interaction. The rhythmicity of interaction seemed as, if not more, important in the development of their relationship as what the mother or the infant actually did. Another important finding was that at three weeks of age infants were seen to respond with concern and distress if presented with a still, unresponsive face. In that situation, the infants endeavoured to draw the mother into interaction but if that failed would withdraw. Trevarthen (1977) has reported similar findings in slightly older infants (seven to twelve weeks), and also noted that mother's deliberate withdrawal was far more distressing to the infant than her temporary, and perhaps quite natural, engagement in conversation with a third person.

In similar work, Trevarthen (1974) examined the 'direction' of the interaction by the two month olds he was studying, and Stern (1974) used analysis of video recordings in the home to examine how the mutually elicited behaviour of each member in turn influenced the behaviour of the other member.

An important feature of the mother–infant 'dialogue' is, of course, the use of 'motherese', referred to earlier in relation to maternal depression. Its features have been described by Murray et al. (1993). This form of speech is familiar to all of us, both male and female. It has a musical quality both in tone and in rhythm. Its pace changes with the infant's response – becoming faster and more high-pitched as the infant becomes excited, and slower, softer and quieter as the child withdraws. It depends on mutuality and harmony in the relationship. It is child-focused and child-directed, and tends to be questioning rather than directive. Its identification and postulated relationship to child development and patterns of attachment serves as a marker for new research which is pulling together individual influences on infants' developing relationships by considering just how each impacts on the pathway to a healthy outcome.

The wider system

Research so far clearly supports an interactive model of mutual influence between mother and infant from birth. Greenspan and Lieberman (1989), however, have suggested that it has not yet addressed the meaning of behaviour. They believe that this is because behavioural units are not interpreted within the total developmental context in which they occur. But, according to Minuchin, among others, times are changing:

> Studies of the mother–child dyad have been the hardest perennial in the developmental field. In recent years, however, the scope of research has expanded, and studies of father and child, siblings, and so forth, are increasingly common. It seems likely that broad theoretical developments outside the field – systems theory, and the twentieth-century alertness to context – have been influential triggers for expansion.
>
> (Minuchin, 1988: 7)

She sees the relation between general family patterns and those of various subsystems as a major question for systems researchers, particularly those studying early childhood, where the main foci have previously been the properties of individuals or dyads.

Criticism at this point in time seems unjust, as a number of groups have already begun to put child development research into a wider context. Richards and his colleagues (for example, 1974c and 1986) are one example. Yogman and Brazelton (1986) too have viewed the family as a system interacting with other social systems in order to try to understand the influence of stress and supports on child development. And, in *Relationships Within Families – Mutual Influences* (Hinde and Stevenson-Hinde, 1988), a number of researchers have presented their preliminary reports on the relationship between individual development and family processes.

Developmental psychologists have begun a very intricate and elaborate dance, going back and forward between the properties of individuals and the properties of families and wider social systems. They have been joined by researchers from other fields, in what could be predicted to be a very fruitful exploration, which should lead not only to a greater understanding of development in context but also to a more sophisticated understanding of developing relationships and their implications for the future.

SUMMARY

Theories from different schools have contributed to an increased understanding of early parent–child, and especially mother–child, relationships. A growing body of research has elaborated and expanded upon the work of John Bowlby on the role which early attachment plays in personality development, and later mental health and capacity to parent.

Full-term babies arrive in the world ready to communicate with, to get to know, their carers, who instinctively respond to their signals and learn to 'fit' with their child. The quality of actual relationships, as well as the infant's perception of them, will influence growth and development. Babies need to be emotionally contained, or kept in mind, by their mothers, who in turn need to be contained by their families, and, in the case of special care infants, by staff in the hospital. Past experience and beliefs will affect each carer's ability to do this, as will their mental health and wider social context.

Chapter 2

The special care baby

Infants and their families have widely differing experiences of special care and neonatal intensive care units. The variation is accounted for by a number of factors, which include the reasons for the infant's admission, the type of delivery, hospital policy about matters such as visiting, rooming in, and parents' participation in caring for their child, and, not least, the family's ability to adapt to the extraordinary set of circumstances which confront them. The perceived experience of each member of each family is the result of the coming together of policies, beliefs, and history with the impact of day-to-day and even minute-to-minute events on the unit. The complex interaction of these factors makes each participant's own experience unique.

There is, then, considerable difficulty in knowing what or how to write about special care infants and their developing relationships in a way that acknowledges that uniqueness. Not only is it important not to appear to make sweeping generalisations or to give a message that seems to either trivialise or dramatise the experience, but it is also necessary to take account of the rapid advances in medical technology and the increasing sophistication in research methodology which lead us to reappraise our understanding of development in this context almost daily.

Many authors have addressed the psychological aspects of neonatal intensive care. Books have already been devoted to the subject. Brimblecombe *et al.*'s *Separation and Special-Care Baby Units* (1978) was followed in 1983 by Davis *et al.*'s book, *Attachment in Premature Infants*, which gave a clear account of the state of the art at that time. Both publications gave clear suggestions for change in both policy and practice aimed at reducing the stress of the experience of special care for infants, their families and those working there. Affleck *et al.* (1991), in their report of a rigorous research project, identified and weighted the contribution made by a number of factors influencing parents', and particularly mothers', ability to cope with the crisis of intensive care. Goldberg and DiVitto (1983) have considered the later development of premature babies in detail and presented this for parents. Another book, *You and Your Premature Baby* by Hudson (1985), is written by parents for parents. Tiffany Field (for example, 1990a and b) is also among those who have written extensively on the subject, and her research findings on the physiological impact of caregiving procedures have been accompanied by recommendations for small changes in practice which could make a huge difference to the experiences of special care infants.

Two recent papers outlined some key issues related to the 'special care' situation.

Patteson and Barnard (1990) reviewed factors adversely affecting the parenting of low birth weight infants, that is, babies weighing less than 2500 grams, and included infant characteristics, parental emotional response to prematurity, and patterns of parent–child interaction. Many studies have suggested that premature infants are more irritable but simultaneously more passive and less responsive. They can also have less predictable sleep patterns. Parents are often unprepared for their arrival which can be accompanied by an 'emergency' situation. They may expect the baby to die, and distance themselves as a result. This, of course, has implications for the development of the relationship. The authors of this paper also considered interventions and possible areas of future research, in which they included: analysis of how changes in the intensive care environment would affect the infants' characteristics and their interactions with their parents; and research into the mechanisms by which infants' characteristics interact with parents' characteristics to alter parenting behaviours.

'The prematurity stereotype' has been defined by Stern and Karraker (1990) as a set of biased beliefs about infants who are born prematurely. It has been shown to influence adults' perceptions of, expectations for, and behaviour towards premature infants in a negative way. The infants may subsequently respond as if in accordance with expectations. These authors have called for research into this issue; in particular, they advocate description of how parental beliefs about prematurity relate to their own perceptions of and behaviour towards their own infant.

It is interesting but perhaps not surprising that most reports emanating from the study of the very young seem to end up talking about the adults involved. Although it is acknowledged and even stressed that the family is a system, and that the mother–child dyad is a subsystem of that system, the presentation of the baby's contribution is usually overshadowed by discussion of the adult's role. This is to some extent right and proper because we know much more about adults' experiences. Adults can communicate them infinitely more clearly than the infant can. Those who do try to present the infant's point of view are often accused of overinterpretation and adultomorphisisation. However, if we do not infer or interpret our observations, we are faced with the problem of how to take account of the neonate's own experience, and therefore how to acknowledge the infant's contribution to the developing relationship right from the word go. Another ready-made reason or excuse for not thinking too much about the neonate is provided by the systemic perspective. Relationships cannot be understood simply by looking at their component parts; the relationship is more than the sum of its parts. It is important to hold on to this idea but I would argue that examination of each partner's contribution in addition to the examination of the whole relationship is important. After all, the mother and the child are subsystems of the mother–child relationship in the same way that the mother–child relationship is a subsystem of the family, and so on.

Thinking about, and trying to empathise with, a special care baby is a very difficult thing to do. It is a painful process, probably more so for professionals than for parents. In a busy special care baby unit, the staff do not have time to focus on the baby as a whole human being. Some people will dispute this, and I know that enormous efforts are made to personalise infants, to talk with them as procedures are carried out, and to celebrate their milestones with them and their parents. But how many staff have the time or are able to make the time to stand by the cotside for even ten minutes, and try to tune into what one particular baby is feeling? How can any of us begin to put ourselves in the place of these babies, some of whom are fragile, scraggy-looking creatures who may be naked and blindfolded, who are connected to tubes and wires to keep them alive, and who cannot be cuddled or loved in the same way as ordinary babies?

The nature of the task of professional carers in this situation necessitates that they put into operation their emotional defence mechanisms in order to do their job, which often involves inflicting painful procedures on their charges. Here, we enter another area of possible dispute (Marshall, 1989). Some will say, and firmly believe, that these neonates, especially the ones who are very premature, do not feel pain in the way that we, the grown-ups, understand it. Many infants are sedated with morphine in order to reduce their restlessness and help them to tolerate their situation, and this must play a part in modifying their reactions to pain-inducing or discomforting stimuli. It is important to acknowledge, too, although it should go without saying, that the things that are done to these infants are, of course, all necessary to preserve their lives and minimise the sequelae of either their early arrival or their potentially life-threatening situations.

DEVELOPING RELATIONSHIPS

The special care baby 'belongs' to its parents, and to the unit. The baby's developing relationship with the person who is to become the primary caretaker, in most cases the mother, is influenced by both the family and the hospital. This developing relationship is critically placed at the interface of these two institutions, and as such is likely to be vulnerable. The quality and strength of the relationships at different levels between these two giants may either facilitate or inhibit the development of this key relationship. The actions of each player on each side will be informed by their own experience of events and by personal, family, organisational (specifically the hospital's), cultural and societal beliefs about child care, prematurity, and the role of medical intervention.

In the rest of this chapter, I will examine the contribution of each part of the system of the developing relationship, beginning with the infant, and then going on to consider the hospital environment and the family, including the mother.

The infant's contribution

As I have already indicated, infants admitted to special care baby units are by no means a homogeneous population. The decision to admit is made for a number of reasons, and may be influenced by hospital policy. Thus, to cite some examples: infants born at full term after a long and hazardous labour may be admitted for two or three days for observation and prophylactic treatment of systemic infection; infants of drug-takers may be admitted for opiate withdrawal (an increasing population); infants born as prematurely as twenty-three weeks gestation will be admitted for intensive life support; less premature babies who are small-for-dates may require nutritional support; and others born either at term or prematurely will be admitted because they have severe or life-threatening disabilities. Only a tiny proportion of these babies will look and behave like healthy full-term babies. Those who do will have only a brief stay.

Premature babies usually make up the majority of this rather special population. I'd like, therefore, to begin by focusing on them. What do we know about them and what constitutes 'normal' are two questions that are often asked. The second is probably impossible to answer. Information about preterm development comes from two main sources: the first is the study of the foetus, and the second is the study of the preterm neonate.

The foetus

Graves (1989) has pointed out that prenatal mental life is the subject of dreams, free association and folklore. Reconstructive reports of this, for example those elicited in the course of psychotherapy, do not shed much light on what actually happens but usefully serve to signal a neglected area of human experience. However, while relatively neglected, prenatal experience had certainly been thought about before recent times, as MacFarlane pointed out when he quoted Samuel Taylor Coleridge (1802): "'Yes – the history of Man for the nine months preceding his birth would probably be far more interesting and contain events of greater moment, than all the three score years and ten that follow it'" (1977: 11).

Winnicott is one of the few psychoanalysts who have considered prematurity. In a paper called 'The beginning of the individual' (1966a), he talked about 'psychology becoming meaningful' during the life of the foetus:

> At some stage or other in the development of the healthy human being there is a change which can only be described by saying that to anatomy and physiology becomes added psychology. The brain as an organ makes possible the registering of experiences and the accumulation of data and the beginnings of a sorting out of phenomena and their classification.
>
> (Winnicott, 1966a: 54)

While reaching the conclusion that the right time for birth was at full term, he thought it was important to acknowledge the evidence for the existence of an individual before that.

The inborn mental apparatus has its origins in prenatal life (Graves, 1989). The psychoanalytic view proposed by the object relations theorists of an intact ego at birth is supported by the research of developmental psychologists who consider that the infant is born 'preadapted' and ready to interact with the environment. In his introduction to an exploration of the functional development of the human foetus, Graves has drawn attention to the evidence across species that 'developing motor and sensory-perceptual systems are capable of functioning before they have completed neural maturation' (1989: 436). This evidence supports a bidirectional structure–function relationship; that is, 'while genes give rise to structural maturation processes, these processes are susceptible to, even dependent on, the influence of function before complete maturation is attained. . .' (Graves, 1989: 436).

Casaer (1993) has recently reviewed research on perinatal brain development. This is of relevance given that most of us would probably agree that the concept of mind, that is, the mental apparatus for both cognitive and emotional functioning, belongs with the brain. Focusing on the period between twenty-four and forty weeks gestation, he considered a number of areas, including general brain growth, and function. Crucial changes occur during the last few weeks of gestation. In premature babies these will occur postnatally provided adequate respiratory, circulatory and nutritional support is present. Casaer emphasises that brain growth is an important variable in assessing risk factors for later psychosocial development. Different parts of the brain are more vulnerable during their periods of rapid growth, and thus cerebral palsy is most likely to be a consequence of an insult around twenty weeks or at the beginning of the third trimester, whereas later hazards can result in problems with temporal and spatial sequencing.

MacFarlane (1977) has drawn attention to work demonstrating the influence on the foetus of different forms of stimulation, for example both smoking and loud noises leading to a change in heart rate, vibration and sound influencing movement *in utero*, and light causing pupillary reaction. The foetal ear can hear, and W. E. Freud has wondered to what extent intrauterine sounds, like maternal heartbeat, breathing and 'tummy rumbles', might 'be thought of as forerunners of "transitional objects". . . or "imaginary companions". . .' (1989a: 473). The influence of sound and rhythm has been supported by experiments after birth, which seem to confirm that the infant–mother relationship begins *in utero* – babies who were played heartbeats at eighty per minute for four days gained more weight and cried less than babies who were not played them. Babies who were played fast heartbeats (at 120 per minute) became upset. The changing pressure of the amniotic fluid as a result of the mother's movements also stimulates the foetus (Graves, 1989).

Both evoked and reflex movement occurs *in utero*, the former beginning at between seven and eight weeks, the latter slightly later. The grasp reflex, for example, can be evoked at eleven weeks, and is sufficient to support the weight of the foetus at twenty-seven weeks (Graves, 1989). The baby touches itself *in utero*, and early on will seem to move away from the touch but later this situation reverses and the foetus appears to explore the touch. Other actions include finger sucking, postulated to occur at about nineteen weeks, and swallowing of amniotic fluid from twelve weeks.

'The functioning fetus' has been described in detail by Graves (1989), and it is apparent that in the prenatal period, the baby has many capabilities. Whether it can then be inferred that mental functioning also occurs is, not surprisingly, a matter of debate. Graves pins his colours to the mast when he states that 'this picture of a "competent fetus" forcibly suggests that our search for the origins and early developmental phases of human mental life must begin with the fetus' (1989: 461), and like MacFarlane goes on to quote the poet Coleridge.

The premature neonate

W. E. Freud described his initial impression of low birth weight babies: 'Their physical development is measurably incomplete, and they were routinely separated from their mothers and subjected to massive medical intervention – infantile experiences that are certainly potentially "momentous"' (1989b: 485). In this one sentence he managed to capture the dilemma facing those who work with these babies – yes, these babies are obviously premature, not yet 'developed', but does this mean that they are unable to 'experience' themselves and the world around them?

Gorski (1983) seemed to have no doubt that these infants do experience their world, inferring that their method of communication about their experiences is initially through their behaviour. He hypothesised that:

> High-risk prematurely born infants exhibit behavioral responses that represent signals for neurophysiologic stability, disorganization, or distress. These cues may precede less subtle, more costly physiologic crises that caregivers commonly recognise as calls for caregiver reaction.
>
> (Gorski, 1983: 258).

If staff are tuned in to what to look for, the infants will communicate with them. At a more crude level, and following behavioural cues, continuously monitored vital signs may also be thought of as communication, for example, increased heart rate, altered skin tone and decreased oxygen tension indicate stress (Field, 1990a and b). Sometimes we forget that we do not always rely on verbal communication to understand each other as adults: the appearance of someone who is frightened or anxious is often our only clue to their mental state.

So what are the differences between a term infant and a preterm infant? Neurologically, they are less mature; they may not be equipped with the usual reflexes of the newborn, which probably serve to assist the infant in the birth process and protect it from noxious stimuli. The sucking reflex in particular appears later, and is preceded by the rooting reflex.

The movements of very premature infants differ from those of their term counterparts. Early on, they may appear jittery, and exhibit many startles, shudders and involuntary movements (Newman, 1981); later, some have been noted to have lower activity levels (Sameroff, 1989). One of the problems in trying to know about any spontaneous activity of these babies is that they are often very constrained by their environment. Their limbs, for example, may be splinted in order to protect intravenous lines, of which there are often several; their ability to suck or cry may be impeded by an endotracheal tube. Newman carried out an observational study of infants of twenty-eight to thirty-two weeks gestation, and noted that after the first week these babies 'seemed to engage in intentional action aimed at maximising contact with the hard surfaces' (1981: 453). She called this activity 'range-finding', in order to reflect its apparent purpose, which was to define boundaries. She noted that the pressure these infants exerted on the surface of their incubator was often enough to make their hand or foot turn white.

A premature baby's sleeping patterns are also different; they have less well defined cycles of deep sleep, which is thought to have a restorative function. Brazelton and Cramer noted that the occurrence of this kind of sleep 'is a sign of maturity and of good nervous system function in a disordered or high-risk baby' (1991: 64). These babies also have difficulty shutting out external stimuli, so that they are likely to wake rather than return to deep sleep when they go into the REM stage of sleep. Related to this is their poor ability to 'habituate', that is, they do not manage to shut off from stimuli like bright light and noise. Term babies will startle but then respond less and less. In Brazelton and Cramer's words, 'these infants are more at the mercy of environmental stimuli of all kind' (1991: 67). This observation seems to contrast with the observation that when handled or stimulated as part of assessment procedures, premature babies may initially withdraw to sleep, frown or, if able to, cry; when pressed, however, they often have catastrophic reactions, such as changes in heart rate or breathing pattern (Brazelton and Cramer, 1991; Gorski, 1983). This is in keeping with Patteson and Barnard's report (1990) that they have a limited ability to control their state, and in particular show less ability for self-quieting or consoling activities. What seems to be apparent, then, is that the infant may try to shut off from external stimulation, but often just can't manage it.

W. E. Freud, among others, has referred to the value of non-nutritive sucking; it 'probably plays a major role in safeguarding continuity of salient stimuli from intrauterine to extrauterine experiences' (1989b: 494). He has also referred to the infant's need to hold on 'in the widest sense' (1989b: 494), and suggested that something to suck might serve to help the infant to do this in the absence of mother.

> On several occasions a co-observer. . . and I offered a very sick baby who was in an incubator a finger to suck. More than once he rallied dramatically: he sucked with amazing vigor and became temporarily far more alert and coordinated than he had been before; sometimes this was accompanied by marked changes in the colour of his skin. Both of us had the distinct impression that his sucking was in the service of holding on, and we felt that the uninterrupted presence of his mother might have assured sufficient alertness for him not to give up and die.
>
> (Freud, 1989b: 494)

Interestingly, Freud refers only to the presence of the mother, and does not infer that the mother should necessarily handle the infant. This is in keeping with

Gorski's (1983) and Wolke's (1991) observations that some fragile infants react with adverse physiological responses to handling.

Patteson and Barnard (1990) have reviewed studies on the temperament of low birth weight babies. These studies are difficult to interpret, but apparently conflicting results can probably be ascribed to different populations under study. Thus, those which report no differences between premature and term babies seem to have focused on older and healthier premature babies, whereas those focusing on very low birth weight babies do support a difference, and suggest that these infants are 'at risk for temperament characteristics which may negatively influence parenting behaviours' (Patteson and Barnard, 1990: 39). A major flaw in these studies, which is difficult to overcome, was the use of parents as the main raters of temperament. Given the stressful set of circumstances surrounding the birth and early life of their children, it would not be surprising, for example, that parents might rate their infants as difficult to handle. Retrospectively, I have heard a lot of parents describe their teenage, formerly premature, children as stubborn, strongwilled and tenacious; and many will proudly attribute their child's resilience and ability to survive the neonatal period to these qualities, which are causing them (the parents) concern now that adolescence has been reached.

Knowledge about the capabilities of, and recognition of the existence of a subjective sense of experience in, these infants has many implications for their environment. On the basis of the outline given here alone, many adaptations could be made which would result in a better fit between the infant and the environment. These will be discussed in a later chapter.

Full-term neonates

As I have said, these babies are likely to be in the minority in a special care baby unit. Nonetheless, the environment will be artificial to them, and they will of necessity be separated from their mothers for much of the time. The characteristics of the sicker of these babies may be similar to those of premature babies for different reasons. Babies with congenital malformations, for example, will require life support in both pre- and postoperative periods, and this will usually be accompanied by significant sedation, which will mask their personalities and communications. Others, who are frail and fragile, may, like premature babies, be too weak to signal to their caretakers.

The hospital environment

The neonate's immediate environment in hospital is the incubator or cot; visual and auditory stimuli from the surrounding room contribute to the baby's sensory world, as do physical interventions from staff and parents, be they gentle touches or procedures of a more invasive nature. Richards has been critical of medical practice in this context:

Neonatology is characterised, by and large, by what Thomas McKeown ... has aptly called the engineering approach to medicine. Illness and disease are seen as disordered physiology, malfunctioning machinery to be repaired. Physiological functions are closely monitored, nowadays almost always by electronic devices. All the vital physiological needs, for warmth, for oxygen, for food are closely controlled – again, often by mechanical devices. In the incubator among the tubes and wires of the monitoring devices the baby is lost as a social being, to her or himself and to his parents. The baby is lost to him or herself because the first step in developing autonomy and so a social self depends on the association in time between the expression of changing need and their satisfaction by a caretaker.

(Richards, 1979: 38)

Others have also commented on how 'lost' and distant these infants seem, for example, Freud (1981), and Szur has noted a lack of 'liveliness' accompanying this:

Inside their incubators, and surrounded by complex machinery, the babies seemed also a little remote and alien. Certainly there was a feeling that the powerful impact of the benign lifesaving machinery might also contain a threat – i. e. of subduing the human liveliness of the people involved with it – the patients, their families, the personnel.

(Szur, 1981: 138)

This observation would perhaps, at first sight, seem to lend support to the lobby supporting stimulation of premature infants. Wolke (1991) has considered the debate about this issue – one group considers that the infant is deprived of appropriate extrauterine stimulation, while another believes the infant is overstimulated in the busy SCBU environment, and needs protection. He has concluded that in most cases the infant is inappropriately stimulated, that there is a mismatch between what is offered and what is needed. This is illustrated in a description by Chaze and Ludington-Hoe:

The infants in our unit were lying on plain sheets. We had hung brilliantly colored mobiles, but they were too far from the incubators, outside the babies' visual range. Pictures of faces were visible to staff and visitors, but *not* to the infants. A radio blared rock-and-roll music.

(Chaze and Ludington-Hoe, 1984: 68)

This particular mismatch probably impinges less on the baby than other attempts which involve the more active input of stimuli to the infant.

Recognition of and attention to an infant's wish to exert a choice on how much he or she has to do with the environment, and in particular, the caregiver, can lead to dramatic changes in progress medically. A specific example cited by Gorski illustrates this point very clearly:

One nurse had been singularly effective in feeding this baby, no one else could get him to suck feeds from the bottle. She alone avoided the aspirates and the vomiting that predictably accompanied feedings. In watching and talking to her, I learned that she disliked the infant. All the other nurses were strongly attached to the baby and, out of sadness and guilt, were trying harder and harder to act as normal parents to him. Whereas they provided as much contact and social stimulation as they could, this nurse clocked her obligatory ten minutes for feeding the infant while holding her hand away from the isolette, looking away from him. And the baby sucked and swallowed the entire bottleful. The baby's father taught me what he too noticed about his son. The infant would maintain eye contact with him only so long as he held him at arm's length. As soon as he held the baby close, the infant averted his gaze from his father's face, increased his respiratory rate, had unstable skin-color changes, and really looked distressed. By designing a care plan with respect to the infant's threshold for sensory overload, we soon effected weight gain, in addition to more positive social behaviors and coping mechanisms in this infant.

(Gorski, 1983: 258)

Daws has referred to the lack of choice these infants have: 'A good way to describe the situation is to say that the premature baby has no rights. He is impotent, unable to influence his world' (1989: 233). Unlike normal babies who have a preponderance of good experiences and develop an idea of predictability, premature babies have things happen to them at all sorts of times, and these things are often painful.

They have no control over procedures or the light or sound that bombards them. Newman (1981) monitored the noise inside the cots of preterm infants. Noise level ranged from sixty to sixty-five decibels, and this noise seemed to obscure certain frequencies and enhance others. Infants were noted, especially during the first week, to be continually aroused and startled by apparently random sounds, and it was hypothesised that this might cause unnecessary and clinically significant energy expenditure by the infant.

Nor do they have any control over the numbers of people who relate to them or for what length of time. Large numbers of caretakers are usually involved. Even in units where a key nursing system operates, infants may have contact with at least twenty different people. Richards (1979) has suggested that the conditions for caretakers to 'get to know a baby's individual patterns' and be 'ready and able to phase their behaviour with that of the baby' (1979: 39) are rarely satisfied. Jones (1982) reported that high-risk premature babies received direct contact care from staff for 6.1 hours per day. Most of this was related to the tasks around general or medical care, which were usually accompanied by personal attention; 3.8 per cent 'additional personal attention' was given. Among other things, the amount of personal attention each infant received was strongly correlated with the nursing staff's preferences among the group. These preferences were related to factors such as prognosis; ethical issues and the sense of success or failure; family–infant and staff–family relations; familiarity; and the accessibility of the infant. 'Preferred' infants received more nurturing and less impersonal care but also, perhaps not to their advantage, were played with if they were awake to the possible extent of sleep deprivation. This study provides some evidence to confirm a well-recognised but not well-voiced dynamic which probably occurs in all hospitals but perhaps more obviously on paediatric wards. In the case of babies, it may well be related to what I described earlier as adultomorphisisation.

Stern (1977) referred to this in the context of ordinary newborn babies. He considered that the early facial expressions of infants merited further study, and described their presence as 'provocative'.

> Any individual differences in facial neuromuscular integration from the beginning may help stamp the nature of ensuing relationships. A singular study bears on this point. Bennett . . . carefully watched the routine morning activities of newborn nursery nurses and their charges. He noted that most infants were quickly character-typed by the nurses, who rapidly and fairly unanimously dubbed one infant as a lover boy, naughty but lovable, and another as a 'simple nice girl, not sexy or flirtatious,' and so on. The nature of the nurses' interplay with each infant was strongly colored by how they saw his or her personality.
>
> (Stern, 1977: 43)

This attribution of personality or temperament may not only result in some infants being favoured but may also lead to imagined conflict with the baby as if it was a toddler, adolescent or even adult. Nurses and doctors sometimes talk about the neonates in a slightly different way from that described by Stern, ascribing them potency for their actions in a playful way, perhaps hiding dismay, anger or frustration. An example might be, 'That little so-and-so just won't take any milk for me', or more sinisterly, 'He's dropped his blood pressure again, the little bugger'. These expressions of frustration, or enactments of conflict, may serve as a release valve which then lets the carers get on with their job, or may be allowed to build up into a portrait of an awkward child, collectively painted and believed in by most of the staff group.

The issue of staff time for infants has been brought up in a different way by Campbell *et al.* (1983), who point out that some babies may be neglected. In their discussion about who should be admitted to special care units, they highlight the disadvantages of admission for well babies. The alternative for mature babies of being with their mother is not only more desirable from a psychological point of view but also from a practical one, as unit nurses will focus most of their time on critically ill infants.

The 'price' of neonatal intensive care

In a very subjective article on ethical dilemmas in this area of work, Relier describes the infant in intensive care as 'the distressed neonate: a human being at the cross roads' (1990: 49). Decisions about how much effort to make, and for how long to support the lives of critically ill infants, are not easy to reach. 'Withdrawing a neonate's life supports and limiting resuscitation efforts are amongst the most complex, tragic and stressful decisions faced by parents and physicians' (Jellinek *et al.*, 1992: 119). So, too, are decisions to maintain life, and of necessity inflict painful and stressful procedures on an infant. 'Technology and research have been driving forces in neonatal intensive care' (Bedrick, 1989: 451). Technological advances necessitate an almost continuous revision of the ethics of such decision-making, and the questions 'at what price?' (Bedrick, 1989: 451) and 'is it worth it?' (Blackman, 1991: 1497) will always have to be asked.

The price of intensive care is paid by the infant, the parents and the staff in these units. A small proportion of the huge number of follow-up studies of low birth weight infants will be reviewed later in this book. For staff, 'an unconscious desire must exist [there] to show that those long hours of effort devoted to the infants' early care have been supremely worthwhile' (Davis, 1989: 143). The price is also paid by society, of course. A number of the recent articles addressing ethical issues also address the financial cost of both intensive treatment and the later support of those who are disabled. This care is expensive but, to date, decisions seem to be made without taking this into account.

The attitudes of parents, doctors and nurses about 'active' treatment of low birth weight infants have been shown to differ. Lee *et al.* (1991) asked parents, paediatricians and nurses whether they thought that active treatment should be offered to potentially severely handicapped VLBW infants. Parents of both disabled and healthy children supported treatment, while doctors were divided in their responses. Interestingly, nurses were most opposed to active intervention; 71 per cent thought it unethical. Almost a third of the 53 nurses in the study objected to parents making treatment decisions, and many supported the use of the hospital ethics committee in advising clinicians directly involved on the making of such decisions. The main interpretation offered by the authors for the findings which related to nurses' attitudes in particular was that a lack of up-to-date information meant that there was a misconception about outcome and subsequent quality of life for survivors. Nursing staff tend to be involved with the infants when they are very sick and, unlike paediatricians, do not have the opportunity to follow up their charges.

This, I feel, is unlikely to be the whole story. Little attention was paid to the fact that it is nurses who are in the front line most of the time, and they who are likely, by virtue of that position, to both witness and be personally subjected to the stress and distress that comes with the almost constant life or death situation.

A number of authors have drawn attention to the anxieties and conflicts borne by staff working in a neonatal intensive care setting (Bender, 1981; Freud, 1981). Low morale can manifest itself in a number of ways, including absenteeism and sickness. It is probably precisely at those times that staff find it hardest to talk about their work and acknowledge the stress of their job. This stress is not only related to the task of directly caring for the neonates but also to how supported and appreciated they feel – by their managers, by the institution, and by parents. They often have to cope with parents' extreme emotional responses to their situation which may involve displays of direct hostility or anger, which are directed at them not because they are to blame but because the parents don't know what else to do, or who else to turn to, or on.

Oehler *et al.* (1991) have reported the results of a survey of neonatal nurses which was carried out in an attempt to ascertain the degree of job stress and burnout. The latter is manifested as:

> Low energy, chronic fatigue, weakness, and weariness are all characteristics of physical exhaustion, and feelings of depression, helplessness, hopelessness, and entrapment are characteristic of emotional exhaustion. Mental exhaustion is characterized by negative attitudes toward oneself, toward work, and toward life. Characteristics of mental exhaustion are detached concern for patients, intellectualization of stressful situations, compartmentalization, withdrawal from patients and co-workers, and reliance on other staff members for support.
>
> (Oehler *et al.*, 1991: 500)

All staff were found to be experiencing emotional exhaustion and feelings of depersonalisation, with some having high burnout scores in relation to their sense of poor personal accomplishment. Job stress was related to perceived lack of support, relationships with physicians, and the ethical dilemmas of the task, and was felt most acutely by less experienced nurses. A number of potential areas for interventions to reduce stress were suggested. Marshall also identified staff burnout as a serious problem, and suggested that 'if we paid more attention to neonatal pain, perhaps we would decrease caregiver burnout' (1989: 900).

Staff members are likely to cope with this stress in different ways. Some, for example, will probably deny or shut out their feelings, and consequently will be able to be enthusiastic in their approach, but a little insensitive to the emotional issues generated by the life and death nature of their task. For others, the job may be seen as merely that. Job satisfaction may be experienced as minimal but they will be protected from the extremes of emotion, often evoked by this particular kind of work. There is no doubt that some staff will, as a consequence of their commitment, find the emotional stress of their job enormous; they may become very closely involved with infants and their families at the expense of their own emotional well-being. Many, of course, will achieve a balance and manage their task with efficiency and sensitivity, providing an optimal level of support to infants, parents, and also their colleagues.

Sensitive and well-supported staff will appreciate the connection between the nature of their own relationship with infant and parents, and the infant's developing relationships. It may be difficult at times, and with certain families, to achieve the right balance here. Staff need to be sensitive to how the mother, particularly, interprets their involvement with the infant. For some mothers, the nurse may be seen as a rival or a threat to their own developing relationship, and extreme sensitivity is then required to support and encourage, without undermining. In other cases, the parent's lack of concern and failure to make appropriate overtures to the infant may leave staff with an overwhelming desire to 'mother' the infant in order to somehow make up for this bad experience. Some will believe that they are better carers than the parents (W. E. Freud, 1981), and again a sense of rivalry has the potential to inhibit the developing parent–child relationship.

The family

The birth of a premature baby is a shock for most parents and usually sets into motion a series of events, which include separation, anxiety about the baby's survival and development, and exposure to an unfamiliar area of medical care (Rosenblatt and Redshaw, 1984). Likewise, the birth of an infant with a congenital malformation or obvious early disability presents a complex challenge for carers (Klaus and Kennell, 1983).

In the context of the family life cycle, the infant's life-threatening illness occurs at a point in time when the parents are in the creative phase of their own lives. They may have already lost parents or grandparents through death but there is usually no expectation that their own lives or those of their children will be threatened. In the context of creativity and new beginnings, the challenge to each family member inherent in the infant's near-death situation is felt acutely.

The nature and course of the illness and its treatment have to be taken into account in any attempt to conceptualise the whole experience of each family. Rolland has considered the impact on families of chronic, rather than acute, illnesses:

> From the family point of view family systems theory must include the illness system. Further, to place the unfolding of [chronic] disease into a developmental context it is crucial to understand the intertwining of three evolutionary threads: the illness, individual and family life cycles.
>
> (Rolland, 1987: 203)

His proposed theoretical framework is also relevant to the conceptualisation of the stress of acute life-threatening illness. It seems particularly apt when considering the sick neonate. The onset of the illness is likely to be rapid, and to occur in some cases even before extrauterine life has begun. In such instances, the family are required to rapidly mobilise their own crisis management skills, and, as Rolland points out, this is in the context of highly charged emotional states.

Reactions to the crisis surrounding the infant's birth are related not only to the circumstances of the birth and the child's fragility but also to past events, which include those of each parent's own childhood and subsequent experience, their relationship with each other, and their dreams and phantasies about their unborn child. The effect on bonding of a premature birth has been reported in some cases to appear to be more related to the presence of family conflict than to the birth and subsequent events (Delucca et al., 1989).

Whatever the origins of the difficulties, there is no doubt that actually getting to know a sick or premature baby is a difficult task for parents. In addition to what they bring with them from the distant past, they are sharply confronted with their own powerful and sometimes overwhelming feelings each time they visit their baby. These feelings relate directly to the baby; that is, they not only have feelings about the baby but they also feel for, or on behalf of, their infant. Feelings *about* the baby are closely related to their own internal emotional state, so that as well as a sense of shared confusion, anxiety and helplessness, mothers in particular may also be preoccupied with memories of the birth, feelings of loss, and a sense of failure. Many parents will have been quite unprepared for the timing of the birth, while others will have been in a state of expectancy for some weeks or since the beginning of the pregnancy, even. In the case of very premature births, both groups will have had little expectation that they would have a live baby at the end of it. This, I think, is probably the case for a number of reasons. Human beings, especially those in the Western world, probably never like to anticipate the best outcome; a pessimistic rather than neutral stance is adopted in relation to both happy and sad events as a defence against the pain of disappointment and loss. Second, although much has been said and written about neonatal intensive care in a way that is accessible to the public, most people think 'it'll never happen to me' (Affleck *et al.*, 1991) and thus know little about what is possible in the situation facing them. People are very ready to sponsor charity events and pop some coins into a tin and then get on with their lives. Third, the events surrounding a complicated birth often take place at an alarming rate, with the consequence that communication is forgotten about, and parents are often in the dark about what the prognosis is. Mothers may often feel even more in the dark because the baby has been delivered under general anaesthetic. She may be afraid to ask whether the infant is alive or dead.

In the case of parents of babies who are very frail or more obviously disabled, it is not only the presence of the disability or the appearance of the baby that may affect how easy it is to get to know them but also the feelings aroused about others' expectations of interaction. Several authors have commented on this. Newman (1981) reported that some parents did not feel at ease handling their babies, despite, and I might add perhaps also because of, staff's encouragement to do so. They may feel compelled to handle their fragile infants, who may in turn react with adverse physiological responses (Wolke, 1991). Bender (1990) has observed that a mother's behaviour towards her infant correlates most highly with her personal perception of her infant's sickness. Nordio and de Vonderweid, among others, have drawn attention to the need to individually assess each parent's participation in the care of their child, recognising that some parents 'need "coping through commitment" while for others "coping through distance" may be preferable' (1990: 108).

The implications of this realisation are at least twofold. The first is the acknowledgement that if mothers, in particular, can feel in charge of themselves rather than helpless and out of control, they may feel more confident in their ability to relate to their own children. If they are given permission, as it were, to go at their own pace they will still feel anxious but perhaps less so than if they feel hurried or forced. They may already feel that they have been hurried or forced, by events and sometimes actually by obstetricians, to give birth too soon. This feeling may be felt even more sharply if the mother has had previous experiences of being rushed: ambivalently into marriage, for example, or into a pregnancy which was unplanned or the result of an unconscious attempt to resolve other difficulties, marital or more personal. A significant proportion of women in this situation will have had previous miscarriages or neonatal deaths, and may not have mourned these fully. Indeed, a number of women will have become pregnant again very shortly after the loss of a baby. For them, the sense of loss and failure related to current events may be muddled up with past loss. At a deeper level, some women may be reminded of a feeling that they had been rushed through their own childhoods. W. E. Freud has given a particular example of the sometimes complex link between feelings of failure and early development:

> On a deeper psychological level, unresolved conflicts from the time of the mother's toilet training may be reactivated: guilt and distress over not having been able to produce 'the right thing at the right time' add to her depressive feelings. With her confidence and self-esteem so shaken, anxieties over being and remaining useless may interfere with normal processes of mourning and recovery. . . .

(W. E. Freud, 1989b: 490)

Second, acknowledgement of the validity of each individual's or family's response to the situation may allow staff to address its meaning *for* them *with* them. Further, it may allow for a more appropriate 'fit' between staff expectations about their level of involvement and the family's actual capabilities. It may also lead to a greater understanding of, and more sympathetic response to, angry outbursts or apparent withdrawal.

The move in the world of family therapy to a reconsideration of the value of acknowledging family belief systems has contributed to a view that it is not just the family's history in itself which is important. It is the relationship between the history, the present, and the belief systems which holds the key to the conceptualisation of each family's, and each member of the family's, ability to cope. Thus, beliefs will have evolved in relation to past events and may be confirmed by current ones. Alternatively, the experience in the present may be so paradoxically opposed to a firmly held belief that the family may be thrown into a state of confusion by the ensuing conflict.

At its simplest, this is illustrated by a family whose experience of serious illness may have been that it was always fatal, that no matter what was done, the course seemed to be fixed and immutable. This may have led them to reaffirm or adopt particular religious or philosophical beliefs, which can be represented by fatalistic statements such as, 'what will be, will be' or 'it's all in God's hands'. Members of this family may have learned both separately and together to cope with the pain of loss by cutting off from their feelings, and also cutting off from any sense of their own competence or agency. Faced with a situation where their own responses may be literally vital to the sick member, they may remain distant and detached and await the hand of fate. Alternatively they may be thrown into a state of confusion and manage to recognise the disempowering nature of their own belief system. They may then be able to re-examine the past with different eyes, either on their own or with the help and support of friends or professionals. Making a different sense of the past may then help them to act in a different way in the present. This is a painful process and may result in more distress in the short term. Opting out of this re-storying of the past before a resolution is reached may result in family members feeling more fragmented and confused, and may contribute to them distancing themselves again. If they manage to rebuild their own defence mechanisms, they may be relatively unscathed, and if they don't they may become angry or depressed. Completing the task is likely to lead to them being more able to support each other, and their sick infant, and even if the infant dies, they are likely to be left feeling more satisfied about their own role.

Parents' experience of the special care baby unit

A number of researchers have asked parents, usually mothers, about their experience of having a baby in a neonatal unit. Some responses are probably particularly relevant to the unit in question in each case but there are also many common findings. As I have already indicated, mothers' feelings and actions in this situation are likely to be influenced by pre-delivery and delivery events, and when asked about their experience, many will in fact begin their story at a point predating their infant's birth.

Rosenblatt and Redshaw's study (1984) is probably exceptional in that mothers were asked about their initial experience in the unit *at the time*, that is, between four and seven days after their premature baby's admission. Many of their subjects had had little antenatal care, and a quarter had had previous experience of foetal or neonatal death or a requirement for 'special care'. Half of the mothers and three-quarters of the fathers had seen or touched their baby within the first two hours, but 10 per cent had not done so by forty-eight hours. Half the mothers and a third of the fathers had held their infant by the end of the first day but a quarter of mothers had still not done this by the fourth day because of the frailty of the infant. Not surprisingly, mothers tended to be much more involved in visiting and carrying out caregiving activities than fathers but fathers' reduced visiting was not found to be related to the presence of other children at home. Fathers who did take on the role of substitute caregivers were most likely to do this if the mother was too ill to visit. The authors commented that 'stereotyped attitudes about the paternal role are probably still too strong for a father to adopt a separate and competitive role by performing maternal duties when his wife is capable of doing so' (Rosenblatt and Redshaw, 1984: 240).

The babies in the study were evenly divided between those who had been delivered vaginally and those delivered by caesarian section. Half of the mothers expressed disappointment about their baby being born too soon, and this was most apparent in those whose infants were born at less than thirty-three weeks. Fathers were often less disappointed because their main concern had been for their partner's safety.

Most mothers were not unduly upset by the procedures being carried out on their infants as they could understand the rationale behind them. This was because of explanation at the time; few had any prior knowledge of the neonatal environment

– as in other centres, the visit to and discussion about the unit as part of antenatal preparation classes was covered too late to be useful to those who delivered prematurely. Mothers did, however, feel superfluous and inept, believing that they could have done more to care for their babies in the unit. The stress of feeling in the way was added to by a feeling that staff often dismissed genuine questions, and at times made insensitive comments. Lack of privacy and amenities were also commented on.

The authors of this study identified practices and attitudes which, in their view, might have led to either a sense of competence and well-being in parents or alternatively, by making them feel stressed or uncomfortable, led to their distancing and detachment, and as a result affected their developing relationships with their infants.

Many studies have addressed the experience in retrospect, seeking information about parental perceptions some time after discharge. Most have reported similar findings to those of Rosenblatt and Redshaw, identifying feelings of inadequate preparation, and memories of a bad experience of labour (Lissenden and Ryan, 1982). A sense of a lack of adequate information, reported in Lissenden and Ryan's study, was related to mothers' feelings that they had difficulty in understanding or hearing what was said to them, and this is likely to have been a reflection of their emotional state at the time. This study addressed a number of other areas. Most mothers reported mixed feelings towards their baby initially but by ten weeks most felt positive. Their anxieties predominantly concerned the baby's medical condition and weight. Seemingly more trivial issues were also identified as very important, and added to their sense of anxiety and confusion. Feeding was one such area; mothers found it hard to express breast milk – they felt inadequately informed about practicalities such as storage and transport, and a number felt distressed that their milk was not reserved exclusively for their baby. Staff comments about their efforts were also felt to be unhelpful. Stewart (1989) has commented on the powerful impact of the environment on parents. In her study, parents' memories of the unit were predominantly positive but a large number also commented on how noisy, crowded, uncomfortable, hot and smelly it was, and on the overwhelming impact of the sight of very tiny babies amidst the complicated life-supporting machinery.

The time of discharge home has also been identified as particularly stressful. The feeling of lack of preparation, and the burden of having to cope alone, often makes mothers feel quite distressed. Affleck et al. (1991) have reported that parents often feel more distressed then than when their baby is in hospital; they relate this to the intensity of their memory of previous events:

A compelling reason why a newborn's intensive care can have a lasting effect on parents' psychological well-being is that they re-experience this event in memory. Some of the participants in our study, including the mothers quoted next, volunteered that the distress ensuing from their memories even exceeded that which they had felt during their child's hospitalization itself.

'The emotional trauma of having your child in an ICU gets even worse after you leave it behind. When it's happening, nobody gives you a choice, nobody asks you if you can handle it or not. When you get home, and begin to remember it, that's when it hits you . . . the full awareness that she had just as much a chance of dying as living.'

(Affleck *et al.*, 1991: 99)

Relating the experience of parents in this situation to that of 'victims' of other traumatic events, the authors suggest that the persistence of these memories may represent continuing attempts at mastery.

In a very detailed and intricate study, Affleck *et al.* (1991) examined the responses of parents to their situation and correlated these with a number of outcome measures, which included the child's developmental outcome and the mother's emotional well-being. Seventy per cent of the mothers in this study had had no warning of a premature or hazardous delivery, and consequently had not only felt unprepared but had had their previously held beliefs and assumptions shattered. One of the authors' key propositions was that in this situation, mothers pursue meaning in an attempt to gain a feeling of mastery and control, which is then correlated with a good outcome, especially if benefits have been identified as arising from the crisis situation. The main implication from their findings, in their view, is that many families are able to cope with 'the crisis of intensive care' without professional help, and this ability is strongly linked to their sense of being in control, and their attribution of meaning to an initially incomprehensible occurrence. However, as they note, some will have a more difficult time. It may be that professional intervention should be aimed at assisting families in their pursuit of meaning rather than not offered at all.

Some specific issues for families

Nordio and de Vonderweid (1990) have referred to 'matters of fact' and 'ideas' in their discussion about the 'epistemology of perinatology'. They 'propose some "matters of fact" we have to deal with and some "ideas" we have to consider' (1990: 104). Their aim is, I think, to differentiate between aspects of the care of premature babies about which there is little choice, and those areas where the exploration of ideas might lead to a better psychological outcome for infants and their families.

It seems important to consider aspects of the experience for parents about which there is no choice, in particular, mother–infant separation, congenital abnormalities and disability.

It is interesting to note that parents themselves seem to make little comment about separation from their infants, even though in many cases this is for a lengthy period. They do, however, often acknowledge that they don't really feel that the baby belongs to them until the time of discharge from hospital. This is perhaps because separation is understood by parents to be essential in certain situations. The necessity for separation will be easier to accept in cases where the infant is dependent on life-supporting equipment for survival.

Much of the early research into the effects of early separation addressed the situation surrounding straightforward uncomplicated births, and led to appropriate criticism of some hospital practices. Recognition of the early adverse effects on the mother–infant relationship has resulted in changes, and full-term babies are now less frequently separated from their mothers in the period after birth. Separation of the very premature infant, of course, is not a matter of choice. There have, however, been changes in practice in this area too; for example, access by parents to their babies is no longer restricted, as it was previously, supposedly for fear of infection.

Richards (1978) has discussed the effects of separation in the context of admission of a baby to a special care unit. Early studies focused on separation as a factor in determining the developmental outcome for the child, and have probably been overshadowed by more recent studies carried out in the context of both improved medical care and policies of open visiting for parents. His points about the impact of separation on parents, however, are still pertinent.

Before the birth of a child many mothers have fears and phantasies that their baby will be abnormal in some way. Admission to a special care unit may serve to confirm these fears; and while increased anxiety levels have been associated with frequent visiting, lack of contact may serve to fuel phantasies about the baby's degree of disability or appearance.

> Occasionally, even when there are only a few minor problems, parents can become convinced that they have produced a grotesque monster, and may then stay away from the baby for fear of having their fantasies confirmed. Often when the baby is seen there is a sense of relief that he is not as bad as they had feared.
> (Richards, 1978: 26)

Mothers who distance themselves from their baby early on are likely to have difficulty adapting later. A separated mother is likely to feel far less confident about her ability to care for her baby, especially if it is her first. Also, her sense that the baby is a stranger is likely to lead to difficulties in interpreting her baby's communications and anticipating her baby's needs.

Richards considered 'that a *prima facie* case has been established that early separation has at least a short-term effect on patterns of mother–child relationships' (1978: 22). The evidence for long-term effects remains unclear but studies have reported links between infant ill health, early separation and child abuse (for example, Lynch, 1975). Douglas (1975) is one of the few who have considered the possible negative consequences of increased early contact with sick infants. In his opinion, parents who care for their children when they are extremely small and vulnerable may become overprotective and engender nervousness in their off-spring.

Some babies will, of course, have congenital malformations, which will not only put them in a life-threatening situation but may also result in disfigurement. These babies may be particularly hard to get to know for several reasons. First, the parents may distance themselves in order to try to protect themselves from the pain of a potential loss. Second, they will probably experience many of the psychological symptoms of loss in relation to their loss of a perfect and longed-for healthy child. They may become depressed and withdrawn as a result. Third, their baby's appearance may actually engender feelings of horror and abhorrence, which they will need help to overcome.

As Klaus and Kennell (1983) point out, two in every one hundred babies will have a major malformation. Parents in this situation often feel very alone, as if this has only happened to them and not to any other family. For families carrying gene abnormalities, each birth will have the potential to evoke feelings of disappointment and despair. The advent of antenatal screening for both malformations and genetic abnormalities has resulted in new dilemmas about whether or not to preserve the life of the foetus but has also offered opportunities for preparation and antenatal support.

Coming to terms with a baby's disability may take a long time but parents in this situation are often repaid for their commitment to their infants. After their initial feelings of shock, denial and despair, they are able to find the baby beyond the disability, and experience the rewards from the infant of their emotional investment. For others, the impact of a diagnosis may not be truly felt until years later. Many parents seem not to hear information offered about their baby at the time, perhaps denying the severity of the condition or unconsciously protecting themselves from the emotional consequence. Some parents will hear only bad news, no matter how balanced an explanation is given, and this may lead to outright rejection. This seems more likely if the infant remains particularly unresponsive even with maturity.

The individual factors which can play a part on how each family responds to the birth of each infant are many in number. Later in the book, I will review some of the follow-up studies which have included consideration of the child's developing relationships. Twin and multiple births, not yet mentioned, will be included.

The uncertainty of what the rest of the baby's life will bring means that the family may have to de-adapt at some stage, either to mourn or to allow themselves and their child to get on with living. Alternatively, they may have to continue to adjust to and cope with chronic disability. Those who cope with the crisis period well may have problems later on, perhaps especially if the child has no impairment. Their style of coping which was adaptive in the early months may be difficult to leave behind. The closeness, the nurturing, the protectiveness which have helped the child to survive may be inappropriate later on. For the families of those who have long-term sequelae, particularly of a life-threatening nature, such as severe epilepsy or bronchopulmonary dysplasia, the uncertain outcome or the inability to predict the future can lead to what Rolland (1987) calls 'idiosyncratic family interpretations'. 'The "It could happen" nature creates a nidus for both overprotection by the family and powerful secondary gains for an ill member' (Rolland, 1987: 205).

The impact of the 'special care' experience is not only immediate. Its consequences seem likely to be felt as each child grows up.

SUMMARY

Each special care infant has a unique history. Events before and around the time of birth, as well as the personal history and beliefs of each parent, will influence the baby's progress physically and psychologically. Uncertainty about what premature or disabled infants actually experience has been replaced to some extent by a growing body of knowledge about the important role which the environment, including relationships, plays in promoting development.

Both parents and professionals may experience the task of caring for a sick infant as very stressful. This may lead to exhaustion or, alternatively, to the erection of defences which act to deprive the infant of valuable and nurturing emotional contact. A family may need to adapt to a series of different challenges to their integrity as the baby's prognosis changes. The future may be uncertain. The 'fit' between hospital and family is important as problems or misunderstandings between parents and staff may have consequences for each one's relationship with the child. For parents, in particular, it is important that they feel that they know what is happening to their child.

Chapter 3

Holding on to meaning

In 1979, I was asked, as a fourth year medical student, to write an essay:

'The invasion of medicine by technology has resulted in the decline of the Hippocratic system. . . . Modern medicine is essentially Cartesian based on the assertion that Man is a machine.' Discuss.

This essay constituted the examination in the subject of clinical physics. It seemed to me at that time to be a rather crazy topic to base a *physics* exam on; however, it intrigued me, and with gusto I set about comparing and contrasting the Hippocratic and the Cartesian approach to medicine. In retrospect, the writing of the essay gave me the opportunity to punctuate my own experience as a medical student, and probably served to crystallise my plan for the future, which was to become either a general practitioner or a psychiatrist.

Ultimately, I chose the latter but it was not until much later that I came to realise just what the examiner was getting at. Of course, I've now 'learned' that there is no way of actually knowing this but the sense I make of it now is related to what I have read about 'new science'.

In this chapter, I will present some ideas from the world of 'new science' which are relevant to the search for understanding and meaning in human behaviour. The fields of medicine and psychology both provide the context for this research and are themselves under scrutiny. For the interested reader, this may shed some light on why I have chosen particular methods to find out about special care babies. A detailed account of these methods is presented along with clinical material in Part II.

Some ideas about knowing from the field of family therapy seem relevant to the subject under discussion, particularly because they permit the uniqueness of each person's experience to be acknowledged but also because possible solutions to the dilemma of how to hold on to meaning are offered. In addition, these solutions offer a way of acknowledging the validity of the different theoretical perspectives presented so far.

Science and research

In recent times there appears to have been a revolution within the scientific community. Historically, it is probably fair to say that in the Western world, the spirit of enquiry around from the very beginning of Man's existence became increasingly formalised in the wake of Descartes, who lived during the seventeenth century. For some reason, and I don't think anyone actually knows what that reason is, respectability within the scientific community became associated with a mechanistic and reductionist approach to knowledge. In some branches of science, researchers seem to have become quite obsessed with the idea that the truth could only be discovered by a rigid and perhaps dogmatic approach characterised by experimentation and microanalysis. The underlying premise was that there is such a thing as objective reality, and that that reality can be discovered. The search for reality or truth came in some areas to be characterised by breaking down the whole into parts. It was necessary to quantify differences observed and the respectable way to do that was to digitalise. By this, I mean that in some branches of science, it seemed that the idea that the whole might represent something in itself was almost discarded, and along with that idea went the acknowledgement that someone's, anyone's, view of the world might be valid in its own right, and that qualitative, and essentially subjective distinctions might be useful. These beliefs were particularly strongly held by those practising in the fields of the physical sciences but as Goldberg and David (1991) point out, those working in the field of social science have on the whole always conformed to a different belief system, more in keeping with a constructivist philosophy. This has been difficult, because:

> the physical sciences – including the new variety – are meant to deal with the most 'real' of worlds, [that] they are 'harder', more concrete and somehow more connected to the outer physical world. In our society 'harder', more concrete sciences are given more prestige than the 'soft', more ephemeral liberal or social sciences.
>
> (Goldberg and David, 1991: 19)

Within these different spheres, research is characterised in different ways. 'Diligent search or enquiry' or 'scientific investigation' (Irvine, 1956: 840) has been interpreted alternatively as 'the seeking of truth through experimentation' or 'the seeking of understanding through observation and description'. Both methods require a human or thinking component, that is, inferences have to be made at the end of the day, but it seems that in the realm of the traditional physical sciences, respectability has been associated with the minimalisation of the role of inference. It appears that the word 'scientific' has become associated in our society more with the experimental approach than with the descriptive. As Goldberg and David (1991) have said, the former has been given more prestige.

My own explanation for this, which perhaps represents my view as a psychiatrist, is that in the Western world, Man has responded to the anxiety generated by feelings of uncertainty by constructing an elaborate defence mechanism. Because we all share the anxiety evoked by our feelings of not knowing, we have come to adulate those who strive to define our world for us, and to offer concrete explanations for every part of it, and every event within it. Each of us feels comforted by the belief that there is an objective reality, it offers us some feeling of certainty, and some sense of security. The trouble is that when one firmly held belief, or the truth as we understand it, is then challenged or upturned by a new theory or explanation, it throws us into confusion. We become anxious and feel lost, and have to decide whether or not to stick with the old truth, or adopt the new version. Alternatively we might try to accommodate both truths but this is difficult unless we have a model in our mind by which to do so.

The revolution within the scientific community, which I referred to earlier, concerns the move away from reductionism and mechanistic explanation by physical scientists such as physicists, chemists and mathematicians. 'New scientists' believe that there is no such thing as objective reality, and appear to have joined their counterparts within the social sciences in adopting a constructivist approach. The relationship between science, the search for wisdom, and philosophy, the love of wisdom, appears to have come full circle. The writings of the ancient Greeks suggest a respect in that community for a holistic approach, and a belief in the necessity of a connectedness between what is known and how to know. In more recent times, science and philosophy have been viewed as the antithesis of each other, and their relationship has been characterised by hostility and antagonism. We now seem to have moved into an era in which they can be seen as more complementary, fitting together, coupling creatively rather than destructively. They might even be described as symbiotic. The process of research, or how we come to know about things, is as valued as its end products.

Science, medicine and psychology

Science has historically always been connected in some way to medicine. One might even say that medicine has traditionally been informed by science. Research and experimentation have led to an increased understanding of how the human body, including the brain, functions; and experimental methods have been adopted in order to ascertain the most effective treatments of certain conditions. The process of diagnosis relies heavily on a scientific approach, a history is taken and observations are made. The ensuing investigations of a more technical nature often represent the hypothesis-testing stage of the enquiry. Treatments too are sometimes offered in order to confirm or refute each possible diagnosis or hypothesis.

Psychiatry, a branch of medicine, has been characterised by a split between those following a more biological approach, who seek to treat psychological disturbance through the correction of the physical problem or chemical imbalance they believe underpins it, and those who choose to address either the behaviour presented, the patient's way of thinking or the hypothesised meaning of the symptoms through 'psychological' therapies. The latter comprises a heterogeneous group in terms of both the theoretical models of understanding and the treatments used. There are similar splits within the discipline of psychology but it is fair to say that psychologists on the whole have more in common with the latter group, which includes most child and family psychiatrists. As Kraemer has pointed out:

> Child psychiatry is a unique branch of medicine. In no other field is there such a variety of philosophies and methods. Furthermore child psychiatry is the most progressive in the use of the multidisciplinary team, so that even calling it a branch of medicine sounds odd to some ears.

(Kraemer, 1987: 1)

This group of psychologists and psychiatrists ally themselves with social scientists, and are likely to have been informed by research in that field. However, when it comes to carrying out research, it seems that many of them have in recent times been caught up in the struggle for scientific respectability, and have sought to apply experimental methods to their subject in an attempt to capture objectivity.

In this field, the debate about how to research, or how to know, appears in different guises throughout the literature. One example comes from the *Journal of the American Academy of Child Psychiatry* (1986) where the debate between Ferholt, Hoffnig, Hunter and Leventhal, and Garmezy exemplifies the issues involved. These authors were considering the area of disaster research, for which there were said to be three major approaches which represented a hierarchy of 'increasing sturdiness and sophistication in the level of scientific research' (Garmezy, 1986: 384) as follows: (a) clinical descriptive, (b) epidemiological, and (c) quasi-experimental. Different ways of resolving the tension between scientific method and clinical relevance were discussed. Two resolutions which were considered to be particularly 'debilitating' were the dismissal of all 'scientific' research as irrelevant, and the invalidation and rejection of many aspects of clinicians' experiences of complex phenomena on the grounds that they are irrational and unreliable. Ferholt *et al.* considered that the belief in 'the inherent supremacy of controlled experiment' (1986: 724) was still widely held. However, by its very nature, quasi-experimental research may only provide data of a more concrete or allegedly objective nature, in contrast to clinical descriptive research which may also take account of the subjective experience. The inference here, I think, is that in order to make sense of human experience, research in this area must include subjective appraisal, and not simply seek to measure what is observed. A more helpful resolution may occur if a broader view of science is adopted – 'scientific realism' then replaces reductionism on the grounds that descriptions at different levels of abstraction and complexity are not interchangeable. Each can be seen as making a meaningful or even valid contribution to the subject under study.

In a plea for a return to cultural or folk psychology Bruner, in *Acts of Meaning* (1990), has traced the history of the discipline. He has described the cognitive revolution which occurred in psychology in the 1950s. Its aim was to replace behaviourism with a more holistic and humanistic science which embraced anthropology, linguistics, philosophy and history. By his account, it seems that the new discipline took off in a different and rather unexpected direction. The initiative, from Bruner's point of view, seemed to backfire – 'From early on, for example, emphasis began shifting from "meaning" to "information," from the *construction* of meaning to the *processing* of information' (p. 4). Discussing the impact of this reductionist approach on psychology, Bruner has stated his belief that the subject 'has become fragmented as never before in its history' (1990: ix). He is critical of the way in which scientists have addressed the 'meaning-making process' and calls for 'venture beyond the conventional aims of positivist science with its ideals of *reductionism, causal explanation* and *prediction*' (1990: xiii). He goes on:

> The study of the human mind is so difficult, so caught in the dilemma of being both the object and the agent of its own study, that it cannot limit its inquiries to ways of thinking that grew out of yesterday's physics.
>
> (Bruner, 1990: xiii)

In his text, Bruner considered meaning-making in more depth, and, in particular, drew attention to the importance of language and narrative, as well as context.

Martin Richards is another standard-bearer for the cause of social or contextual understanding. Two of the many texts which he has edited are particularly relevant to the topic of this book. *The Integration of a Child into a Social World* (1974c) and *Children of Social Worlds* (1986) are texts in developmental psychology, which both have as their foundation the proposition that 'social context is, at a variety of levels, intrinsic to the developmental process itself' (Richards, 1986: 1). Richards himself stated that:

> all [the authors] share a fundamental common belief that the development of children cannot be understood outside the social context in which it occurs. The influence of this context has often been treated as an 'optional extra' in relation to a universal asocial developmental process, rather as icing is to a cake.
>
> (Richards, 1986: 1)

The latter text includes papers by historians and anthropologists, and La Fontaine (1986) ascribes this some significance, citing it as evidence of a changing awareness.

Ingleby (1986) has placed the first book in a temporal context, and has related its origins to the 'critical movement' which arose from within the discipline of psychology in the 1960s. Summarising its implications for developmental psychology, he stated:

> Basically the message was that science was not neutral but value-laden, and we did not like the values that it was laden with. The functions of developmental psychology were likened to those of psychiatry: following the model of 'anti-psychiatry', it was argued that psychologists were employed to bring children into line, to adapt them to their situations instead of vice versa, and to maintain a wholly artificial 'normality'. The goals of sorting, grading and straightening children out had deformed the vision of psychology.
>
> (Ingleby, 1986: 298)

In his discussion, he considered psychology's political context as well as its more general social context. Implicit in his arguments are notions of power and control, and this has various threads which include the issues of gender, class and race.

There are three main themes. First, 'in keeping with its task as an apparatus of social regulation, psychology was seen as propagating spurious norms of development: cultural values were presented as facts of nature' (Ingleby, 1986: 299). Here, he is critical of ethnocentric discussion of '*the* child, *the* family, or *the* mother–infant relationship' (p. 299), and notes that the approach to testing and measurement ignores the fact that any test is in fact simply a social construction. Second, he considers that properties of the individual had held a key position and as such had resulted in a blindness to cultural or social variables. The end-product of this approach was that individuals were seen to be 'blamed' for their condition or situation. Third, he suggests that a positivist approach had been associated with a denial of agency. 'This neglect of agency had helped to obscure the fact that growing up was not simply a matter of acquiring skills, but the site of complex political tensions between children, parents and the state' (p. 300).

The role of challenging the political motives of both those researching and those offering treatment within the human sciences has perhaps been taken on more openly by those writing about their work in the field of family therapy.

Contributions from family therapy literature

The literature in family therapy during the past ten to fifteen years has been littered with references to epistemology, most simply defined as the theory of knowledge. The attempts to resolve the conflict created by the simultaneous desire to adhere to a systemic viewpoint and attain scientific credibility have led to a sometimes confusing presentation of a range of theories drawn from the world of physical science and philosophy.

Historically the origins of family therapy lie in at least two different arenas. On the one hand, family therapy's roots, particularly in the UK, lie in the world of psychoanalysis, and owe a particular debt to the object relations theorists. The application of a psychoanalytic perspective to systemic family therapy is described clearly by Dare (1979). He suggested that 'in order to have an understanding of a family in sufficient detail to generate sensible foci, aims and technique for treatment, three frames of reference are required' (Dare, 1979: 138). These frames of reference are: conceptualisations of the life cycle stage of the family; the historical, intergenerational structure of the family; and the current interactional qualities of family life. In the US, family therapy's origins lie in the work of the communication theorists. The resulting style of family therapy tended initially to be pragmatic, that is, action rather than meaning-focused, and has taken various forms and names, for example, structural family therapy (Minuchin, 1974) and strategic family therapy (Haley, 1976). Both groups have developed and expanded their ideas, and have been influenced in particular by the work of the 'Milan group' (Selvini-Palazzoli *et al.*, 1978, 1980). The influence of 'Milan' and 'post-Milan' thinking on family therapy practice and research has been intrinsically linked to the philosophies of constructivists and social construction theorists, and the ideas emanating from the world of 'new science'.

The relevance of this to the area under discussion in this book is that these ideas seem to me to offer a model by which each level of interaction can be considered without losing a systemic perspective.

Threads of influence

As I have already stated family therapy has drawn on the research and writings of workers in different fields, which include anthropology, philosophy, linguistics and 'new science'. It is difficult to discuss the impact of each area in isolation as they have fed and nourished each other, co-evolving to reach, or perhaps almost reach, conclusions which are shared in parts but still remain true to their origins. In this section, I will present some ideas from these different areas in order to try to shed some light on current family therapy theory. This presentation is by no means intended to be exhaustive. It is also fair to say that I am personally more ready to 'believe' or commit myself to some of these ideas than others.

Bateson (1972, 1979) has offered us a number of ideas, which include the notions of context and circularity, patterns which connect, and the unity of mind and nature. He was concerned with trying to understand how we know about the world in which we live. At one level he saw this concern with how to know as the thing or the pattern which connected all living creatures (Dell, 1985). His crucial contribution to theories of knowledge and the understanding of meaning might be considered to be his notion of information as 'news of difference' (1979: 72), and as context-dependent; and his associated belief that the meaning of any communication is that ascribed by the receiver. This fits well with the view that participants each define their own world, that one cannot 'know' objectivity.

A similar position is reached by a different route by Maturana and his colleagues (Maturana and Varela, 1988; Mendez et al., 1988). As a result of their experiments in the science of cognition, they too concluded that 'there is no such thing as an objective independent reality' (Mendez et al., 1988: 146).

Hoffman has described the change which has had to be made in order to take on a constructivist mantle:

> Constructivism holds that the structure of our nervous systems dictates that we can never know what is 'really' out there. Therefore, we have to change from an 'observed system' reality (the notion that we can know the objective truth about others and the world) to an 'observing system' reality (the notion that we can only know our own construction of others and the world).
>
> (Hoffman, 1988: 110)

In a later paper (Hoffman, 1990), she talked about the difference between constructivism and social construction theory, favouring the latter as a theory useful for family therapy.

> Social construction theory sees the development of knowledge as a social phenomenon and holds that perception can only evolve within a cradle of communication. . . . [It] posits an evolving set of meanings that emerge unendingly from the interactions between people.
>
> (Hoffman, 1990: 3)

This position inevitably leads to an interest in language and social context, and fits not only with the approach of the Milan group who opposed the 'tyranny of linguistic conditioning' (Selvini-Palazzoli *et al.*, 1978: 51), and Cecchin, who later stated that 'it is impossible to be curious when we are "true believers"' (1987: 412), but also with the new second-order family therapy. The latter subscribes to the view that therapists must include themselves as part of the system, and part of what must change. The move away from a directive stance is an attempt to address issues of power and control implicit in the social organisation which separates families, with their problems, from the therapists, with their (value-laden) knowledge and solutions.

Keeney and Sprenkle (1982), who propose an ecosystemic epistemology, that is, a framework of ideas based on cybernetics, ecology and systems theory, have discussed the functions and constraints imposed by language. They have suggested that it is impossible to desist from linear, rather than circular, descriptions of events because of the limitations of language:

> owing to the structure of occidental language, there is no way of avoiding slicing the world into namable pieces. The naming of 'parts' consequently leads one to engage in some sort of dualism, even when one is attempting not to be dualistic.
>
> (Keeney and Sprenkle, 1982: 6)

Despite these constraints, we are bound to use language as our main way of sharing our view of the world, and acknowledgement of this led a reappraisal of systems theory and systemic therapy. Anderson and Goolishian (1988) were explicit in their rejection of a 'Parsonian' view of social systems, which 'implies that problematic behaviour, pathology, or deviance within components of a system represents inadequacies in role or structure' (p. 375). Instead,

> human systems are seen as existing only in the domain of meaning or intersubjective linguistic reality. In the domain of meaning, social systems are communication networks that are distinguished in and by language. That is, they communicate with each other, they are in conversation with each other.
>
> (Anderson and Goolishian, 1988: 375)

Underpinning their theory is a view that meaning and understanding are socially and intersubjectively constructed; that is, they 'refer to an evolving state of affairs in which two or more people agree (understand) that they are experiencing the same event in the same way' (1988: 372). The use of narrative exemplifies this way of thinking, and will be discussed further in Chapter 5.

How does all this tie in with 'new science' and constructivism? Taggart (1985) followed the story in the world of science from the old to the new; that is, from the point when 'true knowledge has been taken to be unconditioned and as such is its own (and only) context' (p. 118), to the point when truth was seen to be 'connected intimately with our ways of looking for it' (p. 118).

The 'new' systemic approach which arises from all this is characterised not by an abandoning of original ideas from systems theory but by an awareness that the boundaries and definitions of any system are where the members choose to place them. Context is similarly defined, not as something outside the system which can be ignored but as something which both influences and is influenced by the system. Taggart's explanation of this is as follows:

> System/context relations may be thought of as a function of the interplay between three closely related operations/concepts – punctuation, closure and boundary. The *punctuation* of a pattern by an observer is an act of *closure* which establishes the *boundary* of a system and, by the same act, calls the system's context into being and fixes *its* boundary. [Thus], the distinctions (models, theories, techniques, etc.) created by these operations are themselves methodological and provisional rather than real and permanent.
>
> (Taggart, 1985: 120)

When thinking about a special care infant's struggle to survive and grow, professionals can, if things are not going well, choose to draw a boundary around the family system. Similarly, parents may choose at different points in time to see the baby as belonging to the hospital. The fact is that infants in this situation are part of a series of ever-expanding systems which fit into each other rather like Russian dolls. There is a real danger that, in failing to acknowledge this, we ascribe blame or responsibility to a part of the whole, and fail to recognise the importance of context, and of relationships, at every level.

Co-constructivism

Rather strangely, it appeared that 'new' constructivist ideas had been taken on unquestioningly by some family therapists, who seemed almost evangelical in their desire to spread the news of their discoveries. Birch, referring to Maturana's work, has asked 'Why so little enquiry, so few questions?' (1991: 371) and offered some very valid criticism, not only of family therapists' acceptance of Maturana's work but also of the work itself. He also identified the dangers of an important systemic phenomenon, that is, the potential mirroring of the therapist–teacher relationship by the client–therapist relationship. What would happen if our clients accepted what we said without question? The issues relate to power and control. In his words, 'The debate is never merely academic, but always moral and political too' (Birch 1991: 372).

Speed (1991) has also discussed the impact of constructivism and social constructionism on family therapy. She proposed that some degree of realism was necessary. A pertinent example supporting this position is the recognition of 'real' abusive relationships within families. As she has pointed out, feminists in particular have been critical of a constructivist approach as it seems to deny the existence of 'real' violence. Similarly, it is important to acknowledge the reality of the special care neonate's life-or-death position, and later, the reality of the family's memory of almost losing a child. The idea that such a family is pathological because the parents are protective of their child, or because the mother and child have a very close relationship, is not helpful, and could be seen as a dismissal of their view of the world.

Speed, acknowledging that some of the ideas from 'new science' are helpful, has offered a position of compromise, co-constructivism:

> By co-constructivism is meant the view that what we know arises in a relationship between the knower and the known. . . . It takes for granted that a structured reality exists but recognises that that reality is constructed or mediated in the sense that different aspects are highlighted according to ideas that people individually or in groups have about it.
>
> (Speed, 1991: 401)

In her view, the implications of adopting this stance are twofold: first, we need to be aware of the influence of our own ideas on how we see things; and second, we have an obligation to carry out more empirical research, that is, to find out about the world out there.

Finding out about special care babies and their developing relationships is, of course, research. The compromise that I have reached in trying to hold on to meaning, and acknowledge the systemic nature of the subject under discussion is to try to see each piece of information *in* context and *as* context. Potentially each context represents a different logical level of meaning. I have found a particular theory useful as a model with which to consider how to reconcile different theoretical perspectives, and the different perspectives of the actors in the unfolding drama of the special care infant.

'The coordinated management of meaning'

The theory of the 'coordinated management of meaning' (Cronen *et al.*, 1982; Cronen and Pearce, 1985; Cronen *et al.*, 1985) has been presented as a possible model by which to conceptualise the structural complexities of hierarchical systems. In presenting their theory, the authors acknowledge an epistemological shift in the field of social science from reductionist thinking to the acceptance that social meanings are context-dependent. Two definitions underpin this theory:

1 Hierarchical Relationship: Two units of meaning are in a hierarchical relationship when one unit forms the context for interpreting the meaning and function of the other.
2 Reflexive Loops: Reflexivity exists whenever two elements in a hierarchy are

so organised that each is simultaneously the context for and within the context of the other.

(Cronen *et al.*, 1982: 95)

The property of reflexivity has the advantage of acknowledging bidirectional 'influence', but may lead to difficulties when trying to determine meaning. If no change in interpretation occurs regardless of which level is looked upon as 'higher' then a 'charmed loop' is said to exist. However, if the interpretation is different depending on which level is regarded as the context, then the loop is considered 'strange'. Some degree of reflexivity is common in hierarchical relationships, and indeed reflexive loops are intrinsic to the process of social interaction.

One of the most recent examples I have noticed of a strange loop was in a film when a famous screen nanny was putting her charges to bed. The children protested that they were not tired, and so she sang to them. The melody was that of a lullaby but the words told the children *not* to go to sleep. The higher level of context was the tune; if it had been the words, the message and the consequences might have been different.

The proposal that 'not all paradoxes are problematic' is fundamental to the theory, and as such represents a move away from earlier thinking, particularly that represented by the theory of logical types. The authors' main criticism of Bateson's work was that despite the theoretical consideration of multiple levels of learning and communication, Bateson actually only worked with two levels, namely, content and relationship.

The advantage of their proposed model is that more than two levels can be embraced – in fact five or six embedded levels of context are proposed. This series of levels may begin with *Speech acts* – 'these are the relational meanings of verbal and non-verbal messages' – and continue through to *Family myth* – 'this refers to high-order general conceptions of how society, personal roles and family relationships work' (Cronen and Pearce, 1985: 72). There can in fact be any number of levels of context or meaning. Each level is 'a place marker for a complex of information at a particular level of abstraction' (Cronen and Pearce, 1985: 72). They believe that analysis of relationships between levels of meaning depends on the availability of information about three or more levels. This is particularly important in relation to the topic of special care babies and their developing relationships, as one of the key concerns relates to the influence of higher level 'messages' on the mother–child relationship.

As stated, the mother–child relationship in the context of the child's admission to the SCBU represents the interface of two institutions, family and hospital, both of which may influence and be influenced by that dyad. The close examination of specified relationships in a small subsystem around that dyad may clarify some of the interactional processes at this interface, and may also raise hypotheses about the relationship of one institution to the other. Similarly, exploration of beliefs held at a family, institutional or society level may shed some light on other influences on the developing relationship.

Systems thinking and the research process

The concept of a truly 'systemic' model of research has been considered with scepticism (Goldberg and David, 1991) and confusion (Auerswald, 1987).

Auerswald considers that the confusion has been created by the 'strange loop' which has arisen from the merging of ideas from physics, from Bateson's model of evolution and from the work of family therapists. This loop refers to the conflict between the epistemologies of 'new' and 'old' science, the former embracing a both–and perspective, the latter an either–or one. The ability of the new science epistemology to permit (theoretically) the idea that there could be more than one reality allows it then to embrace the old Newtonian system as a paradigm within it.

Similarly, Goldberg and David resolve the dilemma of systemic versus linear by adopting a hierarchical model of explanation. Thus, a systemic theory at one level can be deconstructed to a number of discrete linear theories at another. This model effectively deals with a related dilemma, that between methods attempting to lead to 'neutral objectivity' and those with a subjective view. The latter, often associated with the participant observer stance, is said to result in the generation of systemic hypotheses. Interestingly, a recent study on parent–infant interaction has adopted a hierarchical approach to analysis (Fivaz-Depeursinge, 1991).

The concept of ambifinality is useful when trying to hold on to a systemic rather than a linear perspective.

> Any discussion of 'effects' or of how things work in a system is difficult using a language whose bias is linear. In a systemic epistemology, 'causes' are not distinct from 'effects' and the relevant variables cannot be 'isolated' without killing the system. An ambifinal cause is one whose 'effects' are 'context dependent' or 'contingent' on the state of the system in which it occurs.
>
> (Cronen and Pearce, 1985: 71)

It is not necessary to renounce objectivity, but it is important that what is reported is put in context.

Different perspectives on developing relationships

In Chapter 1, I presented some ideas about the development of relationships from different perspectives. It will be apparent that, depending on whose theory we choose to adopt, we might be more preoccupied with some things than others. A Freudian perspective, for example, will leave us feeling very preoccupied with the infant's inner world, while a developmental psychology perspective would lead us to notice features of the dyadic interaction. Depending on whose account we were reading we might find ourselves acutely aware of the race, class or religion of the participants. Most of us probably notice all of these things. In order to permit each theory the same validity as the next, we can consider them in a hierarchy of meaning, which extends from the molecular level of brain functioning through inner world to dyadic, triadic and tetradic relationships, to family and institutional beliefs and to social context.

Similarly, we can observe or listen to different people's accounts about different levels of meaning without having to enter them into a competition with each other. We can allow each its own validity. Our own sense of meaning at the end of the day will be determined by how we choose to fit these pieces together – different participants' contributions might be fitted together like a jigsaw, while information at different levels of abstraction might fit together as a sort of tower. The choice is ours. The point I am trying to make is that one view does not need to be either true or false. We have more chance of holding on to meaning if we refrain from disqualifying some of the contributions.

Of course, the idea of rapprochement is not new, particularly in relation to the schools of psychoanalysis and developmental psychology. The application of an integration of these two viewpoints is probably exemplified by the contemporary practice of child psychotherapists.

Bentovim (1979) considered the possibility of integration in this area favourably but also noted that this was in the face of considerable opposition. However, with the move in child development research to consider the impact of the infant on the caregiver, rather than the impact of the caregiver on the infant, he felt that 'Child development research may well need a set of theories which focus on the subjective phenomena of the experiencing infant to lend a structure to the numerous observations now being described' (Bentovim, 1979: 99). Bentovim identified the use of a cognitive–affective model of development by both groups, which was labelled in different ways. Both groups have also focused on how experience, and especially experience of relationships, acts as a guide for future relationships, and for the development of autonomy.

Urwin (1986) has also tried to reconcile the differences between developmental psychology and psychoanalysis. Like others, she has identified the apparent opposition of these theories, this seeming to be related to different purposes and populations, 'and different assumptions about methodology and scientific truth' (Urwin, 1986: 257). She has also noted, however, that 'considerable borrowing' (1986: 258) has taken place between the two traditions. The shift in emphasis by developmental psychologists to consideration of social context does seem to bring it closer to a broadly psychoanalytic view but, in her view, 'it may require some effort of introspection to perceive a relationship between emotionality and human reasoning' (1986: 265). In contrast, a psychoanalyst would see an intimate connection here.

Urwin has identified complementarity as well as opposition, for example between the work of Piaget and psychoanalytic theory. This complementarity seemed to be taken for granted earlier this century but later, as developmental psychology developed as a discipline in its own right, appeared to get lost. The rediscovery of potential areas of mutual investigation, as described by Urwin, leads to a conclusion that the time for rapprochement is right, and may give both schools the opportunity to offer something to the understanding of the young child and its developing relationships.

The work of Stern (1985), among others, has done much to further the 'fit' between these two particular viewpoints. In a more recent work, Stern (1990) actually presented the world of a young child as he developed, in narrative form. In doing so, he tried to represent in language the inner world, the subjective world, of the preverbal infant.

More recently, systems theorists have tried to 'fit' with developmental psychologists in their search to understand the effects of relationships on relationships (for example, Hinde and Stevenson-Hinde (1988)). Donley (1993) has been critical of attempts so far to approach attachment in a systemic way. She has proposed that the triangle be considered as the basic building block of the emotional unit, rather than the dyad or triad (which she dismisses as a group of dyads). In presenting her case, she has drawn attention to the potential loss of the notion that a system is more than just the sum of its component parts. It does seem essential to hold on to this idea and allow it its validity too. This may be possible within a hierarchy of meaning.

In Chapters 4 and 5, I will focus on two methods of receiving information which seem more systemic than others: the first is the method of psychoanalytic infant observation, and the second is listening to narrative.

SUMMARY

Historically, scientific respectability has been associated with a mechanistic and digital approach to research but more recently, the validity of each person's experience has been recognised and has heralded a re-evaluation of descriptive research. The 'new science' idea that there is no such thing as objective reality is complemented by the acknowledgement of the importance of real events, such as a baby's admission to a special care baby unit, and their often traumatic effects.

A hierarchy of meaning in which different levels of context are seen to be in a complementary relationship offers a way of fitting together different theoretical perspectives on the special care infant. It also offers a way of acknowledging the importance of inner world experience, relationships, and wider historical and social context.

Part II

A clinical perspective

Chapter 4

Observations in a special care baby unit

IN SEARCH OF AN ECOLOGY

The complex nature of the developing parent–child relationship in the 'special care' situation has been emphasised by a number of authors. Jones (1982) considered that the diversity and arbitrary differences in intervention programmes for premature infants, and the conflicts regarding an appropriate model for such programmes, indicated a lack of understanding of the ecology of premature infants. This has been reiterated by Wolke (1991), who has emphasised the need for descriptive studies of the NICU environment prior to intervention evaluating research. Observation studies of an anthropological nature have been carried out in an attempt to provide a more whole and meaningful picture of the neonate's environment (Newman, 1981; Jones, 1982). However, it is more often the case that studies of the special care environment have focused on measurements of one sort or another and, while producing interesting information, have tended to paint an incomplete picture. Psychoanalytic infant observations have been carried out in neonatal units in the context of, and to inform, therapeutic work, and have been noted to be very useful but painful experiences (Freud, 1981; Earnshaw, 1981).

During 1991, I was privileged to be allowed to spend time observing infants, alone or with staff and family members, in a special care baby unit. My aim was to somehow get a feel of what was happening in the unit, and of what the experience might be like for babies and their mothers in particular. Staff, who were a little puzzled by my motives, said that they did not have the time to simply observe, and indeed it was my experience that they rarely stood still. They made comments such as 'It looks really mad – just sitting there watching' and 'I don't know whether to talk to you or not'. On the whole, however, staff seemed to be able to ignore me for most of the time.

During my training at the Tavistock Clinic I had carried out an infant observation, and I wanted to observe and record my observations in the SCBU in a similar way. I thought that this method might help me to hold on to meaning.

What is psychoanalytic infant observation?

A number of authors have written about psychoanalytic infant observation, describing what it actually involves and what actually happens; but few have 'defined' it. This seems to be a hard thing to do without losing some of the sense of the process. Waddell helpfully summarises some of the key features when she states:

> The practice of infant observation derives from a particular way of seeing; one which links the analytic process to the observational method initiated by Esther Bick. . . . It is a method with no claims to impartiality or objectivity. Rather the reverse, it is rooted in subjectivity of a particular kind – with the capacity to look inward and outward simultaneously (an aspect of character described by Wilfred Bion as 'binocular vision'); one that struggles to prevent observation being clouded and distorted through preconception. It is a method which requires the observer to be as minutely cognisant of his or her internal processes as those of the subject of the observation. The method reaches to the heart of the analytic relationship, making particular demands, which are well-expressed in Keats's notion of 'negative capability' – the capacity to be in doubts and uncertainties, not to reach after irritable fact and reason.
>
> (Waddell, 1988: 1)

Infant observation has been an integral part of the training of both child psychotherapists and psychoanalysts for many years. Esther Bick, initiator of infant observation at the Tavistock Clinic, thought it was important for a number of reasons, 'but mostly because it would help the students to conceive vividly the infantile experience of their child patients . . . they would get the feel of the baby that he was and from which he is not so far removed' (1964: 240). Margaret Rustin summarises the rationale for devoting so much time to this activity as 'learning about early emotional development – that is, about the actual baby – and also learning from one's own response to the observations' (1989: 8). Emotions aroused in the observer are important, and should not be regarded as 'a distraction or contaminant' but rather 'an indispensable tool to be used in the service of greater understanding' (Miller, 1989: 3).

The aim of this method is to provide material from personal experience in the observation setting which can be thought about in terms of its emotional significance. It should include a detailed account of what is happening, and sensitive descriptions of the feelings of the participants, including the observer. Supervision, by which I mean later presentation and discussion of the data with a particular analyst or psychotherapist, is crucial in relation to this method, as the observer is freed from having to interpret the data immediately. Subjectivity and a 'neutral' perspective are important but nonetheless the observer, of necessity, approaches the task in a focused way, with some preconceptions and preoccupations. Michael Rustin considers these shared preoccupations, and includes the following:

Interest in the baby's bodily sensations and experiences, which are seen as the basis of its emerging emotional and mental state.

The nature of the baby's relationship with its mother in the first months of life, especially in relation to feeding, but including the whole range of infant care and comfort.

The process of weaning and its meanings for mothers and babies.

The development of the infant's capacities to express and explore its states of mind symbolically, through play, especially in relation to weaning and tolerance of mother's absence; and to the growing awareness of the wider family context.

The mother's reaction to the impact of a new baby and its demands, including the ways in which she may experience her baby as dissatisfied, distressed, enraged or rejecting.

The states of mind and feelings of siblings, especially young siblings, and how they impinge on the experience of baby and mother.

The mother's relationships with other significant adults around her, especially the baby's father, and sometimes her own parents, and ways in which they may provide a supportive context for the early months of childcare.

(Rustin, 1989: 58)

Some of these particular foci are clearly not applicable to the observation of infants in an intensive care setting but are useful to have in mind later.

My own preoccupations included an interest in the baby's bodily sensations and experiences. However, in considering the nature of the mother–baby relationship, it felt inappropriate to use feeding as a key indicator of the quality of the developing relationship, as I had quickly become aware that the feeding of these babies was often a fraught issue. Feeding was not forgotten but there were many aspects to be considered, including the actual nutritional status of the baby; and while true weaning was obviously not an issue with these babies, they *were* being 'weaned' off tube-feeds and on to bottle or breast. They were also being 'weaned' off ventilators and other means of physical support. The mother's way of talking to or about her baby helped me to get some sense of the relationship, as did aspects of gaze and physical holding or touching, her apparent perceptions and attributions of meaning when the baby was distressed, and her reactions to demands. The mother's interactions with other adults were noted, and in the special care setting these included nursing and medical staff as well as other mothers and family members.

In the next part of this chapter, extracts from observations of four particular babies are presented. I have included some information about the context; a fuller story will be told in the mothers' accounts presented in Chapter 5.

OBSERVATIONS

Alan

This baby was born at 26 weeks gestation very suddenly and unexpectedly, to Ms A, a single 20 year old woman. On the day of the birth she was with John, and he accompanied her to the hospital and was presumed by the staff to be the baby's father. It was only much later that the error of this presumption was appreciated.

These are extracts from a first observation at seven days old.

A young couple are sitting at the cotside – she is holding the baby's hand, by putting her little finger in his palm and gently pulling up and down. She looks very pale and nervous, shocked, I think. He looks more solid somehow, kind, supportive, firm. I introduce myself and tell them about my wish to observe. They both nod, the man smiles. They look at me only briefly as they respond, mostly they're glued to looking at the baby. She puts her finger back in his hand, and comments on how strong he is.

Later – the parents have gone.

Alan is lying on his back, head turned to the right, he has a gauze hat on, there is a ventilator tube in his mouth. His eyes are shut. He has a Pampers nappy on. His arms and legs are very spindly and bluish, he has a splint and a drip on his left arm and on his right leg. His fingers seem very long.

He does not lie still for more than a few seconds. Every part of him is moving, his legs twitching then kicking out. His right hand in particular is always on the go. He seems to be trying to hold the tube in his mouth. The hand repeatedly moves up to touch, almost grasp it, then moves away again. He occasionally waves the arm across his body or makes a grasping movement down at his right side. His other splinted arm waves occasionally.

There is a bright yellow teddy in the corner, otherwise nothing personal. He wouldn't see it even if his eyes were open.

His mouth moves a lot, he seems to be trying to suck the tube, it moves round it in a goldfish sort of way, almost like a baby trying to mouth a nipple. He gives three long yawns – his mouth wide and his whole body stretching out. He frequently flexes and extends his toes, and his left leg is often pulled up and across the other leg. It feels as if he wants to roll over or at least be on his side.

The unit is very busy. There is music playing – Rod Stewart's 'Maggie May' followed by Shirley Bassey singing 'Big Spender'! At one point a lot of different things seem to be going on simultaneously. Staff are gathered around another baby's cot and seem rather frantic in their activity. A cleaner comes and goes. Others too. Questions fly across the room. There is a lot of noise. I wonder how much he hears, he seems to be wincing in response to the hullabaloo, or is it just my imagination?

Comments

It's difficult to know what to make of this baby's own experience of what is happening. What do all these little movements mean – the twitching? Is this irritability related to the immaturity of his nervous system; or is it the same as the little fluttering movements that come between the 'kicks' that a pregnant mother feels from her foetus? And what of the mouthing? *In utero* this baby would be taking in and peeing out the amniotic fluid – he would be beginning to know about swallowing; he might even be sucking his hand or fingers. Later on in life, developmentalists refer to nutritive and non-nutritive sucking. It is well recognised by all parents, and children themselves, that sucking fingers, a thumb or a dummy is satisfying and calming. 'Ordinary' babies begin to do this before they are born, and one could guess that it serves the same function then. This fragile baby who is not able to breathe for himself is intubated with an endotracheal tube; that is, he has a *huge* piece of plastic pipe stuck in his mouth. What comfort does that give him? His mouthing may represent a persistent attempt to gain oral comfort. It does not seem coincidental that he moves his hand up towards his mouth frequently. The medical care necessary to keep him alive in this alien environment acts like the restraints used in former years to stop thumb-sucking, and one wonders about his sense of frustration at this. He has moved from a dimly lit, quiet, free-floating, almost weightless environment where he has been free to move – to stretch, to touch himself, to comfort himself – to a brightly lit, noisy place where he is restrained. His strength is weak, his muscles are not ready yet to counteract the effects of gravity the way a full-term baby's are. He is helpless.

There is a question of what information such a short piece of observation can provide about the developing parent–child relationship. Yet even in this snippet, there is a sense that this mother is trying to reach her baby, to make contact with him. I feel that she is looking for some response as she jiggles his hand up and down. She is clearly preoccupied, and this preoccupation seems to be with Alan. At the same time, she seems as if in a dream. Indeed, this is what it probably feels like. People who have been bereaved or suffered a trauma often refer to the first weeks or months after the event as dreamlike. They try to wake themselves up; they think that what is happening is not real.

Research by Murray and her colleagues (1991) supports the idea that a mother's way of talking to or about her baby provides a key to the quality of the developing relationship. This mother is proud of her baby's strength, and her ascription of a sense of potency or agency to her infant is important.

Mother's partner is not in such a dream-like state – he is more solid somehow. There is a clear sense of what his role is from the way he is, his position there beside the mother. He seems to be attending to both mother and child, providing a support for her in her fragile state, and validating her observations and sense of knowing about the baby.

In this observation there is a real sense that special care babies, and this baby in particular, are not immune to what is going on around them. It's impossible to 'know' this, of course, but I know that the noise has an effect on me, and I imagine that this baby's wincing is related to the impact of the noise on him. I perceive the hullabaloo as a stress rather than a comfort. I am very aware of how the music fails to tune into the baby. By that, I mean that synchrony is important. Stern (1977) describes, for example, mothers who without noticing talk in synchrony with their babies' movements. They give the baby a rhythm, either with their voice or with their hand as it strokes theirs, they both alert and soothe, they lend meaning to the baby's experience. Some music is thought to be soothing in itself; somehow I don't think it is this sort of penetrating pop.

This is an extract from an observation at 103 days old.

I'm observing Alan when his parents arrive. 'Dad' tells me that he's had some setbacks, '*They* thought they were going to lose him a few times but he's made it.' Mother comes over, looks at Alan, rubs his cheek and then looks at the monitor.

We greet each other, and she offers to show me the photographs. She takes me through them – they're all there from three days to one hundred. She seems proud but sad: 27 days – his christening; 51 days – he's doing really well at this stage, he's having his first proper bath; a few weeks later – sitting up in his ventilator box, puffy faced, with toys around him, smiling she says, eyes wide open; 95 days – he has been intubated again. Then his 100th day birthday party, they both show me his cards and toys. I say that I'm sorry to hear that they've all been having a difficult time. '*We* didn't think he was going to make it' she says, 'but he always fights back.' I ask her how she thinks he's managing it all. She says she doesn't know, but makes reference to the fact that he's sedated.

Alan looks calm, his eyes are shut and he is still. He has a little hat on, and gloves, a blue one on one hand and a white one on the other. He is covered with a small patchwork blanket. I move back trying to regain my position as observer, and end up standing over to one side of the cot in a place where I can watch the baby. 'Dad' sits on a chair next to the cot.

A nurse comes over and starts to look at Alan's charts, chatting to his mother as she does so, asking how she is and continuing the conversation from there. Her manner is bright and breezy. Ms A shows her the photos. The nurse goes a bit over the top I think, and I feel uncomfortable. 'Oh, look at that,' she says and laughs raucously. Another nurse approaches and says something that I don't catch. 'Ms A knows that I always laugh,' the nurse replies. Ms A is busy sorting Alan's covers in a sort of absent-minded way; she smiles quietly but then over the next few minutes her demeanour changes markedly.

She looks agitated and seems not to be able to be still. The nurse leaves, and Mother's partner offers her a seat which she declines. She's standing not sure what to do; she reaches over and rubs the baby's cheek again, then leaves her hand resting next to his head in the cot. The nurse returns and, as if debating with herself, announces that no, she won't suck him out just now as he's sleeping and everything seems OK. She goes off to a meeting.

Mother stands with her back to the baby facing the monitor and her partner. She still has her hand in the cot behind her. She seems transfixed by the monitor – they are talking quietly and earnestly. He moves over to look at the charts. She does so too. She presses some buttons on the machine, and continues to watch it. She glances occasionally at Alan. He's lying mostly very still and calm. He occasionally wriggles, and his hand reaches up to his tube as if to pull it out. Then he is still again. He doesn't open his eyes.

Mother suddenly starts to rub his chest, then bangs it, six quick slaps in rapid succession. She is not looking at the baby but at the monitor. Again – rub-rub, bang-bang, then stops. They both look worried. She takes her hand out and fiddles with the machine again, then puts it back on his chest, gently this time. She quietly pats him and watches the monitor.

He tells me that the reading is supposed to be more than 90. I continue to watch them watching the monitor. Alan is quiet and still, oblivious to this, his ventilator pumping away. His mother in particular is glued to the monitor and responds to every swing with vigorous rubbing or banging on his chest. This seems to work, but his heart rate and oxygen saturation levels are certainly not stable. The latter goes down to 64, 70, 68 – frequently. *I* feel worried. I say, 'Should you tell someone?' Mother says 'Yes' but stands for another few minutes doing the same as before. Then she purposefully strides over to a nurse and tells her. The nurse looks over and says that Alan looks all right just now – she'll come when she's finished what she's doing. When she comes, his reading is 80. They tell her how low it's been, rather desperately. I suspect they think that she doesn't believe them.

The nurse looks at him and then reviews his charts, then says something. She gets out a plastic cup-like thing and percusses his chest with it very vigorously. His heart rate reading seems very high, I guess that that's not a true reading and probably just reflects her activity, but I'm not sure what the parents are thinking. Then she puts a tube down his throat and 'sucks him out'. He doesn't really respond to any of this, he must be heavily sedated. There's not much sputum or aspirate. The monitor is going crazy. The parents are transfixed. The nurse stops and disconnects the suction tube. Mother asks her if she wants the suction machine switched off. She does. She says that she thinks that will be better; Alan's oxygen saturation level is registering on the machine at about 80. The parents continue to watch the monitor. Alan makes a big stretching movement and wriggles a bit. They don't notice. After about five minutes they leave.

I watch Alan for a further ten minutes. He seems very tranquil and his oxygen saturation level occasionally reaches 94. I leave reluctantly as I feel that someone should be watching over this particular baby.

Comments

With the review of photographs at this visit, Ms A has somehow managed to telescope her own, her partner's, and especially her baby's experience into a few minutes. Alan is now three and a half months old, and he is almost back where he started. He looks very different, he is bigger and looks more like an ordinary term baby in some ways; but he's also very puffy as a result of the steroid treatment he has been given to assist his breathing. There have been two important dates in the last week. The first date, his expected date of delivery, has passed quietly, and the second, his one hundredth day, has been celebrated by his parents, the staff and the parent support group, who sent a present. During his short life attempts have been made to wean this baby from his ventilator. Gradually, he has been allowed and encouraged to breathe by himself. However, he has not managed this step towards independence. In the week prior to his party, he had to be reintubated as he became unable yet again to breathe on his own.

Ms A appears sad, the strain of the last three months shows on her face. She seems subdued and a little empty in response to my question about how Alan is managing. Yet, she is here, by his side. There have been times when she and her partner have visited less regularly but there is no doubt that they continue to be devoted to the baby. At different times before this visit, I had noticed that their use of language seemed to reflect how close they felt to Alan, and perhaps even gave an indication of who they thought he belonged to. In this observation, I am immediately struck by 'Dad's' use of 'they' – 'They thought they were going to lose him'. Alan's mother, on the other hand, says 'we' – 'We didn't think he was going to make it'. These slips of the tongue seem important; he may not have wanted to associate himself with the seriousness of the situation, or may not feel that the baby really belongs to him.

The observation offers an opportunity to observe two episodes of nurse–parent interaction. In the first episode, the nurse enquires how Mother is, and I find myself feeling pleased – the focus is not just the baby, the nurse wants to know about Mum too. My pleasure changes to a feeling of discomfort and perhaps despondency when I realise that this nurse is so cheerful that it would be hard for anyone to say how they really felt. She is perhaps trying to be cheering as well as cheerful. I am not sure how the parents feel. Their infant is critically ill, it is not a very cheerful time, although there have been happy moments during the last three months. Ms A is quiet, responding to the nurse with a smile but also diverting her attention from her to first the baby and then the monitors. I am not sure whether she trying non-verbally to encourage the nurse to focus on Alan or trying to shut her out. Perhaps neither. I wonder how attached the nurse is to this baby; her laughter may be hiding her own sorrow.

The next sequence of events seems to last an eternity; the atmosphere is emotionally charged. Mother's increasing agitation and concern is related to the baby's oxygen saturation readings. Briefly, her worry seems to lead her to focus directly on her baby as she rubs his cheek. Quickly, however, her whole attention becomes centred on the monitor, and in response to what she sees there, she rubs and bangs his chest. She is not able to look at him to see how he is but instead is transfixed by the monitor. I felt that these parents must be expert in knowing what to do in relation to their child on the unit. I didn't question at the time whether the rough stimulation was appropriate, although I did feel alarmed by what was going on to the extent of almost suggesting that they should consult someone. Later, I wondered – this was the only mother I saw doing this. Afterwards, I thought even more about what I had seen. This baby's saturation levels didn't often jump about like this, although they were often on the low side. Is it possible that this mother transmitted her anxiety to her baby? Instead of bringing the infant back towards a steady physiological state, as intended, did her actions in fact knock him further off balance? Research into neonatal stress has shown that both invasive procedures and handling, for example when nappies are changed, are accompanied by decreases in oxygen tension (Field, 1990a and b).

The next episode of nurse–parent interaction is very clinical. I'm not sure if, again, this nurse is very attached to Alan, and is finding his critical condition hard to manage. Or is she just very busy? Or fed up with these parents? Or perhaps she simply doesn't know them very well? Whatever the reasons, I feel that her efficient way of dealing with the situation, and brief reassurance, serve to make this young woman and her partner feel more vulnerable. I note that rather than stay to see what happens next, the couple leave. I feel as if I have been left to watch his monitor, and I oblige.

Daniel

This baby is the second child of Mrs D, an Irish woman, separated from her husband and currently living with her sister. He was born at twenty-nine weeks by spontaneous breech delivery. Her first child, now fifteen months, was also premature.

This is an extract from an observation at ten days.

Daniel is in an incubator. He's wearing a white baby-gro, very white, he has a tube in his nose for feeding. He is lying on his back with his eyes wide open, he has a shock of very blond hair. I am immediately struck by how cherubic he looks, how like a 'real' baby. He seems to look much older than some of the other infants I've seen of the same gestation. His mother is very close, and has both hands inside the incubator. She hovers for a moment and then touches his arm gently. 'I think he's going to be sick,' she announces, to me, I think, though we haven't even said hello. I am surprised that she has noticed my presence.

I introduce myself and explain my purpose. She smiles welcomingly but says again, 'I think he's going to be sick. Just a minute and I'll turn him over'. She opens the incubator and turns him on to his side. She gently rubs his back, 'It's all right, it's all right,' she says quietly. He looks at her (I think he's looking at her) with his bright blue eyes. A nurse is nearby, and Mother tells her about the sick. Then he is a little sick – on to the sheet. 'There – he's done it, he's been sick,' she says with a sense of relief and also satisfaction that she had known just what was troubling *her* baby.

The nurse comes over. 'Oh yes,' she says, 'it's very mucousy – better out than in.' She sounds very businesslike and matter-of-fact. She says that she will give him some suction, and leaves. Mother continues to gently rub Daniel's back and croon to him. She tells me that his name is Daniel. We look at him together. With this mum I do not feel as if I am intruding; she seems very proud of him and seems to give a message that it's all right for me to join her in her adoration. I comment on what lovely hair he has, and she agrees: 'It's really blond'. He is lying on a slight slope in the incubator; she strokes his head. He has a green teddy with a shamrock next to his head, and there are two or three other cuddlies, including a green dinosaur at his feet. His incubator is like a little nursery; I feel he is already Irish. He looks alert and calm.

The nurse returns, and I fetch a chair and sit down. The nurse is busy sorting things out, disconnecting and reconnecting wires, and moving him. She leaves him on his back. His hands are held out. One is held up in the air. He moves his fingers slowly, very slowly, flexing and extending them. His other hand is caught under a wire. He's making all these movements with one hand, and the other one feels as if it's got stuck. I want to say something about it. He seems to want to move this other one, but he can't. She comes back and opens up the front again; the mother is standing watching. 'I'll just put some suction on his tube.' She does this, and finishes with him and then moves away again. She doesn't actually speak. I'm fascinated – have they had a previous conversation or is it just an understanding because of a previous occasion or routine? This mum seems to have a way of knowing.

The nurse brings a chair for Mother, and when she's sitting she gives her a blanket, and then lifts Daniel out on to her lap. Mum is just delighted and she smiles, beams at him. He looks up with his eyes wide open. She wraps him in the blanket, leaving room for his hand to reach out. She holds his hand with a finger of her free hand and jiggles it a bit. 'He's got quite a grip for his size, you know,' she says proudly, she looks very proud. She looks at him. I feel they are very together. Very calm.

A few more minutes pass; she is watching him, he is watching her, they're both watching. She holds his hand or strokes the back of his hand. And then he gives three huge slow yawns, 'Oh, you're a tired little baby. Are you a tired baby? O-o-o-oh, or is it just so-o-o boring.' He gives two short abrupt sneezes and his whole body shakes. He is all snuggled up in the blanket, I can just see his head and his little hand outside the blanket. After a few wriggles, he is still again. Quiet. They seem very peaceful.

Comments

This mother and baby are a pleasure to observe. Not only does this mother seem to be in tune with her baby, she also seems to be in tune with the nurse.

She focuses on her baby with her gaze, her touch and her voice, she lets him know that she is there and that she is attending to him. Her gaze is there to meet his when he is ready, and he actually seems to take up this offer, despite his prematurity. Her voice talks to him and about him, and is musical in its rhythm; that is, she talks 'motherese' (Murray, 1991; 1993). Alvarez has noted that 'so much of the language of these authors who are studying intersubjectivity in the young baby is of a quasi-musical type. They write of rhythm, synchronicity, dialogue, surging, turn-taking, conversation-like exchanges, amplification' (Alvarez, 1992: 83). In this example, the mother conforms to the expectations of all the experts in her way of talking to her baby. She also ascribes him potency or agency, and is clearly bursting with pride even though he has arrived early. She gives no indication of any anxieties about his survival.

She empathises with him to the extent that she knows that he is going to be sick before he is. But this empathy does not result in distress; rather it helps her to comfort him. She remains very calm throughout but in no way seems detached.

Her communication with the nurse is interesting. They do not speak much to each other but they are clearly in tune. The nurse is efficient but also gentle and firm, quietly supportive and understanding. I say this because of what the relation-ship feels like rather than what can be objectively reasoned or evidenced. The mother feels as if she is being 'looked after enough' or 'contained enough' by the nurse, and the nurse feels as if she is quietly confident that she is doing the right things.

The infant in this observation, as I have said, seems older than other babies of the same gestational age, even those born at the same time. He is not at all jittery nor is he withdrawing into sleep. I may have been lucky to catch him in this state of alertness but I have a feeling that it was not just his state that contributed to his togetherness. In part, I think, it was something to do with his mother. I would also guess that he was less damaged. He appears more competent, more able and, most importantly, he appears to be more integrated, more of a person. At this young age, gestationally, he seems to show preadaptation, a readiness to meet the world and interact with it. He seems to be aware of his separateness, and this perhaps can be seen as a sign of an early differentiated ego.

Brian

Brian was born at twenty-nine weeks, the third child of Ms B. His father was Ms B's third partner and although he didn't live with her and her children, she had changed her surname by deed poll to his. Each child had a different father. The year before Brian's birth she had had a miscarriage at fourteen weeks; she had had several earlier ones before that. She had bled from very early in this pregnancy and had been told that she had originally been carrying twins.

This is an extract from a first observation at nine days old.

The charge nurse has suggested that I observe Baby M. He is lying in a cot in the corner of the 'cold' room, swaddled in a blanket with a blue hat on, he's barely visible. After peeking at him, I ask about Mum. 'She's expressing,' I'm told. I feel awkward, and probably look it. The nurse blusteringly reassures me that it's OK to go and see her, and points to where she is.

I still feel awkward. To make my introduction while she is expressing breast milk doesn't seem appropriate, yet the nurse's expectation, I feel, is that I should. I don't want to spy on the baby. I stand and watch him for a bit; he is very still, only the slightest movement and slight sound of his breathing, regular and fast. A red scrunched up little face, eyes shut tight, a tube coming from his nose. I feel that I am looking at him without permission and so, I tentatively make my way round to see his mother.

She is fastening up her bra. I introduce myself, and apologise for intruding. She is unembarrassed and enthusiastic in her welcome. 'I've just finished anyway.' She tells me that she won't be doing it any more, she hates it, her breasts are sore. She then quietly and calmly puts the milk into a bottle and then into the fridge, talking to me as she does so. I tell her about my wish to observe and she willingly consents, saying that there will be a lot to learn. I feel as if she is relieved that someone might appreciate that this might be a problem. 'I'm not used to all this, I have 8lb babies you know.' She tells me that she has two older children, they were big healthy babies not like this one.

She continues talking unprompted. It seems that the more she says the more she has to, and the feeling is of relief as a lot of bottled up thoughts and feelings come tumbling out in a rather disconnected, yet also connected, way. She talks about her children and their attitude to the new baby, about previous pregnancies and miscarriages – 'lost babies' – ending up in the present and remembering Brian's birth. In hospital, bleeding, trying to hang on, never imagining that he'd be a live baby, thinking about and expecting to have another miscarriage, then suddenly having a baby who is alive and who seems to be going to stay alive.

She pauses and looks down. We've reached the cot and she looks calmly at the baby, and in contrast to the outpouring of the previous minutes, quietly comments on how fast asleep he is. I agree with her that he is sound.

This baby has three names on the card at the end of his cot, and in response to my confusion, his mother tells me that one of these is a first name and two are surnames. She changed her name some years ago, but because her hospital record had her old name on it, she has allowed her baby to be referred to by this name, Baby M, even though that is not his name. I feel quite amazed that she has allowed him to be called the wrong name. Ms B goes on to talk again, about the children, their fathers and other things. She says she is feeling quite well apart from her breasts, they are agony and she cannot last for more than a few hours without expressing. She's dripping everywhere, enough milk for lots of babies, he can't take it, it's all going in the fridge. Brian hasn't regained his birthweight yet, and he was so small in the first place.

Brian's breathing pattern changes, there is a sense of him being about to do something – wake up perhaps. He is in a perspex cot, like an ordinary baby, but is on a monitor. The wires come out from under the covers and stretch across to a heart rate monitor, which bleeps away in the background. He yawns and then goes back into a quiet sleep. This seems to prompt his mother, who says that he hardly ever opens his eyes when she is there. She tries to come in every day but has to look after the other children too. Usually she comes in from about 11 until 3 o'clock, and will often return with the children in the evening. Her partner, who is very busy, pops in at odd times, often late at night. Brian opens his eyes for him; there is a tone of resentment in her voice.

Brian stirs again and yawns. He is so wrapped up, it is difficult to see what exactly he's doing, how wakeful. He gives another huge yawn and a wriggle, opening his eyes for a few moments. She tells me she will take him out for a while and see if he will wake up properly before she changes and feeds him (through his tube). She has to test the acid in his stomach before that, and tells me that she hates doing it.

She lifts him gently out and lays him on her lap with his head at her knees and his feet pointing towards her. She looks at him intently. He is sleeping quietly. He makes no response to her first gentle 'hellos'. She cuddles him, cradling him in her left arm and gently rocking him, she is leaning forward 'into' him, and she starts quietly talking to him – 'Hello you, you never wake up for me, do you? Are you going to open your eyes?' She leans back a bit and strokes the side of his face continuing to chat to him. She tells him that he only opens his eyes for his Daddy. He starts to move his lips a bit, making a smacking sound. When she stops touching him he goes quiet and still again. She expresses dismay and tries again, and this is repeated several times. She lays him on her lap again and continues. He stirs, then sleeps, stirs then sleeps, and then with a few yawns opens his eyes and 'peeks' at her, then closes them again. He does this a few times, and then opens them for a bit longer, about 30 seconds. She is heartened and talks more to him. He wakes more as she does this.

Comments

This baby is almost exactly the same age as Daniel, he was born at the same gestation. Yet he looks quite crumpled and red compared to his ward mate. I don't get much opportunity to get a sense of what he's like initially. Instead, I do find out a lot about his mother's experience. This woman spills out her story, without needing any invitation. I did ask the parents of these babies about what had happened but not until after I'd had the opportunity to do a series of observations

– I didn't want to know too much initially so that I could be relatively free from preconceptions. In this case, the mother clearly believes that it is important for me to know things – she thinks 'there will be a lot to learn'. I sense that she is talking for herself too, and the way in which her story comes tumbling out suggests to me that she is feeling very stressed and isolated by this experience.

There is a striking contrast between the way she talks about what has happened and her demeanour in relation to baby-focused activities. There is no sign of feeling flustered or stressed as she calmly puts her milk into bottles, and when she talks about and to her baby, she again feels calm and collected, serene almost. It's as if she's allowed her panic about not knowing what to do in this strange situation to burst through. There is a sense of relief as it does so but also a sense that she knows that she has to be coping and competent for her baby. She's strong on the outside and fragile on the inside.

I discover that Baby M is actually Baby B, Brian B to be precise. Yet he is referred to as Baby M, that is, he is called by the name of Mother's previous partner. She has been unable to correct this. I wonder if there is a need to placate the nurses somehow; would it be wrong to let them know that she has been divorced? Or is this something to do with assertiveness? There is a feeling that it may be difficult to be assertive with hospital staff who have produced a live baby in a situation where she thought that was impossible. Or is it to do with ownership? This baby may not really feel like hers, she may not feel that she has a right to be assertive about his name.

This is a sleepy little baby, who doesn't seem to want to face the world. She calls to him, gently trying to get a response. Her comment about him opening his eyes for his father is brought into her conversation with him as she struggles to reach him. She does not sound as bitter when she addresses him as she did when she told me about it, but there is a note of frustration in her voice which makes me wish that he would wake up and look at her. The baby's role in the interaction, his contribution to their relationship, is emphasised for me by the change I see in her. When he does respond, opening his eyes at first tentatively and then for longer, she responds with a marked change in affect and renews her attempts to reach him. Although he is to be tube fed, I notice that he is smacking his lips as if hungry. I wonder if he is ready to suck, to take his own milk and learn about satisfying this sensation he may not yet know of as hunger.

This is an extract from an observation at sixteen days old.

Ms B is sitting down with Brian in her arms when I arrive and ask if I may join her. She is rubbing his cheek gently and talking to him. His eyes are shut tight.

She turns and tells me that the doctors have told her that there is something wrong with him, she doesn't understand what. He might have some learning difficulties when he is older, she's not sure. They don't know, they're going to do more tests and let her know. She thought he was going to be all right. She repeats this several times before going on to say that everything looks fine, he doesn't have problems with movements or other things. She seems to be trying to make light of it all, yet I feel that she is very shocked and worried. She is well dressed and is wearing make-up, looking bright on the surface. I think that underneath she's exhausted, and wonder what she would look like without make-up on.

A bit later, after she has very gently and carefully changed him:

Brian is lying in his cot, on his back with his eyes shut. He still has a nasogastric tube in place, but she tells me that they've decided that he can have some milk from a bottle. She started feeding him this way yesterday, and is about to try again. She goes to fetch the bottle. He is lying very still, much stiller I think than some of the other babies I've observed. He occasionally moves his hand up to his mouth and down again. I feel that he is awake with his eyes shut, but I don't know.

When Mother brings the bottle, she puts it down and lifts him out talking to him quietly as she does so. She puts him on her lap and tries to lift his head up with one hand. He opens his eyes. She rubs the teat of the bottle gently on his lips. It is huge compared to him, and she comments on this saying that this is the smallest size, and it just doesn't seem right. She encourages him to open his mouth, then strokes his throat, telling me that this is the way to get *them* to swallow. The nurses have told her this – it encourages *them* to drink. There is a feeling that she believes that this is a bit cruel, and I notice that she seems to have to separate herself and her baby from the theory about babies in general.

It's all very difficult. I feel that she has been very calm but now she starts to get a bit panicky about it. She tells me how important it is for him to take it. He's *got to* put on weight. She persists more calmly again, stroking his throat and pushing the nipple into his tiny mouth. His heart rate drops suddenly and the alarm goes off. There is no apparent change in the baby who seems to be lying peacefully with his eyes mostly shut, but opening every twenty seconds or so for a few seconds. It's difficult to look at him and the monitor simultaneously. A nurse comes rushing up and tells the mother that it's too much for him; she should give him a rest. His heart rate has quickly returned to normal but from now on Mother watches the monitor and not the baby while she's feeding. She feels blamed, and I'm not surprised. She says she doesn't know what to do, watching the monitor means that it is more difficult to feed him – she needs to concentrate on him to feed him. From the way she talks, it is clear that this has happened before. She then tells me that he was on medicine to keep his heart rate up, but they have tried without for the last day.

Another nurse comes with some medicine. They've decided to resume it meanwhile. She gives it to him via the nasogastric tube. She is very warm and sympathetic and clearly tells the mother that it is not her fault that the heart rate dropped – not to do with feeding, just a coincidence. This reassurance is given kindly but somehow does not undo what's already been said. Mother asks about continuing the bottle feed, he hasn't taken much but it has taken a long time. She seems relieved when the nurse agrees with her, saying that he's done all right and should have the rest by tube. In contrast to the previous observation, Ms B tells me in a very straightforward way that she is going to test his stomach acid. She lays him in the cot and fetches the necessary syringe and litmus paper. She then proceeds calmly to do the test, put the aspirate back and give him his milk via the syringe and tube. He is now lying flat on his back with his eyes shut again.

Comments

There is a feeling today that Ms B is shocked, stunned by the news that her son may be disabled. She repeats her belief that he is going to be all right several times, and tries not to believe what the doctors have said.

I think that I can see the impact of what's been said on her as she tries to feed Brian. I find myself wondering if she's been told about the importance of nutrition in minimising brain damage. She has certainly been told that he has to gain weight, and to do this, it feels as if she's forcing herself to push this teat into his mouth. As she massages his throat, she refers to what the nurses have told her about premature babies in general. She seems to have to distance herself and her baby from this cruel force-feeding regime. Her panic wells up, and is pushed down again, she is trying very hard to stay calm, and is just managing. She is focusing on the baby, she knows that she has to do this to get him to feed but after his heart rate has suddenly and temporarily plummeted, she switches her gaze to the monitor. Brian has remained calm throughout.

Two nurses give her quite contrasting messages about what has happened. The first serves to confirm Ms B's own belief that what she is doing is cruel, it has caused her baby's heart rate to fall. She knows, even though she hasn't read the research, that her baby has been stressed by her attempts to feed him. Her feelings that she is to blame, that she is not up to the task of looking after this baby, and that she doesn't know what to do, has been confirmed for her by the nurse's sharp words. The warm and sympathetic approach of the other nurse doesn't help, it's too late.

This woman has two children, she is already a mother, and has demonstrated to me that she is a sensitive and appropriate one to this baby. But she cannot hang on to her competence in this situation. She feels deskilled and ill-prepared for the task of bringing up this child, and each setback seems to make her feel more daunted. Her upset about the news from the doctor this morning has not really surfaced yet but must be making her feel even more doubtful.

Towards the end of this extract, surprising evidence of mum's confidence and ability appears again. A task which daunted her a week ago is now carried out with ease. I notice too that the isssue of her breast milk is not raised. She has stopped expressing as she said, and seems to show no regrets about this. I find myself hoping that he is getting the milk she has expressed in his tube, but I don't know.

Catherine

Catherine is the fourth child to be born to Ms C, a Nigerian woman. She has also been given an African name which means 'It's in God's hands'. Ms C's first child, now seven years old, was born at twenty-eight weeks gestation, and her third, three years ago, was born at twenty-two weeks and died shortly after. She was admitted to hospital with a placenta praevia at nineteen weeks, and bled 'on and off' for the next five weeks when, because of the risk to her, the baby was delivered by caesarian section.

Catherine was not planned, and Ms C only realised that she was pregnant at three months. She had separated from her husband by this time. Ms C went home when the baby was less than two days old, saying that she would not return for a week. This caused great concern in the unit but she did come back, eight days later.

This is an extract from an observation at twelve days.

The baby is in the 'hot' room. She is in an incubator, and is being ventilated via an endotracheal tube. She has a drip in one leg and one arm. These are splinted and bandaged. She is lying on her back, naked, with her legs open. Her skin is very dry and flaky, and looks as if it has broken down at her wrists. She has a little white gauze hat on, and her tube is held in place with a gauze bandage but unlike some of the other babies she does not have a bandage across her eyes, which are closed. I notice that she is never really still for a second. Her limbs are constantly twitching, and superimposed on these very fine movements are frequent 'bigger' movements, a flexing of her free leg or arm. There is no sense of rhythm about these movements which come in irregular bursts. When she flexes her arm and moves her hand up, it is as if she wants to pull her tube out.

Comments

This baby was born at twenty-four weeks gestation. Observing her makes me feel more distressed than observing other infants of a similar gestational age, and I struggle to make sense of this.

I think it is probably related to several things. First, her aloneness – although I had managed to ask this mother's permission to observe, I did not have the oppportunity to see her with her child until later on. I knew that Catherine had been without her mother for most of her life so far, and I was also struck by how unnoticed she was in the unit. By that I mean that, in most of my observations, staff would inevitably be 'doing something to' the infant under study. However, in this baby's case, I spent three-quarters of an hour alone at her cotside. Nurses were attending to her, observing from a distance, looking at her monitors, and sometimes resetting them after an alarm had sounded. They glanced at her, as if to check that the monitors were 'telling the truth', but other than this she was alone with me. Second, this baby seemed more exposed than the others, her nakedness, and the prominence of her genitalia in relation to her malnourished-looking and painfully thin body made her seem more exposed and vulnerable. Third, I really felt that I had no idea what this baby was experiencing. I could only identify with what I felt to be a physically and emotionally painful experience, and I, for once, tried to doubt the accuracy of my perceptions. I think her skin played a part in this: there was no tough coat to contain and protect her, and no clothing, and the redness and apparent soreness at her wrists, for example, seemed particularly excruciating. I wondered if her skin was like this because of her nutritional status or because it wasn't yet ready to be in this dry environment.

The lights are bright, and again her skin does not seem to protect her. Her eyes are closed but I doubt that her paperthin eyelids will shield her from their stimulation. Even though she has now been in the world for twelve days, she is still showing a lot of involuntary movement, twitching almost constantly. As in Alan's case, I am struck by the direction and purposiveness of the 'bigger' movements, which to my mind are somehow directed at trying to replace oral discomfort with comfort. Or perhaps, she is just trying to pull herself together – I find myself thinking that the way she is lying, stiff and stretched out, is very different from the position of a foetus *in utero*.

This brief extract is from an observation at thirty days.

Mother sits by the cot looking preoccupied, staring ahead of her most of the time. She is silent, and occasionally looks down at Catherine and touches her hand.

Catherine is still in the incubator, with tube and intravenous lines in place. She has a nappy on, it looks huge, and a vest. She is quite still, but occasionally seems to shiver, one leg in particular twitches more often. Her hand reaches up occasionally as if to do something but then falls down again by her side. Her eyes are closed, I guess that she is sleeping.

Comments

This mother seems as alone as her infant. She appears shocked and numb, detached, even though a month has passed since the birth. Her tentative reaching to her infant does not really feel as if it's intended to make emotional contact, although it may be thought to offer some sort of comfort. The baby of course is not really available for this mum to get in touch with. Her gross movements are slightly less intentional than on previous occasions, and this makes me think that she is asleep. She is still quite twitchy, and does not really seem to be resting peacefully. I doubt whether she ever has the opportunity or the ability to sleep deeply, and I suspect that for her there is little chance to utilise deep sleep's restorative functions. I wonder how or if this mother and baby will ever get to know each other.

WIDENING THE LENS

I want to go on now to consider special care baby units as a whole, to try to give a sense of the context in which babies struggle to survive and grow, and parents and babies try to get to know each other.

There is an immediate problem in widening the lens, my lens at any rate, to take in each whole environment. First, the layout of such units varies but inevitably includes a spread of separate rooms, some more busy than others. Units I have worked in or visited have had between two and six main areas for the care of the neonates, plus an assortment of other rooms for different purposes. Although these are often partitioned by transparent walls, it is only possible to register what is happening in one or possibly two of these at a time. The implications of this for staff may be that they are not always aware of everything that is going on or everything that has happened. Given that any one of them may be approached in passing to be asked about one child by parents, other visitors or staff, good and regular communication is obviously essential. For parents, particularly as their child becomes well, the spin-off is that they are spared having to notice life-threatening events involving other infants.

Second, the task of trying to observe the whole is immediately sabotaged by a subjective interest in the particular. Curiosity is naturally aroused by particular events or conversations while trying to scan the whole environment. So, on occasions when I set out to carry out an institutional observation, I was often drawn to specific events which fascinated me from afar. Similarly, at times when I was observing one baby, I could be drawn to another or become transfixed by some background feature, most often the noise.

It is, however, possible to some degree to extrapolate the method of infant observation to provide data about the institution.

Institutional observation

Observational studies differ from empirical research in that they aim to be synthesising or synthetic; that is, 'they seek to identify a holistic coherence and recurrent patterns' (Rustin 1989a: 56) rather than analyse by a process of breaking the subject matter down into component parts.

The notions of pattern and context have been explored by Bateson, who offered what might be called definitions. He helpfully stated that 'without context, words and actions have no meaning at all' (1979: 15), and 'offer[ed] – the notion of context, of pattern through time' (1979: 14). 'Creatura' cannot 'be understood until differences and distinctions are invoked' (1979: 7). Understanding of the whole, of the connections between people and events cannot really be reached without looking at similarities and differences, which make up patterns. 'It is patterns which connect' (1979: 11). Many people would consider that Bateson, a philosopher and anthropologist, captured in his writing the essence of human existence and proposed a way of thinking about it and making sense of it. His work has been applied to areas beyond his own fields of expertise; for example, to family therapy and consultation work. Others might say, as Bateson himself does at the end of *Mind and Nature*, 'So what?' (1979: 221). In many ways he didn't say anything

particularly new, but he did describe a way of thinking which probably characterised sociologists, and their methods of study.

The method of ethnographic study by sociologists carrying out field work in
their various subjects bears a close resemblance to what I am calling institutional
observation. Famous studies in the field of human experience have used a participant–observer method of data collection and a descriptive style of reporting, and
have had an impact on many people's view of the world or understanding of
particular situations. Examples are the work of Goffman who, in *Asylums*, presented
a view of 'the social world of the hospital inmate' (1961: 7) and Mead, who used
the method 'of observation of the children under normal conditions of play, in their
home, with their parents' (1975: 218) to inform her seminal text, *Growing Up in
New Guinea*. Bruner (1990) has discussed these methods favourably in his plea for
a social or cultural approach to psychology.

What is the difference between ethnographic research and institutional observation? In short, it is the recognition and acknowledgement of the feeling invoked.
The subjectivity of the observer is both accepted and valued. It becomes legitimate
to notice some things and not others, to accept that human curiosity will always
lead to a focusing on particular events, and to accept that human memory will select
only some aspects of an experience for recall. As in the method of infant observation, the observer's emotional response to the data is considered to be a source of
information rather than a contaminant.

General observations

The milieu of a special care baby unit will probably be familiar to most readers.
Nonetheless, I will describe some features of it. While of necessity being in my
own shoes, my purpose is to try to put myself in the shoes of parents, in particular
to try to notice what they might notice, and also, to consider what it's like for the
professionals – in this environment day after day, shift after shift. As I have said:

> There are different rooms, referred to as 'hot' rooms and 'cool' rooms. The cool
> rooms are hot, and the hot rooms are very hot; the temperature in the offices is
> slightly more bearable. On my first proper observational visit, I had to take off
> my cardigan, and I was still too hot.
>
> The rooms are bright, lit with strong, raw lighting; and they seem stuffy and
> airless, even though they are ventilated. There is a smell of cleanness.
>
> There is noise, lots of noise, steady beep-beep noises, erratic buzzing alarm
> noises that pierce through the other noise, the noise of talking amongst staff, the
> noise of chinking and clanking connected, I think, to procedures but somehow
> seeming too loud to actually be such delicate tasks. In the background to all of
> this is music, scratchy pop from the radio, interrupted by the DJ's voice every
> three minutes or so. The cheerful DJ talks oblivious of his listeners. The Radio

1 sob story at about 11 o'clock seems insensitive but captures some of the nurses' attention.

There is a feeling of being crowded in the hot room. Even when intermittently it is almost empty of grown-ups, there still does not seem to be much room. The machines fill the space, the babies are lost, they are so tiny in their cots each surrounded by several machines. Parents are perched on high stools nearby, looking uncomfortable and precarious. Maybe I just think that because I always feel that if I stop thinking about my position for a moment while sitting there, I'll fall off. Some stand, perhaps sharing my feeling about that. As I continue to feel hot and uncomfortable, I notice that one nurse seems a bit weak and wobbly and has to be escorted from the hot room; I hear two others tell her she needs to have something to eat, she says that she hasn't had the time.

A bit later. I am absorbed in watching a nurse attend to one particular infant. The nurse swabs his mouth and washes round it with a little cottonwool ball, then prepares to insert a nasogastric tube, but just as she is about to, she is distracted. She turns her attention to a couple in the corner who want to know if it's OK to take their baby out of his incubator. In the few moments that she is away a doctor comes and takes blood from the baby, quickly, efficiently, but without any social overtures. The nurse returns and carries on with her task, inserting the tube, oblivious, I am certain, to the fact that someone else has just zoomed in and out and performed another invasive technique.

Comments

The experience will be familiar. Once I got used to it, the noise, the heat, the brightness and the feeling of being crowded all lessened. However, the importance of the auditory environment in SCBUs has been well documented. Newman (1981) observed that in the first week especially, infants were continually aroused and startled by apparently random loud sounds, and hypothesised that unnecessary energy expenditure might be compromising the infant's clinical condition.

It was reassuring but also a bit worrying to see one of the nurses temporarily overwhelmed. More worrying, though, was the lack of communication between staff about what was being done to one of the babies. This did not seem like deliberate *mis*-communication, more a case of *non*-communication. It has been shown that these infants are stressed by procedures in a measurable way ($\uparrow$ cortisol levels and $\downarrow$ oxygen tension) (Field, 1990a and b). As this stress is such that it might compromise the infant, this episode worried me.

It was a peaceful evening in the cold room. Several parents were visiting, and all were engaged in activities of different sorts with their babies. Some feeding and changing, others sitting watching their babies sleeping. The music was light and classical, soothing I felt. Suddenly a nurse came rushing in and approached a couple with their baby. She started to unplug a piece of equipment at the wall and take something out from under the baby. I think it was probably a temperature monitor. She told the parents after she'd begun this frantic activity that they were expecting a baby to arrive soon and needed this equipment. Her explanation was rushed and it felt as if she was in a panic. One of the student nurses in the room seemed to pick up the panic, and started talking about how awful it was – 'Is this what it's all about?' she asked her colleague.

A few moments after the first nurse had rushed off, another one came in and very calmly went over to Daniel's mother and explained that they had to take his cardiac monitor away now. She conveyed a sense of calmness, the unspoken message seemed to be that he wouldn't need it any more anyway. There was no sense that she left the mother feeling confused or upset, which I think may have been the case with the first.

Comments

I was very struck by how the different approaches of the staff left the parents feeling more or less contained. I learned later that this scenario often took place. Monitoring equipment was not necessarily removed when it was not required with the result, it seemed, that parents were often left feeling deprived and worried.

Some specific events noted during observations

Sometimes, I was also drawn to attend to conversations between professionals, which I thought should be more confidential but *were* being heard, if not noticed by everyone in the room.

Two doctors were carrying out the evening ward round. The nurse-in-charge had said that she was too busy to join them but did come and go, participating on and off in the discussion.

They review the baby's charts together. The conversation sounds fairly routine and although the baby is in an obviously fragile state, there is no immediate crisis. The most striking feature is that although this baby has an obviously female name, and is lying naked with her genitalia exposed and 'floodlit,' she is constantly referred to as 'he' by both male and female doctor.

This was not the only occasion on which babies were ascribed the wrong gender, and although on one occasion a nurse was seen correcting another nurse, I did not witness a mother doing so.

A nurse says she is very tired, has been on duty for ten days, another four to go. Then I realise from the conversation that she has been doing agency work on her days off – I wonder how that makes the parents feel.

This conversation was not 'wrong' but I wondered how parents would experience it, as I was aware that rather than being less likely to mind, my stance as observer might mean I noticed more as I was not so preoccupied with one baby.

I want to go on now to present some of my reflections on the experience of observation. In doing so, I will present some further observations, and I think these will convey more of how I felt about the experience than what will have been elicited from the extracts I have presented so far.

REFLECTIONS ON THE PROCESS OF OBSERVATION

In order to observe babies in the unit, and to observe the unit itself, I had to negotiate a place for myself with the staff – I had to get permission to be there. It was not difficult to get this permission but it was difficult to get on with the actual observations. I felt that I could understand this.

Initial negotiations were encouraging but I felt that there was a discrepancy between what people said and what they allowed me to do. These inconsistencies in the responses of professionals may have been related to the functioning of the unit, and possible anxieties about being scrutinised. Clearly it would have been unwise to read too much into things but it is important to acknowledge the understandable ambivalence of staff to apparent psychological investigation by an outsider. One illustration of this concerns the explanation of my task to staff.

I explained my wish to observe to the consultant and to the clinical manager. It was then explained to some other staff in the weekly psychosocial meeting and, in response to a further request, to nurses as they worked in the ward itself. Following this, and in response to some questions I asked about the way the unit was run, I was invited to attend a management meeting as an observer. When I arrived, it was evident that the staff at the meeting were not expecting me. The 'inviter' was late, and on arrival asked for a further explanation of my task to be given to the meeting; she then dismissed me, arranging to meet me at a future date. Other staff at the meeting were amused and puzzled as, while waiting, I had explained my role as observer to the meeting. The next meeting was postponed, and when it did occur a further opportunity to explain my role to ward staff was offered.

During my visit to the unit I attended the psychosocial ward round. It was striking but completely understandable that most of the discussion focused on the infants who were doing less well, and about whom there was a lot of anxiety. One in particular became lodged firmly in my memory. The case was described as 'not atypical', although it should be noted that maternal death is rare. It serves as a dramatic example of the complex circumstances often surrounding the birth of these babies.

The baby was born at 25–26 weeks, after a hazardous labour during which his mother had died. His medical progress was erratic, and if he survived, there seemed little doubt that he would be significantly disabled as a result. His father, who was African and not married to the mother, was being threatened with expulsion from the country as his immigration status was unsatisfactory. Further he had neither permanent accommodation nor the finances with which to appeal against his deportation. He was devoted to the baby, but had little materially to offer him. Social Services were planning to place the baby with foster parents on discharge.

The context was in some ways set at this point – I remembered the bad news, the horror stories rather than the success stories. This trend continued throughout my attachment to the unit and was later discussed with the consultant who felt that this was not a skewed perception but was part of the reality of the unit's memory. Despite having a prominently placed noticeboard with photographs of unit 'graduates' who were doing well, the talk was mostly about those who didn't make it or did less well.

During the period when I was spending a lot of time in the special care baby unit observing the same babies sequentially week after week, I had the opportunity to discuss my more personal thoughts and feelings with my superviser, and with a child psychotherapist who worked in a special care baby unit. The latter had also applied the method of infant observation to try to find out about the experience of these babies. I recorded my observations afterwards but she told me that she had found it impossible to sit and observe an infant without taking notes. She described using the notepad and pen as a barrier, a defence against the idea that doing this was seen by others as mad. She felt that the idea that a person could be interested in just looking at a baby did not feel comfortable for some parents and staff. I have already made reference to some of the comments made to me while observing, for example, 'It looks mad, just sitting there watching'.

On each of my early visits, the nurse-in-charge was a different person who, while knowing about my plans, had to be offered yet another explanation. This need to explain on each occasion added to, and perhaps was also fuelled by, my initial doubts as to whether my observations would contribute anything useful to what was already known about this situation. In the context of psychotherapeutic work, the therapist needs to be uninhibited in a particular way in order to 'get in touch'. I found it hard to be uninhibited, to be just myself, and this of course raised a further doubt in my mind about my purpose. Nonetheless I did complete the task, which was not solely to record what was happening but was also to monitor my own feelings throughout. Some of these have been presented as part of the discussion of the observation material; further reflections on my experience are presented here.

Early on, I was concerned about my feeling that I was intruding, invading the privacy of the experience of parents with their babies, and even invading the baby's own privacy. In relation to the frantic activity and the number of people around at any one time, this was odd. However, none of them were actually focusing for any length of time on the emotional experience of the participants. For the professional carers, the task in most cases is to keep the babies alive, to physically care for them, and to support the parents. I was shocked when one nurse approached a baby I was observing and told me that she was going 'to perform his care'. I asked her to repeat what she had said, 'I'm going to perform his care,' she replied. The words suggested something very mechanical and detached to me but I am sure that they were not intended in that way. The expression was probably one commonly used by nurses but I wondered what it conveyed to parents. I doubt that they would be as sensitive or prickly as I was about the rather behaviourist use of language. Indeed, I often wondered if my experience in the unit was somehow false. I asked myself constantly if I was overreacting or being judgemental about things that didn't really matter. I still fear that professionals reading these observations will interpret my reflections as critical or judgemental. They are not meant as such. It is clear to me that they represent one particular way of looking at the situation which is probably different from everyone else's. As such, though, my observations have their own validity, and along with observations from different perspectives – those of the nurses, doctors and parents – form a more complete picture.

Returning to the question of my intrusiveness, in one of my early observations, I actually believed that my presence had driven the parents away. In more straightforward 'ordinary' infant observation in the community, the negotiation about the observation is usually done with the parents first and sets the scene more clearly for what is to follow. In the instances in the unit when observations were clearly prenegotiated, away from the cotside, subsequent feelings of intrusion were markedly less. Practically, however, it was often difficult to take parents away from the baby to explain my purpose more fully. I also felt guilty; I did not want to 'waste' parents' precious time with their baby. In supervision, I was helped to remember that both parents and professionals believe that infant observation can be valuable in its own right. By focusing on the baby, by noticing the baby, the observer helps the mother to do that, and this has a positive effect on the developing relationship. In some cases, mothers also report feeling cared for and 'mothered', at least in phantasy, by the observer who is genuinely interested in her and her baby. Holding on to the belief that observing helps did in fact help me to be less overwhelmed by my feelings of intrusiveness.

At times, each of us probably imagines that we know what it is like for the parents of a very sick baby. I was quickly and sharply reminded of the fallibility of that belief when I found myself early on struggling with my inability to put myself in certain parents' shoes. For example, I felt embarrassed, stupid and awkward after asking one set of parents what age their baby was when he was born. Until that point it was clear in my own head that a premature baby's age was its gestational age. But these parents couldn't understand my question. Professionals working in the field will have two ages in mind for each baby, the gestational age, and the age since birth. Mostly they'll refer to gestational age and indeed the charts at the end of each cot record the baby's age as '27, 28, 29 weeks' and so on. Some time after this incident I was able to confirm my belief that some parents do think in these terms often up until the child goes to school or beyond. But clearly some do not. This was a shock for me, an almost unthinkable realisation that left me with questions about how *these* parents understood their child's development. I wondered if it might help them to think in these terms too.

It will be apparent from one of my accounts that I found the music in the 'hot' room quite disturbing. The music in the 'cool' room felt more appropriate. I struggled to make sense of this particularly when my superviser's immediate response to my report of music was, 'That's good'. For me, the music had a rather harsh and penetrating feel to it. I found myself thinking that it was incongruous, not quite right. It reminded me of my teenage years but I was acutely aware that most of the parents were much younger than me. I wondered whether it reminded them of anything or comforted them, or whether in fact they noticed it at all. For the babies, I felt that it was just whizzing past them, touching them only in an intermittent and unpredictable way. It seemed to me to be rather frantic and jumpy rather than harmonious, melodic and soothing. I wondered what difference the perspex cot made. Did it act like the amniotic fluid in the womb, muffling sounds from the outside? Was it a more or less effective barrier? I was aware that the background heartbeat, which *in utero* acts as the context for all other sounds, was now absent. I wondered whether in fact the music was there for the staff rather than the babies. Was its purpose to comfort them or to act as a diversion for them from experiences which they found difficult?

I observed babies in the unit for a period of about four months. I became very attached to or, perhaps more accurately, preoccupied with two particular babies. One of them remained in the unit for almost that entire period until his death. Despite trying very hard to only watch the baby who was the focus of each current observation, I found myself constantly drawn to looking at Alan. I had decided not to attend the psychosocial ward round or ask for specific pieces of information until I had made at least four observations of each baby. My aim was to prevent the observation material from being 'contaminated' in some way by too many precognitions. However, I did find myself asking about Alan's progress. On some occasions nursing staff and parents would quite spontaneously tell me about things that had happened. On one visit I heard about a baby who had died, and was given some of Alan's alarming history. Brian had also become unwell. I often felt quite distressed about what I was told but on this particular occasion, I found myself some thirty minutes later having to leave the unit early without completing one observation or going on to my second planned one. I felt unwell and couldn't attribute that to my own physical state before the visit or to the heat to which I'd become accustomed. I was reminded of just how hard it was to be there. It was hard for me, a relatively independent person who barely knew these babies, and a doctor who hadn't had difficulties coping with life-threatening situations when an active participant in the giving of essential care. I thought I understood why nurses had 'to perform care' and the like, and I wondered more about the emotional defences needed to work in such an environment. I thought about the parents. Did they feel sick and have to leave or did *their* role and bond with their baby help them to stay?

As I have said, I wondered at times if I was being inappropriately oversensitive to particular issues. One of these issues was gender. I know that when friendly comments are made by passing strangers about ordinary babies in their prams or pushchairs, the infant is often ascribed the wrong gender. In the unit, I felt that it should be different. These babies were known to staff, and helpfully had their names plus an 'M' (for male) or an 'F' (for female) on the charts at the end of their cots. Yet somehow this was often not remembered or not noticed. What surprised me more was that parents felt unable to correct doctors who, even when holding the charts in front of them, got the gender wrong. Of course I too was unable to correct these mistakes, which I witnessed frequently. I think that my status in the unit made it difficult for me to know how to act. Confirmation of my 'lack of status' was confirmed when on one occasion, I was ushered out of the room during the ward round.

I was also particularly sensitive to the issue of privacy in general, rather than in relation to my own feelings of intrusiveness. I knew that it was important that each baby was clearly visible to staff, and that it was necessary that urgent access in cases of emergency was not impeded. However even for the more well babies it was hard to get some privacy. I had observed some parents apparently trying to create a private space for themselves and their babies by sitting with their backs to the room in little groups facing the walls. A staff member told me that the actions of one couple who had repeatedly done this, taking their baby into the corner of the nursery and trying to shut out the rest of the world, had been interpreted as hostile by the staff.

This issue of lack of privacy seemed particularly relevant in relation to feeding, which is often experienced by mothers and babies as a struggle even when the baby is a fit full-termer. Most of the babies in the unit progress from tube feeds to either breast or bottle, and the transition period is often difficult. In this context, I watched mothers trying to feed their babies on the unit in full gaze of everyone. For mothers who were breastfeeding this seemed to me to be quite a hard thing to do. My own experience was that I had fed my own babies in front of other people once I felt we'd worked out what to do, and how to be comfortable with each other. I knew that in the early days, I was not the only mother who struggled as the milk either wouldn't come or, gushing, went everywhere but in the baby's mouth. I observed one couple and their baby, who was not very preterm, in the corner of the 'hot' room. Mother was wearing a nightdress not best suited to breastfeeding and had to squeeze her breast out over the top of it. She sat holding her baby, with her partner and a nurse at her side, looking embarrassed and exposed and, I suspected, feeling physically quite uncomfortable. She could not get her baby to latch on, and seemed to become upset as she continued in her efforts. Babies in the unit are encouraged to the breast even if there is little chance of actual breastfeeding. They can get close to their mother, have skin-to-skin contact, and theoretically get the idea of the breast and of the relationship. Yet in practice, I wonder just what feelings each is left with; after all, how many women, even new mothers, feel comfortable about exposing their breasts? In the actual feeding situation, mothers have, especially in the beginning, to allow themselves to become absorbed with the task. This is necessary to stimulate the milk flow, as well as to attend emotionally to their infant. In Western society if not elsewhere, it is a necessarily private experience.

And what of the infants' privacy? It is difficult to know how aware these babies are of what goes on around them, and indeed of what happens *to* them. Some will say that they are not very aware but there is evidence to counter this viewpoint. On an evening observation of a baby in the 'cool' nursery, where the lights were dimmed and soft music was playing, I saw him immediately recoil when a bright light was put on in the next room. He had noticed it even though he was only one week old, and the equivalent of twenty-nine weeks gestation. His noticing left me thinking not that people shouldn't put on lights but that perhaps it was important, where possible, to be considerate. I had noticed, for example, how, when the nurses were going to do something to a baby, they approached in a measured way, often making themselves known to the infant, talking quietly and carrying out the necessary procedure. They seemed to be both introducing themselves and preparing the baby for what was to happen. This was in contrast to the doctors whom I observed, who seemed to just zoom in and out, like fighter aeroplanes, performing some act or another on the way, not taking the time to 'join with' the baby. This seemed like an invasion of privacy but not only that, I wondered what effect it had on the babies' physiological functioning. Research evidence about the stressfulness of procedures, as well as my own noticing of a possible relationship between the emotional stress of the mother and the physically shown stress of her baby, supported my own belief that this issue of privacy was not simply one of social behaviour but had wider implications.

SUMMARY

Psychoanalytic infant observation is a way of finding out about the experiences of babies and their worlds. Personal feelings encountered in the observation setting provide important information about the emotional experiences of the participants. Institutional observation similarly accords importance to the observer's feelings at the time, and thus differs from ethnographic research. In this chapter, I have presented and discussed my observations of special care infants and their environment.

Chapter 5

Stories from a special care baby unit

We rely heavily on language to share our own experience of the world with others. We are also constrained by language in our thoughts – yes, we do 'feel' things, and have 'non-languaged' experiences but almost immediately much of that experience is 'thought about'. Our thinking is 'in language'. When we are not able to 'code' our feelings in our heads, we often become distressed and confused, more so, I think, than when we are merely confronted with our inability to share our emotional experience with another human being.

Language is a tool with many limitations but it is also a medium which offers possibilities. These possibilities for 'learning' about the many ways in which the world is experienced, or indeed the unique way in which the world is experienced by each of us, are more likely to be realised if we desist from classifying and coding what we hear. Of course, we will always classify what we hear to some extent. Part of the process of empathising probably involves classification, in that we match experience heard about to a story from our own lives and then experience our own feelings about it. We do this unconsciously. Our unconscious feeling state is also influenced by projections we receive from the story teller. Empathy involves the process of 'transference', as well as that of classification and matching. Projective identification, a kind of communication that is *not* dependent on or constrained by language, plays a central role.

Some of our quests for understanding, particularly in the 'scientific' arena, have had coding as their hallmark. The hierarchy of 'increasing sturdiness and sophistication in the level of scientific research' proposed by Garmezy (1986: 384), for example, suggests that some people believe that rated or digitalised descriptions are more valid than 'stories'. However, we don't even need to rate or code in order to lose some of the sense or meaning that may have been intended. Selvini-Palazzoli *et al.* (1978) have discussed the difficulties in trying to reconcile the nature of living systems with the constraints of language. They have referred to 'the tyranny of linguistic conditioning':

we are imprisoned by the absolute incompatibility between the two primary systems in which the human being lives: the living system, dynamic and circular, and the symbolic system (language), descriptive, static, and linear.

In developing his species-specific characteristic, language, which is also the tool of tools for the organisation and transmission of culture, man has to integrate two entirely different communicational modes: the analogical and the digital. Since language is descriptive and linear, we are forced, in order to describe a transaction, to use a dichotomisation or to introduce a series of dichotomisations.

(Selvini-Palazzoli *et al.*, 1978: 52)

In pursuit of 'the world of circularity' (1978: 53), the Milan group set out to explore particular types of therapeutic intervention which were 'characterised by the common effort to overcome the linguistic barrier' (p. 53).

Acceptance of the fact that we live in a 'languaging' world has led to other developments, both based on and independent of the work of this group. These are on the whole characterised by an emphasis on the value of narrative and description.

Narrative

The recognition of the usefulness of narrative has led its application in recent years both to therapy (for example, by White and Epston (1990) and by Sluzki (1992)), and to research (for example, by Sherman (1990)). For Bruner it has offered an opportunity for a return to a cultural or folk psychology. In his own words, he has sought:

to reemphasise a critical point about the organising principle of folk psychology as being narrative in nature rather than logical or categorical. Folk psychology is about human agents doing things on the basis of their beliefs and desires, striving for goals, meeting obstacles which they best or which best them, all of this extended over time.

(Bruner, 1990: 42)

Whatever view one might take of historical forces, they were converted into human meanings, into language, into narratives, and found their way into the minds of men and women. In the end, it was this conversion process that created folk psychology and the *experienced* world of culture.

(Bruner, 1990: 137)

Folk psychology is not so much a set of logical propositions as it is an exercise in narrative and storytelling. It is supported by a powerful structure of narrative culture – stories, myths, genres of literature.

(Bruner, 1990: 138)

Narrative, like infant observation, is hard to define. The *Chambers Twentieth Century Dictionary* defines it as 'that which is narrated: a continued account of any series of occurrences: story' (Macdonald, 1972: 876). But in recent literature, it has tended to be defined by its context and its properties. This is perhaps fitting. Bateson was highly critical of how and what children were taught about definition:

> There is a [parallel] confusion in the teaching of language that's never been straightened out. Professional linguists may know what's what, but children in school are still taught nonsense. . . . That is, they are taught at an early age that the way to define something is by what it supposedly *is* in itself, not by its relation to other things.
>
> (Bateson, 1979: 17)

He proposed that it was 'the context that fixes the meaning' (1979: 16).

The context of each narrative or story is a network of stories; it is also time, place and person. Each individual's construction of experience and events reflects their own belief system, which may be indistinguishable from that of their family or the society in which they live. There are different levels of stories which both influence and are influenced by current experience and the story about that experience. Sluzki has referred to this as an 'ecology of stories':

> Our social world is constituted in and through a network of multiple stories or narratives (the 'story' that our social world is constructed in or through multiple stories or narratives being one of them). This ecology of stories, with different degrees of dominance at different moments and in different contexts, establishes the frames within which we become aware of ourselves and others, within which we establish priorities, claim or disclaim duties and privileges, set the norms for appropriate and inappropriate behaviour, attribute meanings and order events in time. . . . From this perspective, language is not representational; what we call 'reality' resides and is expressed in one's descriptions of events, people, ideas, feelings, and experiences. These descriptions, in turn, evolve through social interactions that are themselves shaped by those descriptions; discourse provides the frames within which social action takes place. . ., a statement that echoes Bateson's notion that the Mind is social.
>
> (Sluzki, 1992: 218)

Each story, then, 'is embedded in a complex network of reciprocally influencing narratives' (Sluzki, 1992: 219). The story defines the context, and the context defines the story.

The temporal context of narratives has been emphasised: 'narrative incorporates the temporal dimension' and 'requires the location of events in cross-time patterns' (White and Epston, 1990: 3). Place can be interpreted in its broadest sense or in its narrowest. A similar set of events may be interpreted or storied very differently in one part of the world from another. The scene has to be set wherever. The context of 'the person' reflects the individuality of each narrative but also takes us back to the ideas proposed by the social constructionists and links together different levels of context. For example, a person's religious, political or ethical views provide a context but are also owned at a very personal level, that is, they are that person. So that, for a woman, her story may be influenced by how she sees women in general in society, by her political beliefs about what being a woman means, but her story is also *her* story as a woman, and as an individual who happens to be a woman. Gilligan has suggested that 'development in women is masked by a particular conception of human relationships' (1982: 25), but goes on to acknowledge the reflexive relationship between the perspective of women, and the account of their development: 'since the imagery of relationships shapes the narrative of human development, the inclusion of women, by changing that imagery, implies a shift in the entire account' (1982: 25). This is a specific example of what Bruner refers to as the 'method of negotiating and renegotiating meanings by the mediation of narrative interpretation' which he sees as 'one of the crowning achievements of human development in the ontogenic, cultural, and phylogenetic senses of that expression' (1990: 67). White and Epston see narrative not only as a key to meaning but also as the means by which we shape our lives: 'persons give meaning to their lives and relationships by storying their experience' and 'in interacting with others in the performance of these stories, they are active in the shaping of their lives and relationships' (1990: 13).

In his own words, Bruner has been 'at great pains to argue that one of the most ubiquitous and powerful discourse forms in human communication is *narrative*' (1990: 77). He has presented what he believes are the properties of narrative. The first of these is 'its inherent sequentiality' (p. 43). Bruner argues that the constituents of a narrative are meaningless, and that meaning is only conferred on them by placing them within the overall sequence, which of course is the task of the listener or interpreter. The second property is 'that it can be "real" or "imaginary" without loss of its power as a story' (p. 44), and this is evidenced by the use of stories in both works of fact and works of fiction. A third feature is 'that it specialises in forging links between the exceptional and the ordinary' (p. 47). This is of crucial importance, and where our drive for meaning-making seems to have a central position. Not only are we able to find new explanations for things which don't fit with our well-rehearsed version of how the world is or should be, but our ability to do this suggests that our view of the world is never fixed, and that we will always have in our head a possible world where the extraordinary *is* the ordinary. Our ability to generate meaning out of exceptions to the rule might be seen as the exceptional act which constitutes the rule of how to be a person. Bruner sees this third property as more than that, also describing it as a function: '*The function of a story is to find an intentional state that mitigates or at least makes comprehensible a deviation from a canonical cultural pattern*' (p. 49). In Bruner's terms, narrative's fourth property is 'dramatism' (p. 50) by which he means its ability to invoke in the interpreter moral dilemmas. This is connected to a further property which he describes as '"dual landscape"' (p. 51); that is, there is always a tension between the protagonist's world or version of reality and that of others in the story. Just as the story is embedded in a network of stories, so too are mutiple stories embedded within it.

The potential of narrative to be used therapeutically and for research purposes seems essentially to hinge on the idea that the story told is only one of a number of possible stories which could be told. In White and Epston's words:

> The structuring of a narrative requires recourse to a selective process in which we prune, from our experience, those events that do not fit with the dominant evolving stories that we and others have about us. Thus, over time and of necessity, much of our stock of lived experience goes unstoried and is never 'told' or expressed. It remains amorphous, without organization and without shape.
>
> (White and Epston, 1990: 11)

So that, 'those aspects of lived experience that fall outside of the dominant story provide a rich and fertile source for the generation, or re-generation, of alternative stories' (White and Epston, 1990: 15).

Byng-Hall (1973, 1988) uses the language of myths, scripts and legends to apply a similar idea to the therapy situation. Family myths are defined as 'those family role images which are accepted by the whole family together as representing each member' (1973: 244). Family scripts 'prescribe the pattern of family interaction in particular contexts' (1988: 168). In a similar but perhaps more digital way to the way that narrativists refer to alternative stories, Byng-Hall refers to parents' alternative scripts as: 'replicative' – 'in which the same style of parenting [as that of previous generations] is adopted' and 'corrective' – 'in which an attempt is made to correct the mistakes that were felt to have been made by their parents' (1988: 168). Family legends are 'those colored and often colorful stories that are told time and time again – in contrast to other information about the family's past which fades away' (1988: 169).

> Legends are continually being re-edited by altering the metacommunication or reshaping the content in order to build up a story that fits present family attitudes. The past is usually seen as creating the present, not the present molding the past.
>
> (Byng-Hall, 1988: 169)

The acknowledgement of reflexivity offers the potential for therapeutic rescripting.

The potential to use narrative as a research tool as opposed to just a way of finding out about how individuals and families see the world has been discussed by Reiss, who refers to 'the represented family', that is, 'each member's experience of the family' (1989: 199), and 'the practicing family' or 'the observable, external, and patterned coordinated practice in family life' (1989: 193). Sherman's account of an attempt to use narrative in research attached particular significance to the inability of some of the participants to recall stories about themselves as children, or 'to come up with any stories that touched family identity issues' (1990: 256). How people tell their stories as well as what they tell does seem important, and might be particularly so in relation to traumatic occurrences. In these instances, stories function 'to highlight, dramatise, and conserve the vividness of significant family transitions and stressful events' (Reiss, 1989: 208), and as such might be considered to be adaptive. Affleck *et al.* (1991) have placed significance on the way that mothers, in particular, of special care babies tell their stories and attribute meaning, again seeing the ability to find meaning in such circumstances as an essential component of an adaptive as opposed to a maladaptive response.

Acceptance of the idea that stories are constitutive, that is, that they shape lives and relationships, leads us to accept each individual's agency (or vice versa), and also seems to imply a particular view about matters such as power, and pathology:

> If we accept that persons organize and give meaning to their experience through the storying of experience, and that in the performance of these stories they express selected aspects of their lived experience, then it follows that these stories are constitutive – shaping lives and relationships. . . .
>
> From this it can be seen that the text analogy advances the idea that the stories or narratives that persons live through determine their interaction and organization, and that the evolution of lives and relationships occurs through the performance of such stories or narratives. Thus the text analogy is distinct from those analogies that would propose an underlying structure or pathology in families that is constitutive or shaping of their lives or relationships.
>
> (White and Epston, 1990:12)

Stories are told in order to both come to terms with and to shape experience; to pass on information; to re-edit; to share something; to coevolve; and to amuse and capture the imagination. They are tools in the task of meaning-making, serving both story teller and listener or interpreter.

While it is 'true' that 'narrative can never encompass the full richness of our lived experience' (White and Epston, 1990: 11), it does seem to provide opportunities. Each story has its own validity and offers a momentary chance to capture that elusive thing called meaning.

Questions

In order to find out about how mothers and staff viewed their experience in the unit, I had to ask them questions. Questions themselves have been the topic of articles about therapy and about research.

Referring to the context of systemic interviewing, Selvini-Palazzoli and her colleagues talked about circularity as 'the capacity of the therapist to conduct his investigation on the basis of feedback from the family in response to the information he solicits about relationships, and therefore about difference and change' (1980: 8). Tomm (1985) took this idea further, and divided circular questions into two categories:

1 Descriptive circular questions – whose aim is to lead to an understanding of the system; and
2 Reflexive circular questions – whose aim is to facilitate therapeutic change.

My aim was the first of these, but as Tomm has also stated:

The intent of a question does not, of course, guarantee its effect. However, it is impossible to ask a question without having some effect. . . .

Some questions will 'stick' in family members' minds and have an impact for far longer than we suspect. Questions asked with a descriptive intent may, of course, also have a generative effect.

(Tomm, 1985: 37)

He recognised that questions could be addressed at different logical levels, and that 'there may be multiple levels of context. . . . With each new level the number of connections that are possible increases enormously' (1985: 39).

White (1988) has also discussed the usefulness of questions in eliciting family narratives. Again, this is seen as having therapeutic potential, and is in keeping with the view that narrative is constitutive (White and Epston, 1990).

Questions asked of the mothers were addressed at different contextual levels; for example, I did ask them about some features of the baby's behaviour, and I also asked them about family beliefs and past experience. More important, however, in my opinion, was their response to my initial neutral invitation, 'Can you tell me what happened?' For two of the mothers whose accounts are reported here, this invitation resulted in an uninterrupted flow of information. Ms B, as will be seen from the extract of observation material about Brian, needed no invitation. She poured out her story right from the moment I met her. I did not really need to ask her questions, even about some beliefs, past experience, and the impact of her relationship with Brian on other relationships; most of it came tumbling out.

Questions asked of staff about these particular babies on the other hand produced a much more guarded response. Some seemed reluctant, for example, to comment on the developing mother–child relationship or how mothers and fathers got on with staff. My impression of this reluctance or wariness was that it was qualitatively quite different from the easy sharing of feelings and impressions that goes along with the clinical task, and occurs, for example, at a formal case discussion or ward round. In these situations, the necessity of considering such things is almost unspoken, and discussion of interpersonal relationships on the unit goes on as part of the work. I have no doubt, therefore, that the response was related to my particular role as an observer in these cases, rather than as a therapist. My sense was that the staff did not wish to appear to make judgements about these women. Nonetheless, they did share some of their observations with me.

THE MOTHERS' STORIES

As a result of mothers' differing styles of interaction with me, and differing responses, particularly to an invitation to recount what had happened, their stories are presented in very different ways. Two are short, one is longer but seems very disconnected, and one was so long that it required considerable editing. Already the discerning reader will realise that what are about to be presented are as much my stories as the mothers'. This is also more obvious in that two are mostly recounted in the third person, while two contain a lot of directly quoted material.

It is important to say that in my search for stories about special care babies, I had fully intended to ask couples, and not just mothers, for their accounts. My attention had been drawn to just how neglected fathers were, by mothers in this context, and by staff. However, I rarely had the opportunity to meet fathers and, as will be witnessed by these particular accounts, 'marital' relationships seemed to be vulnerable at this time in these women's lives. The only account that was given jointly was that of Ms A and her partner.

These accounts are presented here without additional comments. In Chapter 6, themes from these stories and observational material will be woven together, and considered in the context of a wider group's experience.

Ms A – Alan's mother

Alan's birth was unexpected in more ways than one. His mother hadn't planned to be pregnant, and didn't realise that she was until quite late on. She had split up with the father of the baby, and never discussed him with anyone in the hospital nor revealed his identity. She had always had a stormy relationship with her mother and step-father, and left home around the time the pregnancy was discovered, she did not say why exactly. She was living in accommodation for the homeless, a bed and breakfast place. She had attended very few antenatal appointments.

Her story began with the account of her labour. On the day that Alan was born she was walking in the park with a friend when she suddenly realised that she was in labour. A few hours later, Alan arrived. The staff at the hospital mistakenly thought that his gestational age was about four weeks less than it was. He was actually born at twenty-six weeks. His birth weight was 1076 grams. No attempt was made to resuscitate him initially but did get under way when they realised some two hours later that he was still breathing. He was then rushed to the neonatal intensive care unit of another hospital. The friend went with him and was presumed to be his father. It was only later that the error of this presumption was appreciated but he quickly became the mother's new partner and supported her throughout the baby's time in intensive care, which lasted some six months until his death. In her words, the whole thing had brought them closer together.

Alan's mother felt very angry about his beginning but really didn't know who to be angry with. After some difficulties during the first few weeks in being able to commit herself to frequent visits, she became devoted to him, and together she and her partner spent long hours at the cotside. She felt quite isolated in the unit, at different times feeling that the nursing staff were distant and at others feeling very supported by them.

> They're great, very honest. I was quite shocked but now it's good. They tell us everything. It helps. It's better to know. They don't just tell us what we want to hear, but that's good.

She felt unsupported by other parents, and attributed this to how she looked. Despite the fact that she was twenty, she acknowledged that she looked much younger. She felt that other parents were making judgements about her based on their perceptions. On one occasion, she had been told by another mother that she was too young to have a baby. She retorted, 'Who do you think you are, anyway, my mother?'

She was desperately committed to her baby and was determined that he should survive. She described him as a little fighter just like herself.

I was in a special care unit, but I was always fighting. He's always fighting it too. He's very active. I was like that when I was a kid. He's so strong.

She was determined that she would not abandon him: 'I won't abandon him, no matter what anyone says'. She had been a premature baby herself, born when her mother was only sixteen, and said that she had been abandoned, spending her first two to three years in hospital. She had never been close to her mother, and resented her remarriage to a man who had later abused *her* (Ms A). She did not say so but the impression was that she had been abandoned more than once, perhaps into care later on.

As a teenager, she had been one of the older children in the family with a number of step-brothers and sisters. Her life had not been happy. She was often asked to care for them. She fought with her parents and did not achieve well at school. During Alan's time in the unit she received little help from them but did not seem to want it.

Her relationship with the baby grew stronger as time went on, and towards the end of his life, this seemed to be in spite of or because of her increasing feeling of isolation.

Ms D – Daniel's mother

Daniel too was born somewhat unexpectedly at twenty-nine weeks, although the surprise did not seem too great a one. He weighed 1300 grams. Ms D started off by telling me about the birth of her first child. Because the first baby had been premature, she hadn't really expected to carry this baby to term. Her good experience with her first child meant that she felt very positive about Daniel, his survival and her potential to manage. Although she had split up with her husband, she did seem to think that they would get back together again; and while distant geographically from her own mother, this woman had a supportive network of relatives and friends around her. Her sister, in particular, looked after her son while she visited and generally allowed this mother both the time and the emotional space to attend to her baby. The lack of detail and connections offered by this woman in response to my invitation seemed to convey a sense that all this was natural and best just got on with. Even her separation from her husband didn't seem to make much difference to how she saw herself as managing.

As she seemed to anticipate, all went well with Daniel, and he was discharged home at about thirty-five weeks.

Ms B – Brian's mother

Brian was born at twenty-nine weeks, weighing 1220 grams. His mother began her story by telling me about her previous miscarriage. She had had an episode of bleeding at about nine weeks, and later too. It turned out that the baby had died at thirteen weeks, but she did not miscarry until about twenty weeks. She was ill, tired, pale, feeling rough, then she miscarried. They found out that the baby was dead shortly before he was born. She got pregnant again at almost exactly the time that the lost baby was due. She said that she had always wanted to have three children. This time, she had started to bleed at fourteen weeks and was hospitalised until twenty-seven weeks. In hospital, they'd told her that she had lost his twin already. Contractions had started suddenly on the day before his birth, and after initial treatment at one hospital she was transferred shortly before his birth to one where there were cots available in the neonatal unit.

This woman had had a lot of experience of being in hospital, she'd had six miscarriages, the last of which had been just before she conceived Brian. Her family too had been 'plagued with illness', all except her mother who was intolerant of illness and quite unsupportive. Brian's mother said very clearly that she hated hospitals, and based that on her own experience and that of her relatives, 'the only time any of them went in, they never came out'. As a child she had been very close to her grandparents both of whom had died in this particular hospital, her grandmother when she was eleven. She spoke of her belief that she might die.

I had all this bleeding. Any books about pregnancy had said bleeding was serious. It was an unknown, a fear. People were being light-hearted, I didn't know if it really was nothing serious, or if they were trying to stop me from panicking. They threw a blanket round it, I didn't know how serious it was. When they said they'd induce me at thirty-five weeks, I thought well, obviously they're not going to risk my life beyond that. But I *was* risking my life.

They seemed mainly interested in the baby, they treated me like an incubator. If someone had said I had to have a termination, I'd have been upset but I would have known that they were thinking about *me*, I wouldn't have risked my life any further. I felt they weren't thinking about me at all. The woman in the next bed asked for a termination, and they gave her one at twenty-three weeks. She was a business woman, she said she couldn't waste all this time in hospital, she had appointments on Monday. I was two weeks less pregnant than her, *I* wanted a termination, I kept thinking 'how long can I go on like this?' But it was so terrible, I couldn't have done it.

When the baby was born, I'd had twenty four hours of pains, and I went to the hospital. I wasn't going to have a baby, I was going to have a miscarriage. I waited till the point of no return, and then I went, I said to him (her partner) to stay at home, not to come. There would be no happy event to celebrate. I was two centimetres and they decided to send me to the other hospital. The labour suddenly went very quickly, I was seven centimetres, and I could tell that they knew I was going to lose it. His heartbeat went down with every contraction.

There was no paediatrician. Suddenly he was born, they told me it was a boy, but no one said whether he was alive or dead. And then they all went out of the room, they took him out of the room. I didn't know what had happened, I wanted to know, I thought if I shout I'll know, and then I thought it's better not to know.

Later they came and said 'Would you like to see your baby?' I thought they were going to show me a corpse, but he was alive. I thought that he was dying. There was no explanation. I thought he's definitely dying. There will be no champagne and flowers, how would I tell his father. I was upset, I rushed out, and when I came back a few hours later they'd moved him. I thought he wasn't there, but he'd done so well they'd put him in a cot. I wasn't able to ask if he was going to live.

Later she *was* able to ask, and she had to keep asking. When she wasn't with him she'd think the worst, imagining things like 'What if he died when I was having breakfast?'. She went on to discuss communication generally; she didn't think that they told her the truth, sometimes she didn't even think they knew who she was. She hadn't been there for some of his investigations and she had said that she wanted to be. She was sure they were keeping something from her. This had been reinforced by her experience of the bad news. One minute he was OK, the next they were telling her that he had brain damage, but they didn't know how serious it was. He had more scans. And then two weeks later, someone asked her if she was feeling better, relieved, and she hadn't known what they were talking about. They'd forgotten to tell her that it looked as if he would be all right.

Around this time they were talking about discharge and asked her to stay in for twenty-four hours. She had a row with one of the doctors. They didn't seem to realise that she had to be at home. Her mother had taken the girls under pressure when she was in hospital but was not offering to step into the breach again. She'd said to her before that she'd made her bed and would have to lie in it. And then, she was being told that she had to stay in; it was the final straw. She blew.

Hospital was a difficult place for this woman. It evoked strong feelings in her, and it seemed that she evoked strong feelings in the staff:

There's something about hospitals, a feeling of isolation, you feel like your identity has been taken from you.

He's lost his identity. I'm waiting for the day when they say he doesn't have to come here any more, and then I'll say he's mine. The corridor in that place goes on and on, it's like walking up the aisle, I feel I'm never going to get there. Every time I go there, I think that someone's going to tap me on the shoulder before I get to the exit and say, Where are you going? . . . At home, I thought it'd be OK, but I keep thinking that they're going to take him back, that I've got him on loan.

When I was in hospital waiting, I wanted that indefinite helpless feeling to end, I wanted to have him earlier, but now I'm glad I didn't, seeing some of the other babies born only a few weeks earlier. I asked one of the other mums 'Do you feel he's yours?', and she said the same thing. We thought that when we got them home it'd be different, but unless they're there to say it's OK, I feel I might be doing something wrong and I feel blamed.

When I was pregnant, I knew that I'd love him when he came out. And when he was born, I was happy, and only concerned about him being OK and getting him home. Now I resent the fact that he's so clingy, and I blame the hospital for that. Not per se, but they don't pick them up when they cry. They'd leave him crying. He cries now, sometimes I feel persecuted as if he's doing it to get at me. He confuses day and night, he cries, he's brain damaged.

She sounded very despondent and negative, about him and about the hospital. We started discussing his surname, which was still being mistaken by the hospital.

When he was born there was a lot of confusion. I did tell them, but there always seemed to be some confusion. *And* they used to say 'she', even when he was dressed in blue. One time I was holding him in my arms and a nurse said 'She's due for her feed' and then I found myself saying 'she'. I was going to let it drop but then I noticed that one particular nurse did it to others too. I thought, I'm not having this. You know on some days you're more assertive than on others. She still did it later on, I don't know if she realised. I wouldn't have bothered but I hadn't had a boy before. I knew that I wanted people to know that he was a boy but then I thought, it's just me being overreactive.

I asked about her family's beliefs about and experience of looking after small babies, and she told me that currently none of her relatives were in that situation. She was an only child, close to her grandparents and her aunt, whose two children were her age. Her mother and father had divorced when she was only a toddler. The only apparent advice or disapproval came from her mother, and her mother-in-law:

My mother says things like, dip his dummy in honey – I don't do it. I did with my first, but not now. She thinks she knows better than I do, but I hang on to my own ideas. My mother-in-law feels she knows everything. She has strong views on things, but I don't take a great deal of notice. I let it go in one ear and out the other, because she has strong views on everything.

She discussed the relationship between relationships in her family and in the hospital easily. Her two older children had always been closer to her when things weren't going well between her and her partner. She felt that her previous partners, while helping with practical things, didn't have a strong emotional bond with the children. She has always had to compensate in all sorts of ways for their lack of commitment, for example by being strict and setting limits, as well as being close and supportive. She described Brian's father as different, more emotionally in touch but less practical, also more strict.

I know what every scream is for, and when he's there I have to stop him from getting annoyed with him. The baby pushes us apart and he pushes Brian and I together. We split up for a while when he was in the unit. I resented being in the hospital all the time and I took it out on him. I thought he should have been there as well. I knew he couldn't do anything. I hated being there so much I wanted him to suffer too.

The nurses were looking after him more than I was. Some were really pushy, saying that I should do everything for him but I couldn't. I wasn't afraid of them but I resented it. It wasn't because they were wanting me to get to know him. They were too busy. They weren't by my side helping and reassuring. The emphasis was on little things. They wanted me to dress him, with all these tubes, I was afraid I would break his leg or something. They didn't show me, I resented it. I preferred them to do things. I didn't think that them doing it challenged me as a mother. I felt more supported if they were attending to him.

I used to dread leaving, not just because I'd miss him or because something would happen but because *they*'d notice and make a comment. I used to wait until there weren't many nurses around and then leave. It was OK with some of them. One time I came he had been moved and was back in one of these big incubators, he had a chest infection. When I asked why, one of them said that he'd probably got it from one of the girls. They were blaming us!

I used to dread feeding him. The first time I did it, I asked 'How do you wind him?' The nurse looked at me in total astonishment and said 'How would you wind any other baby?' I just wondered if there was another way. I did it tentatively, wondering if I was hurting him. I would hold him on my shoulder and pat him, he would settle down. One nurse was really nice, she would tell me that he knew it was me. I didn't believe her but she did make the effort to make me feel that I was doing something constructive.

It was important to talk to him – I did it with all of them. We used to sit and I'd be talking away to him, I used to tell him everything. I was reassuring him that he'd be all right, that I was here and I'd make sure that he was OK. Maybe it was more important to me than it was to him. I wasn't just going to sit there staring. A lot of people did that. Initially there wasn't even a flicker of an eyelid, later he did respond. It's important to talk to them whether they're premature or not, the relationship stems from that. My mother never had it with me. I was always afraid to ask her things in case she would tell me off. My daughters know that they can ask me anything. I couldn't go to my mother.

I did all that and then he'd open his eyes for his father. He even admitted that he forgot we had him. He'd ask me where I was going, and I'd say the hospital. Oh yes, he'd say. My whole world was revolving around the baby and he'd forgotten we had him.

I asked her about the girls, their relationship with Brian.

The youngest didn't like him, she resented all the time I spent in hospital. He's more of an intrusion now that he's home. The older one likes to look after him – it's a sort of maternal adventure for her.

Having Brian at home was in fact an enormous strain for this woman. He'd been discharged at about three months but even at six months she found him clingy, irritable and very difficult to cope with. She acknowledged the strain on the rest of the family. She was protective of him in the face of their complaints but at times felt very persecuted by him herself. She had help from Social Services. Someone would look after him twice a week so that she could rest or catch up or spend time with her daughters.

Questions about his future and the degree of any disability remained unanswered.

Ms C – Catherine's mother

Catherine's mother was admitted to hospital at nineeen weeks with a placenta praevia.

> I was bleeding, the whole time in hospital I was bleeding. After five weeks, I was still bleeding. And I was praying – there was nothing that they could do. You were bleeding, fearing for your life, trying to have courage. The baby kept kicking. In me, I was praying. Calling my God. Challenging my God.
>
> I didn't want my pregnancy. I didn't know that I was even pregnant. I discovered at three months, I went to the doctor and he did a pregnancy test. It was positive.
>
> This is my fourth baby. My seven year old was the same, he was born at twenty-eight weeks, he's all right. The third one was born at 22 weeks, she died. I said that I was never going to have another one.
>
> I keep thinking that she's going to live. I was really bleeding, but she was kicking, really kicking. It's been like that. She had no feeding line for the first four weeks. She's doing fine. She's a surviver, a real fighter. She's gone through hell. I feel for her. She's seven weeks today, she's gained a lot of weight, but she has a little problem with her breathing. She's still ventilated, if they try to take her off, she drops her breath.
>
> Now she opens her eyes. She knows my voice. It tells her how small she is. When I tell her what she should weigh, she opens her eyes, she knows she is special. The nurses have a special relationship with her. It helps. I don't have much time, they're here all the time.

This woman's previous baby had died. She said that that experience had helped her with this one. But at the time she'd had to forget it. There was nothing that she could do:

> You couldn't help. Premature babies, no matter how small they are, behave the same. They have breathing problems. They think that they're still inside. Their heart rates go up and down.

There was a feeling that she saw herself as a failure in her family's eyes:

> I'm the only one in the family who has premature babies. They fell for me. All the others have full-term babies. I'm the only one who doesn't. My mother had

no problems, she had two boys and two girls, and she did everything, you know the washing, the work, all the way through.

If they want to be alive they will be. No matter how much you attach yourself to them, they decide themselves, if God says. . . . Even if no one's looking to see her, to see if she's here, she's in the world. I believe that once you are born to live you will live. If the baby's destined to be alive she will be whether you come to see her or not. Really, God takes care of little babies. He'll decide.

This mother stayed away from the unit for eight days soon after Catherine was born.

I wasn't feeling well, I'd lost a lot of blood, I thought I was going to die. They looked after me. I was taking all the special food, and being massaged. I had a very rough time. I was afraid for my own life.

In response to my question about whether the baby had missed her:

I don't know if she knows who I am, I can't carry her, I can only touch, she may know. . . . Where I come from, you can only try your best. No one has the power to heal but God.

Catherine's mother acknowledged how helpful she found her beliefs.

Late in the story, she said that she was separated from her husband, but did not say why. He had been happy when he heard about the pregnancy. For her, the baby brought them back together. He had visited, she felt that he was very keen on the baby and that that was a good thing.

Catherine was 740 grams when she was born at twenty-four weeks. She died nine weeks later. Having survived an abdominal operation, and having successfully been weaned off the ventilator, she suddenly deteriorated and did not respond to medical intervention. Her mother was in Africa at the time visiting her family.

THE STAFF'S PERCEPTIONS

About the babies and their families

Not surprisingly, of the four babies presented, Alan was the one to whom most of the staff became very 'attached'. This was in part related to his long stay on the unit, and in part, it seemed, related to their perception of his mother as young and vulnerable. They felt that she too needed to be taken care of. An added influence was his difficult beginning. Some of the nurses spoke to me spontaneously about this; they felt angry about it, and there was a sense, too, that they wanted to make up for it. Right at the beginning of his stay there was concern that his mother might not visit much, and the nursing staff gently helped her to make a commitment to her child. As his life went on, they recognised the strength of the bond that she had made with him, and this created a different anxiety for them. They were almost constantly in doubt about whether she was hearing or understanding their explanations about his medical state, the fragility of his condition. At times, some had grave doubts about the heroic efforts that they were making to keep him alive. This was especially the case when he had had a setback, and seemed to go back to square one. They recognised that at times like this, his mother seemed to become more sharp with them, more challenging, but also seemed less emotionally available to discuss both his progress and how she felt about that.

Towards the end of Alan's life, when he was continuing to deteriorate, they found it difficult to support her, and she distanced herself from them. There was a sense for some of them that she had detected their uncertainty about the ethics of prolonging his life, and had, as a result, decided to shut them out.

During the time that Alan was in the unit, there were periods when the staff perceived their relationship with this family as good and periods when they felt it was not so good. Losing Alan was painful for the staff but his death also brought a sense of relief, which was more easy for some to acknowledge than others.

Brian's mother was another woman who evoked quite strong feelings in the staff group. In contrast to Ms A, whom they saw as fragile and vulnerable, most of them found it hard to be sympathetic towards Ms B. I say most of them, because one particular nurse actually had a very good relationship with Ms B, and interestingly both recognised how special it was. Others responded to her curt and defensive manner in kind. Most found her difficult to work with, and for some reason were unable to hold on to the idea that her brusque manner might in fact be camouflaging her distress. Brian's mother's sense of being judged by the nursing staff, and her sensitivity about their comments, seemed almost to constitute a self-fulfilling prophecy, from which it became difficult to break away.

I felt that the staff were more puzzled than challenged by Catherine's mother, Ms C. Again, there was initially a lot of concern that this mother had abandoned her baby. However, in the same way that Ms C believed that there was little that could be done to change things for her daughter, so too, the staff seemed convinced that there was little that they could do to make any difference to this woman's relationship with her child. Catherine never really became well enough to give any feedback to the nurses caring for her, and this made their task even harder. Additionally, numerous attempts were made early on to establish a feeding line but each was doomed to disaster. This difficult beginning, in that the staff knew what would help her but were unable to give it, seemed again to be associated with an ethical dilemma for several nurses. A sense of wanting to save this baby, and perhaps at times feeling bad because they could not do any more, seemed to add to their confusion. In some cases, a sense of impotence seemed to lead to a distancing from this mother–child pair.

In contrast to all of these, the nurses' perceptions of Ms D was that she was easy to relate to, and cared for her baby naturally. Their fit with her seemed optimal; they felt appreciated by her, and were able to be close or distant without feeling any need to justify their position. *They* did not feel persecuted by *her*, in the way that they did by Ms B, for example. Like me, they felt less concerned about her circumstances than they were about those of other mothers. They saw her as a 'good mum', whose ability to relate to and care for her child did not seem to be affected by potentially traumatic life events. As a result, they did not feel anxious or offer extra support, and while this felt appropriate, it may have left this mother feeling more vulnerable.

About caring for a special care baby

The staff had a strong philosophical belief in a child-centred approach. In other words:

> that the service should fit the needs of the child and not the needs of the workers. Not that we should be assisting the parents or that the parents should be involved in decision-making but a much stronger statement than that, which is that we recognise that the parents are the primary carers, and we're here to support them. We're trying to do more than work in partnership with parents. In neonatal intensive care, it is impractical that parents should do all the caring but that doesn't mean that we should forget it or stop discussing it.

The importance of good communication with parents about all aspects of the baby's care and condition was emphasised. This included an appreciation of the necessity of communication about detail, in particular. So that, for example:

> moving the site of a baby's cot – you must phone the parents and tell them otherwise they walk in and see an empty space – they always think that their baby's dead. Parents also experience the move from the 'hot' room as a crisis, for some it's the moving away from the very posh and sophisticated equipment. For others it's not that but it's important nonetheless.

Some, particularly medical staff, had noticed that they seemed to remember to communicate bad news, but took it for granted at times that good news was passed on. There seemed to be some 'rules' that they knew about but parents didn't; for example, if a baby died, a senior member of the medical staff would seek out the parents to tell them, they would never be left not knowing. Some knew that parents had been left not knowing the good news for several hours after the birth, for example, and thought that this should not have been the case.

Communicating with parents on a day-to-day basis, however, was made more or less easy by how available the parents were both physically and emotionally. These two aspects came together in a particular way as staff noticed how available different parents were while actually in the unit. A member of the medical staff noted:

> The parents themselves are so different – some parents, the minute they're in the unit, their eyes follow you wherever you go. They're waiting for you, just waiting for the moment when they catch your eye. Whereas other parents sit facing the wall, and they sort of look into the corner when they see you coming, and you have to tap them on the shoulder and sort of go round to get any kind of eye contact or make any kind of contact at all with them.

There was a belief, held most strongly by the more senior staff, that it was:

> better to tell people what was going on than not to tell them. And if that worries them or upsets them then somehow you've got to deal with that.

There was also a belief that 'communication should be carried out as a routine procedure'. This encompassed an acknowledgement that emotions might get in the way of the passing on of information. This seemed especially true of the task of informing people like GPs, health visitors and others of a baby's death, when the pain of the loss might lead to forgetting, particularly when tasks to do with living babies provided a ready 'diversion'.

The stressfulness of the nurses' task in caring for a special care baby was most readily acknowledged by senior staff. They recognised that being in the front line was difficult for everyone, especially in situations where the struggle for life, or good quality life, was almost constant. This was seen to be coped with in different ways. More senior nurses would question ethics, and be open with colleagues about their doubts and uncertainties, whereas some less experienced nurses were less willing to acknowledge these aspects, and would at times distance themselves from families to protect themselves from the emotions aroused and the questions that might come their way.

Very few staff members felt that their relationship with a mother might impact on her developing relationship with her infant. This was in the context of a group who readily identified the importance of the early mother–child relationship, and who acted early if they were in doubts about it in any one case. Nursing staff found it hard to put up with parents who were angry or seemed demanding, despite the intellectual recognition that the birth of a very premature baby might be traumatic and hard to recover from, and might arouse many strong emotions. Similarly they had high expectations of parents, mothers in particular, even though they knew that it might be difficult for them to make a commitment to a baby whose chances were not good. Some did not seem to understand that parents might feel nervous about physically caring for a very tiny baby, and again this was in the context of intellectual knowing. It was, however, often acknowledged that how easygoing a parent was influenced their relationship with them and with their infant.

Importantly, the putting into practice of a general philosophy of care for babies and their families was variously not recognised at all to be influenced by personal factors or appreciated in a number of different ways by different individuals who were more or less ready to acknowledge that a parent's personality might influence the staff–parent relationship, and in turn the developing parent–child relationship.

About staff morale

There was a recognition that, as in any institution, morale was lower when there was uncertainty or an expectation of change. NHS reforms had evoked anxiety in many staff, and this was related both to a general feeling of uncertainty about what the future might hold, and to the impact of more subtle changes in the style of management which had already impacted on task performance at every level. These were perhaps felt more acutely by this group of staff than others as there had been much media attention given to the ethical dilemmas and the very high costs involved in neonatal intensive care.

Morale was also seen to be affected on a day-to-day or week-to-week basis by the mortality of the client group. Thus:

> When you have a run of babies dying, morale goes very low, in doctors and nurses and probably other people as well. And certainly, low morale is connected with poor recruitment and poor retainment of staff. If you have a bad patch, you'll find that a lot of students don't stay.

Staff seemed to be constantly caught in a dilemma. Historically, as they had got better at treating babies, and were more certain of the outcome, the ethical dilemmas about treating, say, a twenty-eight weeker had almost been resolved, and the personal stress in relation to this had lessened. But with each step forward in the unit's capability, they were faced with further dilemmas. Doubts and stresses emerged, or re-emerged, as even younger and even more fragile infants were presented for treatment. The implicit and necessary reward of a sense of almost 100 per cent satisfaction and achievement was always tantalisingly out of reach. While caring for 'the tinies' was felt to be a legitimate and essential task, it may have affected staff morale in an unrecognised way.

SUMMARY

Language both constrains our description of our experiences and offers opportunities. Acceptance of the fact that we live in a 'languaging' world has been associated with an increasing recognition of the value of narrative in both research and therapy. Each story has a context but can also be the context for a reappraisal of past events or beliefs. Stories are the way in which people give meaning to their experience and shape their lives. This has been recognised to be an important part of an adaptive response to a crisis, such as a baby's admission to intensive care. In this chapter, the stories of staff and mothers of special care babies have been presented.

Chapter 6

Observer and observed

Making sense of the experience

Most of the families whom I have met in the context of my work in neonatal intensive care, special care or high dependency units have not only been facing the crisis of having a child with a life-threatening illness but have also been struggling with social adversity. I use this term to cover a range of additional stresses, which include poverty, emotional deprivation and adult relationship difficulties. The four mothers and babies presented in Chapters 4 and 5 are most like those I am asked to become involved with as a child and family psychiatrist.

These families are not only most at risk but they are also the ones most likely to have premature babies. The outcome studies on premature and low birth weight infants consistently report a correlation between outcome and social class. Even before they are conceived, these infants have the odds stacked against them. Of course, premature babies are born to well-to-do and middle-class families but, on the whole, their story is likely to be a different one to that told so far. There is no doubt that they too have a stressful and often harrowing time which lives with them for years afterwards but they also seem more often to have a supportive network of people around them. My impression is that most of them also find it easier than low income families to make use of parent support organisations.

For all families, however, it seems clear that what they make of their situation, and how they cope with it will be strongly influenced by their past experience and beliefs. Of course, that will be related to what sort of a person they are; they will have both shaped and been shaped by their own stories. At the time of the infant's birth and admission to special care, the parents' own strengths and vulnerabilities may immediately influence their propensity to make good and potentially supportive relationships with staff. For babies who are destined to spend months in the special care unit, the quality of their parents' relationship with hospital staff may be as important in determining their outcome as the parent–child relationship itself. Its beginning may be crucial if a facilitative rather than rivalrous partnership is to develop.

The observational material presented offers an opportunity to witness this important partnership in action but a fuller interpretation of the significance of what has been observed can only be reached once the stories of mothers and staff members around each infant are also included.

Is it possible to weave the different parts of each story together in a way that makes sense? Is it legitimate? The answer to these questions is probably 'yes' *if* the weaving makes sense to the participants. Being able to make sense of an experience and give it meaning is recognised to be an important predictor of both initial adaptation to 'the crisis of neonatal intensive care' and psychological outcome for both parents and child (Affleck *et al.*, 1991). Some parents may create their own meaning or may be helped to do this by friends, family or professionals. Similarly, staff may have insight into the complex mix of factors that influence their own abilities to support some families more easily than others or achieve insight through discussion and exploration of their own feelings with colleagues.

Before trying to make sense of the experiences of the babies, mothers and staff so far presented, I think it is important to consider some general themes which have arisen in discussion with parents and staff. These themes form the context for the developing parent–child relationship. For parents, they are the pieces of their jigsaw which have to be fitted together, the things that have to be made sense of.

THEMES

Of mothers

A disproportionate number of very young women from deprived backgrounds become mothers of special care babies. They have insecure attachments to their own mothers, and may have become pregnant in order to try to make up in some way for their own feelings of deprivation. They want their babies very much; their phantasies are that their baby will provide something for them that they have not had; many talk of 'having something of my very own' or of 'having someone to love'.

Another group, of older women, will have had miscarriage after miscarriage, and will continue to conceive in the hope that their next baby will survive. Many put themselves in life-threatening situations in order to have a baby. They do not allow themselves the time or space to mourn for their lost babies. Again, there is a sense that these women's desperation has its roots in emotional deprivation, that they are trying to have a baby in order to meet their own needs. I believe that all babies are conceived in order to meet adult emotional needs, particularly women's, but in these cases this drive is even more powerful and at times becomes destructive of other relationships. For these women, the birth of a live infant may be experienced as an unexpected but successful outcome.

For many women, the context of the pregnancy will be more ordinary, and a premature birth will be an extraordinary event. Nonetheless, many of them also do not expect to have a live baby. This is especially the case if the pregnancy has been in jeopardy from a relatively early stage. How ready they are to be mothers will vary. It seems in some ways to be easier to take on the mantle of 'new' motherhood if they have already worn it. This will, of course, depend on what their previous experiences have been. For some women, the ability to be a mother seems to be invalidated in their own eyes if their infant is very small, fragile or obviously disabled. It is as if their mothering capability is suspended by the experience of having a baby who does not fit with their expectations.

Babies who arrive suddenly with no prior indication that things are not right will themselves be disadvantaged by the lack of opportunity to treat them for prematurity before birth. Their mothers too will not be ready. They have been deprived of time to prepare emotionally for the event of delivery itself, and, in the case of first time mothers, to surrender their individuality and replace it with maternal preoccupation. For most of these women, the birth is accompanied by a sense of failure at some level, failure as a woman and as a mother. They experience loss of a longed for and, in phantasy, perfect child, whether or not their baby is obviously disabled.

A number of women seem to think of their pregnancy as a near death experience. They have been frightened, not only for their babies but also for their own lives. Most will have been unable to confirm or refute this, unable to ask at the time and unable to ask later just what risks were taken. And, as is the case at the time of the birth and when the infant is in intensive care, they have made assumptions that no communication means the worst of all possible imagined scenarios.

During the initial weeks and months that their infants are in the special care baby unit, there is an almost constant expectation of loss. Each visit to the unit is accompanied by anxiety, and if the baby has been moved, the first thought will often be that he or she has died. The spectre of disability also haunts these mothers. There is a real sense that the outcome may not be fully known until years later, and this, of course, is often the case. There is confusion about how to behave towards the infant, and a real feeling of not knowing what to do, both physically for and to the infant *and* emotionally. The expectation of loss, the feeling of inability to care for their child, the baby's physical appearance, and the sense of being peripheral and superfluous in the unit all contribute to a difficulty in owning their babies, which many say continues even after discharge.

At an emotional level, it seems that the past is thrown into sharp relief by the current crisis. So that, for example, in the case of a mother who has already experienced loss, especially of a child, there will be a real question of how much commitment she can make to this baby. Perceptions of past and present relationships may be altered in the context of current stress and distress. New mothers, like those whose full-term babies are born in a straightforward way, may suddenly find themselves remembering their childhood and their relationship with their own parents. Many will feel judged by their internalised parents, and as a result may feel unable to accept support from their mothers. Another source of stress and confusion is thrown into the melting pot.

The support they are able to obtain from their partners is also variable. A number of influences come into play. At a practical level, choices often have to be made about how the family will organise itself to cope with the crisis. The resulting division of roles between parents often means that they have little time to spend with each other. Mothers often find it difficult to make a commitment to both father and baby, and when there are other children too, their partner often comes last. The distancing in the marital relationship may also be affected by how the mother is feeling about her role in the events that have led either to the child being born too soon or with a disability of some kind. Many will feel that they have let their partners down, that they have not given him a fit and healthy child. They may also feel angry or depressed, and all of these things may make it difficult for them to allow their partner to comfort or support them. Of course, this is not always the case. Many couples may be brought closer by the circumstances, and may support each other very effectively, and this is likely to be associated with a strong commitment to the baby. The quality of their previous relationship is likely to be important; in some cases where the relationship has been shaky, and required a great deal of work to keep it alive, it appears that that work is often put on hold temporarily while the infant is sick. It is as if the mothers make a decision about how much stress they can cope with; if the stress of their relationship with their partner outweighs the support they get from it, they may decide to separate or distance themselves for a while.

Of fathers

Fathers often feel left out, or even shut out, when their child is admitted to special care. Many will have seen and may even have held their infant before their partner but their involvement is often not sustained in the same way as the mothers'. After an uncomplicated birth, fathers often take up the traditional role of nurturing their partner, and attending to the practical side of family life. They sometimes feel jealous of the mother–child relationship, irritated by their partner's preoccupation, and envious of the attention that their baby is getting. In the special care situation all of these feelings may be exaggerated. Some will be as devoted and attentive to the baby as their partners, while others will find that their main role is in caring for their other children. Some will feel lost, they may feel uncomfortable in hospital surroundings, and they may have been shocked by the experience of the birth. They will often be less upset about the life-threatening nature of their infant's condition, and this seems in many cases to be related to their concern for their partner, their belief that she might have died, and their relief that she has survived.

There is no doubt that despite philosophical statements, unit staff often find it difficult to give fathers a role in the same way that they give mothers a role. Fathers often have to fight for their place. They have to be determined, say, to give their baby a feed or change a nappy as, in the mother's absence, they will rarely be encouraged to do this. The sense is that despite intellectual enlightenment, the female professional carers do show a lack of sensitivity to gender issues.

Interestingly, fathers seem to find their place more easily in the case of twin births, especially if these are first babies. They are given a different opportunity to have a role, perhaps because rivalry with the mother is less of an issue.

IN PURSUIT OF MEANING

I'm going to go on now to offer *the sense that I have made* of the experiences of these particular families. That is not to say that it is different to the meaning attributed by the participants, but my position as an observer and listener perhaps enables me to make some more specific links in each case than it may have been possible or bearable for them to make.

Brian

Brian's mother was not prepared for the birth of a live child. In her own words, she was going to the hospital 'to have a miscarriage'. Her obstetric history was terrible – she had had many miscarriages in the past but for some reason she had an idea in her head, a wish, to have three babies, and so she kept trying. She had already conceived a child with Brian's father. The loss of this baby seemed to have been even more traumatic than the loss of previous babies, and she had not fully mourned for her baby before she had replaced it with another inside her. Brian's conception at the time the first baby was due did not seem to be a coincidence. Nevertheless, she had felt hostility towards him and towards medical staff when she felt that his life was being put before her own. She had both envied the woman who'd had her pregnancy terminated, and been appalled by her own wish to follow a similar course of action. Her ambivalence was acted out when she finally went into labour. She waited until there would be no going back, until she was sure that the baby would be delivered, before going to hospital.

Her anguish then at not knowing whether her baby was alive or dead must have been considerable. She may have believed that her actions had led to his death. She was not told that he was alive. Her comment about 'no champagne and flowers' suggested that she felt she'd let her partner down too. She thought she was going to be shown a corpse, and instead she was introduced to her son, alive but fragile.

She was not only shocked to discover that he was alive but also shocked by his size and appearance. She knew that she could be a good mother but her sense of competence was shaken. This was not one of her babies – despite having had so many miscarriages, she thought of herself as someone who had bouncing eight pound babies. Her shock, her disbelief and her feeling of being deskilled all made her feel very vulnerable on the inside. Unfortunately, she was one of these people who became more brusque, more abrupt and more demanding when she was feeling fragile. Somehow she rubbed the nursing staff up the wrong way.

For me, the past provided some clue to this. She had never had a good relationship with her own mother, and continued to find both her and her mother-in-law intrusive and critical. She felt persecuted by the nurses, she felt that they were watching her, judging her and criticising her. With the exception of one nurse, she felt that they were unsupportive and demanding. She reacted to this sense of being judged with hostility, and by doing this seemed to almost force judgements to be made about her. Her relationship with her mother seemed to be played out with the nurses, and none of them recognised this. Some did suspect that she was very fragile underneath but her manner made it difficult for them to reach her.

Her beliefs and past experiences of hospitals compounded this. The woman she had been closest to, her grandmother, had died in this very hospital when she was only eleven. Her experience was that people went into hospital and never came out. During this pregnancy, she had thought that this was to be her fate too.

Despite all this she did spend time with her son, she talked to him, she let him know that she was there. She did this in quite a different way to the way that she talked to me. With me, she was all over the place, spilling out her story and her feelings at every opportunity. With him, she was calm, collected and containing, most of the time.

The observation material, particularly that illustrating how difficult she found him to feed (p. 87), also gives a glimpse of how devastating a nurse's criticism was to this woman. However, there was a sense that the tension in the nurse–mother relationship served, over time, to galvanise her commitment to her infant. She felt rivalrous towards the nurses, and was glad that there was a shift system because it meant that there was less opportunity for him to become attached to them. The rivalry, and her inability to accept their way of doing things also seemed to be related to transference issues. This woman had decided to be a different kind of mother to her children than her mother had been to her. She rejected her mother's advice, and at times also rejected the nurses' advice. When she did do things their way, for example, when she massaged Brian's throat as she was feeding him, she seemed to dissociate herself from something she thought of as cruel, saying that it was *their* way, and implying that it was not hers.

The staff, in turn, recognised that this woman did evoke strong feelings in them but were unsure what sense to make of them. The failure to let her know that her son was not as disabled as had been first thought was an oversight but was probably also a reflection of just how hard it was for people to talk to her. However, it served to fuel further hostility, as did other things like her sense that they blamed her for his decreased heart rate and his chest infection or her acute awareness of how often one nurse referred to him as a girl.

This woman had looked forward to being able to own her son but still found that difficult after he was discharged. In many ways, even then, he was still the hospital's baby and not hers. My own prediction was that her sensitivity to him, her commitment and her resilience would get them through the hard times, and he would have a reasonably good outcome but I'm not yet in a position to confirm this.

Alan

Alan's story is also striking in that it is clear that his mother too had decided to reject her own mother's way of doing things. Her memory of her own early experience of being abandoned in hospital, which may have been fact or phantasy, was seen by her as important in feeding her own resolve not to abandon Alan. Her commitment to him was strong but there was also a sense from the observations that she struggled to know how to relate to this baby. This was especially marked when he was more ill. In more than one observation, she seemed transfixed by his monitors and, like other parents, could not relate to both baby and monitor at the same time. Some of the information suggested that she was acting as a 'good enough' mother but at other times it felt as if she knew that no matter how hard she tried, she could not tune into him. He was, of course, a hard baby to relate to. However, on more than one occasion, I wondered if her anxiety had in fact contributed to his unstable condition.

Her relationship with staff seemed to vary, and again, her own relationship with her mother may have been important in determining how she responded to them. They felt that she needed caring for but I think that at times her sense was that they were talking down to her. The staff's 'attachment' to Alan influenced their relationship with Ms A. Their personal ethical dilemmas about his care increased not only with each setback but also with their increasing 'attachment' to him as a person. This was managed in different ways but towards the end of his life some nurses seemed to distance themselves from the more emotional aspects of their task. Ms A, sensing this, also distanced herself. Just at the time when it was really important for her to be supported enough to consider the facts about his deteriorating condition, and the ethical implications of keeping him alive, she withdrew. It was as if she could not bear to consider the distress being inflicted upon him in order to keep him alive but also could not bear to be party to any decision not to resuscitate him. Both the mother's and the staff's determination to fight on with this baby was undoubtedly influenced at an emotional level by the distress they felt about his beginning.

Catherine

This baby's story serves to illustrate two important aspects of influence on developing relationships. The first is the role of 'high order' beliefs. Catherine's mother's belief was that God would decide this baby's fate, no matter what she did. The consequence was that she felt more able to stay away and look after herself than some mothers might have. And when she was with her very fragile baby, she felt that she didn't have a role. She sat by the cot, and did not really try to reach her infant in the way that others did. She told me that she talked to her but instead of telling her how strong she was, this mother told her baby how small she was. This relates to the second possible influence, which is on both the relationship and the infant herself. This idea about influence is tentatively posed, as it is unpalatable in some ways. It is the idea that if the mother believes that she can influence the outcome then she will. She may call the baby gently into life or 'claim' her, and by doing this she will actually keep her alive and bring her into the relationship.

In Catherine's case, it is unlikely that an alternative approach by her mother would have made a difference, but with a baby whose chances were more even, I wonder what effect the belief that it was 'all in God's hands' would have had.

The staff responded to this woman with both curiosity and confusion. I felt that they were unnerved by her beliefs, and found them difficult to respect. After all, they had made their profession the saving of babies; they worked hard and endured a lot of personal stress to do their best for very fragile infants, who would not have survived at all otherwise. How could they afford to make sense of the belief that their actions didn't matter? Some chose to see it as a defence mechanism, and indeed it might have been that. This woman had also lost a previous baby, and from her own account seemed not to have mourned properly. Distancing herself from this infant may have been an attempt to protect herself from further pain.

Daniel

Daniel's mother also had strong religious beliefs, of a different nature to Ms C's. They did not seem to impinge on her relationship with her baby in the same way. He was more mature and healthier from the outset, of course. Her past experience helped her not only to be confident in her ability to mother him but also confident that he would survive. I learned little about this woman's own childhood but had a sense that she had had a good early experience. She seemed secure in herself, and was emotionally containing of her infant. The nursing staff liked her and related to her calmly and unambivalently, as if they too felt more secure and confident in her presence. Their relationship was both of being contained and of containing.

THE IMPORTANCE OF FIT

In each of these cases, the fit between parents and staff was important. A good fit in Daniel's case facilitated the easy working together of parent and nurse for his benefit. In Brian's case, however, an already ambivalent mother–child relationship became even more stressed at times as a result of the tension in the nurse–mother relationship. This stress was ultimately associated with a very strong commitment by the mother, but it would not have been hard to imagine a different outcome.

There seem to be a number of factors which potentially contribute to how well parents and staff get on. These include the infant's condition and prognosis, each parent's personality and style of coping, and the staff's sense of potency, to mention but a few. Beliefs and assumptions about beliefs are also important. These operate at different levels.

For example, high order beliefs might be presumed to be the same, but in fact may be discovered to be quite different, as in Catherine's case. The resulting confusion has both different and similar consequences for staff and parents. For staff, their ability to carry out their primary task of maintaining a baby's life and quality of life is not affected, but their confusion may make it difficult to offer someone like Catherine's mother the support that they believe she should have. On the mother's part, she may accept their life-saving interventions as well-intentioned, but may not be able to assist in any way. She is unlikely to be able to seek support from the staff, because she recognises that they have different beliefs from her own.

Complementarity of beliefs, on the other hand, offers more opportunities for working together. Communication can be clear and unambiguous, and dilemmas can be shared. The relationship has the potential to be mutually supportive from the outset.

At a more basic level, lack of fit is evidenced by the example of a parent's assumptions that 'no news' means bad news. This is in complete contrast to what staff accept as ordinary practice; that is, that bad news will be given as soon as possible by someone important.

Another basic assumption held by staff in special care units is that it is important to encourage parents to take an active role in caring for their baby as early as is practically possible in order to promote their relationship. They are well used to handling tiny and fragile infants, and expect parents to do the same when the babies are fit enough. In doing this, they also make an assumption that mothers are not sick or unwell, that the experience of childbirth is part of life and should not be pathologised. I think there is a potential discrepancy with parents' beliefs and views in each of these assumptions. This discrepancy again leads to a lack of fit, which sometimes manifests itself as open conflict.

As I have suggested earlier, many parents do not feel at all confident in their abilities to care for their baby, and may feel deskilled in the presence of a tiny and fragile infant whom they find it hard to identify with and own. They may recognise but not comprehend inner feelings of hostility towards the child, and may distance themselves from the physical tasks of caring as a result. Mothers, in particular, may feel shocked by their experience for weeks, months or years, and may be unable to view themselves as healthy or whole if they have had, in their eyes, a near death experience. Failure on the staff's part to recognise this may leave them feeling very concerned that a mother appears to be rejecting her child. Their construal of her actions as rejection has the potential to push her further away.

Many mothers of special care babies experience what can only be described as emotional turmoil in the postnatal period. Most will probably meet the diagnostic criteria for post-traumatic stress disorder. In these instances, it is my belief that a view of their experience of childbirth as ordinary has the potential to lead to a mismatch between staff expectations and actual maternal capability with consequent confusion rather than complementarity.

This lack of fit may affect the relationships around the infant in a number of ways, and as a result, will impact on the infant's own developing relationships and ability to begin to make sense of these. The infant needs to be contained in order to be able to grow emotionally, and to begin to think and know about the world. A mother can only provide this containment if she too is contained by her family and by staff in the unit. While a mismatch of beliefs may not provide the most fertile ground for a containing relationship, if these differences are recognised and addressed the barrier may not be insurmountable. More problematic are assumptions about beliefs, which are not confirmed or refuted. The mother–child relationship may then get off to a shaky start, and have difficulty recovering, with consequent effects on the infant's development and subsequent capacity to form relationships.

SUMMARY

Many mothers of special care infants are disadvantaged by their social context, which may include poverty and adult relationship difficulties. Not only are they likely to have less actual support, but they may be less able to make use of the support offered to them. In all cases, the circumstances of the birth will have been traumatic and may take some time to recover from. This is likely to affect mothers' developing relationships with their babies, their partners, and with staff. The latter may also affect and be affected by the mother–child relationship. Past history and beliefs also influence relationships.

A good fit between parents and staff is important. Recognition of different assumptions and beliefs offers an opportunity for complementarity rather than dissonance. Similarly, clear communication should lead to more satisfactory relationships and outcome. The stress of the neonatal intensive care experience impacts on child, family and staff, and it is tentatively proposed that in some cases the quality of the mother–child relationship, in particular, may actually influence the infant's viability.

Chapter 7

Jenny and Elizabeth

In this chapter, I'm going to present some observational material on two babies, at the age of about seven months. The first is Jenny who was born fifteen weeks premature, and spent her first ten weeks in the special care baby unit before going home. Her mother's story was a long one and some of it is also presented. The second, Elizabeth, was the subject of regular observations as part of my infant observation course. I have known her for many years. She spent only two days in special care before joining her mother on the postnatal ward. Her mother's story serves to draw attention to the fact that even more straightforward births can have an impact on developing relationships.

Both mothers remembered some very precise details of their labour. This is not unusual (Elkan, 1981). However, it is not often acknowledged that for most women, the events surrounding the birth of their children often remain vivid for many many years, and may colour their personal relationships in a particular way. Relationships with hospital staff or other health professionals may also be affected by this experience. For some, the memory of childbirth evokes resentment towards their child or, for different reasons, towards their partner; for some, it motivates protectiveness and concern for the child. Many women experience a curious mixture of these feelings, which it is often difficult to make sense of.

JENNY

Ms J was a professional woman in her thirties, who had had her second child by emergency caesarian section at twenty-five weeks gestation. She was in a stable relationship. This observation and interview took place when the child was six and a half months old.

Observation

Two pieces of observation material are presented:

> Ms J opened the door and greeted me in a friendly manner. She showed me into the kitchen where the baby girl, Jenny, was lying in a pram. She turned her back

on me, excusing herself saying that she had just been in the middle of playing a little game with the baby and wanted to finish it. I learnt that she had just had her nappy changed and that this 'little game' often followed that. 'Jenny loves it,' her mother told me. The game, a sort of peek-a-boo, was delightful to watch. The mother hid her face behind her hands and leaned over the baby making little cooing and ba-ba-ba noises; she then opened her hands with a great expression of surprise; and finally, shaking her head back and forward in time to more progressively quickening ba-ba-ba noises, lowered her face right down to the baby's tummy and blew on it making a loud raspberry sound. Jenny, quiet at first, gasped and giggled with increasing excitement as the game went on but also paused in momentary snatches of silent anticipation before both the un-covering of the face, and the final contact of Mother's lips with her bare tummy. After the crescendo, both panted quietly waiting in anticipation to find out what was to happen next. Mother seemed to have now decided that the game was over, and she bent slowly to pick up Jenny and give her a firm but gentle cuddle. I felt almost a sense of relief from the baby who had enjoyed the game so much but was now glad that it was over.

Later:

Jenny was sitting in a baby-seat on the kitchen table watching us intently some of the time and seeming quite self-absorbed at other times. She became a bit restless, moving about in her chair, turning her head to one side and trying to suck on her fingers. She moaned a little. Her mother, who was sitting at the table, got up and went over to the other side of the kitchen to prepare a bottle of milk for her, and while doing that explained that she'd had problems breastfeeding her first child. After expressing breast milk for seven weeks, she'd become increasingly depressed about what a small amount she was producing for such a huge effort and had stopped. Her experience of bottlefeeding her first child had been good, and so she had found the decision to bottlefeed Jenny relatively easy to make. She spoke to Jenny as she lifted her out of the seat and sat down with her on her knee to give her the bottle; the baby gurgled in anticipation. Ms J sat upright on the kitchen chair with the baby sitting on her knee, back against her chest, facing towards me. She held the bottle in front of the baby, who took it quite happily pausing only once or twice during the feed. I was astonished to see this mother feeding her baby like this but neither of them were indicating that they minded or thought it odd.

Comments

The first extract describes a very ordinary episode of mother–child interaction. The possibility that it had been 'put on' for my benefit was considered only to be quickly dismissed as most of the rest of the observation confirmed the impression that this pair had a very good relationship, and that the mother was devoted to her daughter. This mother demonstrated a number of things both about the relationship and about what she knew about babies. She seemed to realise, for example, that it was important for babies to have a complete experience, to finish the game. Winnicott said that 'By allowing your baby time for total experiences, and by taking part in them, you gradually lay a foundation for the child's ability eventually to enjoy all sorts of experiences without jumpiness' (1964: 78). The game itself is a classic part of any caregiver's repertoire, and as Stern (1977) has pointed out, this kind of sequence is built into a large array of the social activities in which a mother engages her baby. He considered that the crucial feature of this maternal attention-holding behaviour was the accompaniment of the presentation of the face with a display of expression. He speculated that the repeated disregard by mothers of adult spatial conventions may be important in preparing the infant to tolerate later intimate behaviours such as kissing and snuggling.

The integration of separate behaviours is also important, and is demonstrated by this mother. Her 'facial display' and movement are accompanied by vocalisation, gaze and touch. Although the game is primarily directed by the mother, the baby is able and allowed to tune out and withdraw. I sensed rather than actually witnessed this 'tuning out', and guessed that the mother had too in a much more certain way. The 'reciprocity' of the interaction (Brazelton et al., 1974) is demonstrated by the increasing frequency and pitch of the baby's vocalisations, she 'giggled with increasing excitement as the game went on', and also her 'momentary snatches of silent anticipation' which fit so well with her mother's behaviour.

In contrast to the first extract and the rest of the observation up to this point, the second extract portrays a scene which, had it been witnessed alone, would have caused me to question the quality of the mother–child relationship. Feeding, breast or bottle, is regarded as an opportunity for intimacy and strengthening of the mother–child bond. One of the important features of the feeding situation, according to Winnicott (1968), is that of baby and mother looking into each other's eyes. The observed way of feeding, which did not seem strange to either of them, afforded no eye contact whatsoever. My curiosity about it was roused by its incongruity, rather than anything else. This apparently out-of-tune way of feeding occurred in the context of an apparently good relationship, confirmed further by the mother's anticipation of her baby's need to feed before she had become too distressed. Earlier, she had lifted the baby from her pram carefully, thoughtfully, lovingly, and again, when lifting her from her chair had talked to her, making eye contact and helping her to wait for her bottle, yet she sat her on her knee in an apparently uncontaining and disconnected way.

When I asked the mother about her way of feeding Jenny, she said that that was the way she had seen the nurses feeding her in the unit and had just carried on. She added that 'with her it's been fiddly sometimes' – the baby had wanted to feed but had difficulty latching on and settling. She had tried other positions too, but none of them had been successful. Her answer helped me to make sense of an otherwise nonsensical observation. Her explanation fitted with her beliefs about her baby and the experience of being in the unit, but also raised several further questions in my mind. I wondered why this woman who was caring for her second, not first, child should feel so bound to doing things the nurses' way. Did she feel uncomfortable being so close to the baby who had, during pregnancy, put her in a life-threatening situation? Or was this related to her disbelief at having a live baby? I wondered if she was finding it difficult to 'own' her baby, and therefore felt that she had to continue to feed her the nurses' way.

The mother's story

In response to my explanation about my interest in the relationships of special care babies and, in particular, their relationships with their mothers, Ms J immediately asked if my aim was to try to improve things. She went on to say that she thought that the developing relationship would be affected by what happened antenatally:

> I imagine that quite a lot of it is influenced by feelings in the pregnancy and labour. There will be a big difference between someone who just suddenly goes into labour with no problems before, and someone like me, who had lots of problems and was bleeding for months. I'm on the side of: isn't it amazing that I've got a baby out of all this. You know, rather than: what a shock it is that the baby's come early. Psychologically you sort of go through different processes if you're preparing yourself for a miscarriage.

Ms J started her story by comparing her pregnancy with Jenny to her pregnancy with her first child. She had had a lot of nausea and vomiting during the early stages of her first pregnancy, but then was very well the whole way through:

> Jenny was planned and I was very pleased to be pregnant. We'd only just decided to stop using contraceptives, I was pregnant straightaway. An interesting thing was that I had no symptoms at all for the first three months – no nausea, no tiredness – I was full of beans. I couldn't believe it, I was absolutely fine, I was doing rather a lot, but I felt very energetic. There were no problems. Then I had the first bleed at fourteen weeks, just when I was at the point of thinking, 'Oh good, everything's OK'. I was starting to tell people that I was pregnant.

She went on to tell me about being admitted to hospital, bleeding a lot, she thought. This eased up after three or four days, and stopped after eight or nine. She went home to bed, and then was given the all-clear by the doctor, and returned to work. One week later the bleeding started again. Ms J told me that she had been really busy, not only back at work but doing a lot of other things too:

> I felt a bit fed up. If they'd said to me take it easy, I certainly would have, but I thought it would be all right.

But then, like other women, she seemed confused:

> Mostly they think that once it's happened, there's no evidence that resting will stop it.

Like others, too, I had a sense that she had felt guilty, and had not completely resolved this.

She ended up in hospital again for a few days, and then at eighteen weeks she was admitted for the rest of the pregnancy:

Not to the antenatal ward, but to the gynae ward. It was horrible, everyone's having miscarriages, the whole mentality is miscarriage. Women have either had one or are threatening to have one.

I was very upset after speaking to one woman who'd just lost her baby at twenty weeks. The pregnancy was going on longer and longer, and as it did, I was realising things I hadn't really thought about. I would have to deliver this baby normally, and it was going to be dead. It was horrendous. Anyway, they did transfer me (to the antenatal ward) at twenty weeks. Things never really settled down, one minute it looked like it was going to happen, then off again. I had more ultrasound investigations, and I had to have blood.

Then, there were three crises, one at twenty-one weeks, one at twenty-two weeks, and one at twenty-three weeks. All meant I had to go down to the labour ward. It looked as if I was going to lose the baby, I was pouring blood.

I got to twenty-five weeks. The awful part is that when I was down at the labour ward at twenty-three weeks, they were treating it as a miscarriage. I wasn't particularly expecting anything, I still wasn't expecting a live birth. The threshold was twenty-four weeks; at twenty-four weeks, I'd get the paediatricians.

I'd seen the SCBU before, they'd taken people from the antenatal wards. I can remember thinking that it would mostly be for the other people. For some reason, I really didn't think I was going to need their services. I didn't think it would come to that; I thought I was going to lose the baby. I'd been told by one of the doctors early on that I would either lose it then, or everything would be normal. For me, in my mind, the issue was going to be getting over this part, the bleeding, then it would all settle down.

Anyway, it was very good that I'd seen it. When I was twenty-four weeks, I had three visits from paediatricians to talk about the SCBU and what might happen if I did have a baby and things like that. So that was good. One of them gave me . . . well, more or less fished about, you know, this is current policy, this is what we do. Now that you've got to this stage, current practice is to pull out all the stops to save the baby, *if you want us to*.

So, that's a bit heavy isn't it? It's so awful, the time between twenty-four weeks and twenty-eight weeks. It's that month that you're thinking it's a very dicey business. I just said, well, I'll have to put that decision back to you. It's up to your discretion. If the baby's born and you think she's going to make it then go for it.

I asked if brain damage or disability was discussed:

They underplayed that a bit. There was more discussion later, when it looked like she wasn't brain damaged, than there had been before, I think.

At this point, I felt I had to ask Ms J if it was difficult for her to think about what happened and to talk about it:

No. It's something that happened. So far everything's been positive. She was seriously ill, but – (pausing to look at her daughter) – I've got a really nice baby.

Ms J went on to talk about the final labour. A few days before, contractions had started but had stopped again in response to treatment (Ritadrin given via an intravenous drip). On the day that Jenny was born, she felt that things were different:

That day was really different. I knew. Everything about that day was different. I was getting real. . . . First of all I just thought I'll see what happens. I was getting contractions and I was looking at the clock on the ward. On the other days, you're trying to identify them. Because when you're an antenatal patient, you're there all the time, and you can't constantly call the midwives. You think, will I call them, you're sort of judging it, so I was judging it. I didn't want to seem as if I was panicking, but I was always aware that the sooner that people knew that something was happening the better. So I looked at the clock for about twenty minutes, and bang on every five I was getting a very odd sensation which wasn't really a proper contraction. It was just all very odd – something's going on – I didn't think that I was being neurotic, I thought, something's really going on here. It was odd at first, that was all. So when they put me on the monitor, her trace was terrible. That's basically what led them to do a caesarian section in the next two hours. They said that her trace was extremely bad. They did it two hours later. And I was getting lots of pain by then, by two hours later. I was getting lots of pain, I was in agony by two hours later. It was tearing away, the placenta was coming away. I had a general anaesthetic, it was horrible, I'd never had one before.
   When I saw her I cried. I saw her the next morning, a live human being, I was extremely emotional. It was very helpful that I'd seen the SCBU. I knew where she'd be when I woke up, what it would be like. She did really really feel like my baby. I didn't feel alienated at all. She had quite a strong little grasp.

This mother's story which began historically with the previous pregnancy, and had as its initial focus the events prior to Jenny's birth, included a lot of spontaneous information about family history, relationships and beliefs.
   She interrupted her account of the events surrounding the birth to tell me about the impact of what had happened on her son, aged three. Even before going into hospital, she had been relatively unavailable to him, as she had to rest – she couldn't pick her son up or allow the boisterous toddler to jump on top of her. Then, of course, she was physically absent in hospital, with only short visits from her child who went to nursery during the day. Her husband, who worked full-time, had to

take responsibility, to become his 'main person'. This led to something which Ms J regarded as positive:

> He took it very well. Basically what he did was he treated him like his Mum, and he became the main one. He actually called him – he used to call him – 'mummy' and he used to call me 'daddy'. I felt really good about that. I thought, he's getting all his emotional needs taken care of really, he's OK.

After Jenny's birth things became more difficult for them for a while, partly because Mother would spend all day with the baby, and then they would all visit together in the evening. That upset her son's routine. Once they felt that he really knew that he had a baby sister, Ms J would often babysit while her husband visited Jenny. The consequence of that was that Ms J and her husband saw very little of each other.

Ms J's ability to cope throughout this period seemed to be related to a number of things, not least her partner's changing role. She told me that during her childhood, her own mother had been almost constantly unwell, engendering in her, perhaps, a familiarity with illness as well as a certain resilience. She also linked her ability to cope with her professional training and career as a carer, as well as with her own personal belief system.

We started to talk about beliefs after Ms J told me of how she was influenced to some extent by superstition. She felt this might be related to her religious upbringing, but was in contrast to what she held dear as a sort of philosophy of life, which was that she believed that 'everything that happens is the result of your own actions'. Early in her pregnancy, a mystic had predicted an important sequence of events for her on a particular date, which turned out to be the date of Jenny's birth. She had been quite affected by this, and had often thought about the prediction during her pregnancy.

In the weeks before the birth, she had adopted a particular way of being. Believing that any increase in energy levels in her body might cause more bleeding, she sort of switched off, deliberately not trying to do anything. This included avoiding being upset or crying but instead remaining as calm as possible. She compared this to emotional detachment being used as a protective measure.

I found it interesting that this woman who believed that we were masters of our own destiny had also been so caught up with superstition, which really represents a completely opposing belief. However, her description of her developing relationship with Jenny confirmed for me that she really thought that what she did mattered. She had spent hours with her baby, talking to her, stroking her and singing to her, calling her into life and into a relationship with her.

ELIZABETH

Elizabeth was born by caesarian section, two and a half weeks overdue, after a long and difficult labour. Her mother, aged 37 years, was a professional woman having her first child following a late miscarriage in her first pregnancy. Her husband had been married before and had older children who lived with their mother.

The mother's story

The first visit

I first visited Ms E when Elizabeth was three weeks old. She lay sleeping in her basket while we talked.

Ms E's story began with an account of her labour, which she recalled in graphic detail. Elizabeth's date of delivery had been confirmed early in the pregnancy by ultrasound scan but as that date came and went the obstetrician had said that it wasn't definite. Two weeks later, Ms E's waters broke and labour began. Two days later, she still hadn't made much progress and a decision was made to try to speed things up, first using a pessary and then by intravenous induction. By the evening of the second day Ms E was feeling demoralised and physically exhausted. She was given an epidural anaesthetic, and had a caesarian section the next morning. Elizabeth was admitted to the special care baby unit for two days, because of worries about infection after such a long labour. She was taken there by her father immediately after the delivery. Later, she joined her mother on the postnatal ward.

Ms E was accepting of what had happened but also expressed disappointment. She told me that the baby had managed to turn herself round early in the labour, and was also very long, so that even in the operating theatre the doctors had some difficulty in getting her out. Her main concern was that the experience had been very traumatic for her daughter. She had thought that breastfeeding would be difficult in these circumstances, but in fact they'd managed to establish that very well despite the practical difficulties. They'd needed lots of help as both were on drips, Ms E also had a catheter and was still very tired and weak. Elizabeth had had to be placed in her arms as she was unable to pick her up.

At this point in her account of events, she paused, and looked at the baby lying sleeping in her basket: 'I have to go over sometimes to make sure she's not dead'. Elizabeth was described as a contented baby, who was easy to look after except at night. She will only sleep if she is in her parents' bed. Even at this early stage, there was a link between this and her birth in her mother's mind. She spoke about Elizabeth having dreams, sometimes waking with a cry as if having a bad dream, as if remembering her birth.

Ms E told me that she had been pregnant last year but something had gone wrong and she had lost the baby. There was no doubt that this had contributed to her anxieties about Elizabeth, who was a cherished and much wanted child.

Later

Throughout her first year, Mother voiced anxieties about how damaging the experience of birth might have been for her baby. In the first few months she often referred to her waking with a start and crying, as if remembering her traumatic entry into the world. Later, when it seemed as if Elizabeth would never sleep through the night, I felt that Mother's anxieties often made it difficult for her to bear separation from the child.

Despite worrying a lot about her baby, she led a very full and active life with her in the early months. When Elizabeth was twenty weeks, her mother recounted a recent worrying episode which had left her feeling upset and also a bit embarrassed. She had been out in the car with Elizabeth, and she would not stop crying, screaming louder and louder, and not responding at all to her mother's efforts to comfort her. Ms E had become more and more frantic and had eventually taken her into the casualty department of the nearest hospital, convinced that something was very wrong, at which point Elizabeth had stopped crying.

Elizabeth's difficulty in sleeping at night had persisted, and shortly after the hospital visit, Ms E told me that she was not sleeping much by day either. She looked worn out, while Elizabeth always seemed quite lively. I felt that as the time for Mum to return to work approached the situation got more tense, and Mum got more depressed. She was upset because she'd told the baby to 'shut up' one night. It had worked and she'd gone to sleep but this hadn't made her mother feel any better. Ms E was very aware of the relationship between how she felt and how Elizabeth was.

Observation

This extract is from an observation at almost seven months. Her mother has been back at work for a week. She is at home as it is a public holiday.

I greeted Mother who met me at the door, and then went into the kitchen where Elizabeth was sitting in a baby chair clipped on to the table. I said hello, and she immediately responded with a smile and an outstretched hand in which she held a wooden brick which she dropped on the floor. As I walked round behind her to sit down, she leaned back and tried to keep sight of me, rocking vigorously and almost seeming to push her chair out from the table. I sat down next to her. She continued to look at me and offered another smile and some babbly chatty noises. In front of her were some wooden bricks of different shapes and colours, and a rattle. She stretched out in front of her to reach and pick up one brick after another. She pulled each one to her, pushed it away again sometimes several times, put it in and out of her mouth, and then slowly and deliberately dropped it to the floor. She did not immediately move on and fetch another but continued to look down after each one for what seemed like an eternity. Sometimes while doing this she would rock vigorously, and sometimes before letting go of the brick she would look at me, then it, then me again, solemnly, and definitely giving the brick more of her attention than me.

This extract is from an evening visit, a week later.

Mother answered the door and took me into the kitchen where her husband was preparing dinner. Elizabeth was sitting at the table in her chair and offered no protests when her mother departed upstairs. She greeted me noisily and appeared to be in a playful mood. As I sat down next to her, she continued to watch her father closely, occasionally hurling a brick in his direction. She played with the wooden bricks on the table, banging them up and down very hard, becoming more and more excited, laughing and swinging her legs vigorously. Then she seemed to quieten, becoming quite intense, and very slowly pushed each brick to the edge, and then off the table. She gazed down after them, shouting when she got to the last. Father picked up the bricks and gave them back to her saying, 'Here you are, you noisy girl', then picking her up and giving her a cuddle. Then he swung her round him and through his legs, and put her back in her chair affectionately.

Later, Mother has bathed Elizabeth and dressed her ready for bed.

Once that was done, she carried her through to the bedroom. She switched the television on, saying, 'Elizabeth won't go to sleep without the noise of the TV in the background'. She sat up on the bed and prepared to breastfeed her. Elizabeth seemed tired. She started to feed, then stopped. She stopped and started several times, occasionally looking over at me. I felt uncomfortable and suggested that I was maybe a distraction (I guessed to Mother, who had been talking almost constantly about her return to work, rather than to her baby). Mother stopped talking and concentrated on her feeding baby, allowing her some time at each breast. Elizabeth finally fell asleep, and Mother gently, tentatively, lifted her and carried her through to the bedroom.

Elizabeth was sick as this was being done, regurgitating her milk, which came down her nose as well as from her mouth. 'Oh dear', Mother was speaking to her gently and sympathetically, cleaning her up, then cuddling her close to her body. She took her into the bedroom where she had left only a nightlight on. I stood outside the door. As she put her down, the baby started to cry a little. Mother picked her up quickly, and tried to reassure her. Elizabeth quietened as soon as she was picked up, and cried again as soon as put down. She tried again, and then spoke to Elizabeth, 'Oh dear, you've woken yourself up'. She lifted her again and carried her downstairs. I left.

Comments

These extracts provide material about two related areas, the baby's developing understanding of 'comings and goings' and her attempts to control these, and separation at bedtime, another sort of 'going'.

In both observations there are clear examples of the baby taking control of the 'coming and going' of her wooden bricks. She pulls them to her, pushes them away, pulls them back, and so on. Finally she drops them over the side, either dramatically or slowly, almost tantalisingly, and watches after them knowing where they have gone but often unable to see them. Her rocking back and forth is also a way of making things come and go, nearer and further, nearer and further. There is concrete evidence of the development of, and the baby's experimentation with, the concept of 'object permanence'.

Stern (1977) has linked this to the beginning of the infant being in a relationship rather than simply interacting with her environment. He linked object permanence to the infant's consolidation of an internal representation of Mother. Others would date the development of this relationship to an earlier time but also point out, as Winnicott has done, that 'It must be remembered that what first appears at an early age needs a long period of time to become established as a more or less fixed mechanism in the child's mental processes' (1966b: 7).

The coming and going is also symbolic of the mother–child separation, a painful issue for this family at the time. Winnicott (1964) linked this type of play to weaning, and to the development of the baby as a person. The latter is demonstrated by Elizabeth as she carefully ensures that first she has my attention, and later her father's, as she plays her game. She includes each of us in the play, experimenting by relating to the brick and the person alternately, and seeming to will us to attend to the object and her ability to make it disappear. She plays with the distance and interest of the adults, in addition to her toys. Stern (1985) has referred to this as the baby's development of a sense of a subjective self.

This mother's continued anxiety about her baby's experience of birth and her distress at returning to work seem to make it difficult for her to let go of Elizabeth at bedtime. She gives her the breast even though both of us probably guessed that the baby might not have 'needed' it. By helping her to fall asleep in her arms she avoids the trauma of separation prior to sleep. The television, too, is thought by Mother to be important, Elizabeth's experience of separation from the daytime world almost being masked by the background noise. It is an awkward time, I feel that Mother is desperate to speak to me (as she has done throughout our relationship) about how stressed she feels, yet this seems to interfere with her ability to attend to and settle her baby. Also, I am sure that she wants to be seen by me to be doing the 'right' thing, and this may have interfered with the way she put Elizabeth to bed. It is apparent nonetheless that her guilt and anxiety about the separation (by day and by night) make it difficult for her to bear any slight crying from the infant. I feel guilty about leaving punctually at the end of the hour as it coincides with an opportunity for Mother to confide in me. I feel distressed, not by what actually has happened but by the feelings stirred up in me. I feel I have abandoned Mother just as she feels she has abandoned Elizabeth.

Follow up

Elizabeth's night-times got better as she grew and developed. The relationship between them was very special, and made more so by events which followed, which included several more miscarriages, before another child was born by elective caesarian section. The family discovered that Mr E was a carrier for a gene abnormality. This provided an explanation for the lost babies, but also served to make the two who had survived very special. The issue of whether or not the girls were also carriers had to be addressed, thankfully with a positive outcome. The fact that the genetic testing and counselling was not carried out until the time of the pregnancy with the second surviving child had meant that the parents had had to go through a lot of heartache relatively unsupported. This area in itself is of relevance to developing relationships.

Ms E continues to wonder about the impact of Elizabeth's birth on her development. Now at school, she is a lively child who is always bumping into things. Her mother wonders if this is related to her traumatic beginning.

SUMMARY

In this chapter I have presented some observations of, and stories about, two older infants. The account not only re-emphasises the importance of mothers' experiences around the time of their children's birth, but also serves to give some concrete examples of aspects of each child's psychological development and important features of parent–child relationships. Jenny's account illustrates reciprocity in action, and raises questions about feeding and 'ownership' of the baby. Elizabeth's gives a very typical example of how a child strives to master 'object constancy', and also illustrates the consequent issues for separation.

Part III

Outcome and intervention

Chapter 8

The future

How each special care baby gets on as they move through childhood and into adolescence has been studied primarily in relation to their growth and development, so that, from the early 1960s onwards, there have been regular publications of follow-up studies of low birth weight infants in particular. Most have concentrated on the physical and cognitive sequelae of prematurity and, not surprisingly, the findings of these studies have changed over time as the early care and treatment of these infants has become increasingly sophisticated. A few studies have addressed the topics of later behavioural and emotional difficulties, and relationship problems.

As I have already discussed, there are a huge number of factors which have the potential to influence the outcome for each child, and while correlations have been found between specific factors and specific outcomes, the pathway of influence has not always been able to be clearly delineated. For example, there is an association between intraventricular haemorrhage (IVH) and delayed acquisition of language but all children who have an IVH will not end up with the same measurable communication difficulty, and children with language delay may not have had a brain haemorrhage at all. The pathway is influenced by a number of other factors, which will probably include social class, probably one of the most reliable indicators of outcome identified so far.

For emotional difficulties and frank psychiatric disorder, the influences are likely to be even more difficult to specify. They will involve factors operating at different levels; at one end of the spectrum genetic and 'within-brain' factors will be important, and at another contextual issues within society will play a part. Somewhere in the middle, actual family functioning both before and after 'the crisis of neonatal intensive care' will impact on the child's developmental and psychiatric outcome. Every special care baby can probably be thought of as 'at risk'. Some, like children from very deprived and chaotic backgrounds (Rutter and Rutter, 1992), will show a remarkable resilience in the face of adversity.

Rutter's (1987) description of trajectories with opportunities at different points in time to create possibilities for new experience and a different outcome is very relevant to the topic under discussion. Gorell-Barnes (1990) has applied this model to family therapy research findings and discussed the possible implications for the practice of family therapy. The systemic idea that 'minimal deviations in or changes in living systems, if amplified, can, over time create much larger changes in the system in which they occur' (Gorell-Barnes, 1990: 17) is one way of describing the 'knock-on' effect of early difficulties. These 'knock-on' effects are unpredictable, partly because of the individuality of each person's, each family's, and each network's way of functioning, and partly because at any point in time yet another variable may bump things in a different direction.

The effects of relationships on relationships

Rutter has drawn attention to the complexities implicit in consideration of the 'functions and consequences of relationships' (1988: 332), and has discussed possible mechanisms by which one relationship can influence another. Contemporaneous effects may be mediated in a number of ways. In discussing these effects, he cites as an example 'the association between marital support and good parenting' (1988: 333). First, a third factor may be influencing both relationships in question, and thus making it appear that one relationship is affecting the other. This factor might, for example, be an attribute of an individual rather than a characteristic of a relationship. Second, one relationship may only influence another by virtue of its being part of the general environment, that is, it is not a specific feature of the relationship in question which actually makes the difference to the outcome. Third, the observed effects may not be related to the here-and-now relationships, but be based on expectations based on previous experience. Fourth, 'one relationship may have an effect through altering the meaning of other relationships' (1988: 334) both present and past. The fifth mechanism stems 'from the function of the social group as a group' (1988: 334), and leads Rutter to support an ecological perspective. Sixth, he has suggested that the process resides not in an individual characteristic, but in *changes* within an individual rather than within a relationship.

Considering the mechanisms by which early relationships might influence later ones, he makes similar criticisms of the interpretation of associations so that, again, a third variable may come into play, a characteristic of an individual might be important or there may be a continuity of environmental influences. The possible processes by which an early relationship influences a later one are, he believes, likely to reside in the process by which 'the qualities of a dyadic *relationship* become transformed into some aspect of *individual* functioning' (1988: 335), which is then carried forward to other relationships. Included in possible mechanisms for the latter are Bowlby's concept of inner working models. Rutter's conclusion, however, is that a number of mechanisms may operate in mediating the different effects of relationships on relationships.

Continuities and discontinuities

Research into continuities and discontinuities, normal and abnormal development, and the mechanisms by which resilience or vulnerability are determined continues to try to clarify important issues pertaining to emotional development and the development of relationships. Luthar (1993) has recently reviewed research on resilience, and has noted that the issue has been approached from two angles so far, enquiry into direct effects, and elucidation of moderating effects. This has led to some confusion but has the potential for complementarity if a common language is reached. Like Rutter, Luthar advocates a move forward from research which focuses solely on outcome to research which addresses the processes by which an outcome is reached.

At the present time a number of these studies are under way but it is probably fair to say that process research is still in its infancy. In particular, the mechanisms which determine outcome for special care infants have been hypothesised but not yet confirmed or refuted.

Later in this chapter, I will consider these possible mechanisms. First, I will review some of the many papers about special care infants. The focus will be on those which are more relevant to the child's developing relationships and psychiatric outcome.

FOLLOW-UP STUDIES

Lukeman and Melvin (1993), reviewing research on the preterm infant, have urged caution in the interpretation of follow-up studies. In their paper, they discussed methodological issues in detail, and found that it was difficult to draw any general conclusions from the wealth of studies which have been carried out, mainly because of the heterogeneity of populations selected for research. Cross-study comparisons were considered to be difficult to make for the same reason. Coupled with the recognition that medical expertise in this field is advancing at an incredible rate, with consequent effects on neurodevelopmental outcome in particular, it is difficult to know how to interpret what is on offer in the literature. Also, earlier studies have focused on cruder outcome measures, while more recent ones are using increasingly sensitive research tools to detect more subtle cognitive and motor difficulties in particular. Particular topics and some key papers from different time periods may be useful to consider.

Preterm neonates

Physical and cognitive outcome

While the survival rates of VLBW infants has improved continuously over the last thirty years, and the prevalence of major disability, such as cerebral palsy, has remained steady, there is increasing concern that 'hidden' disability has not been detected (Abel-Smith and Knight-Jones, 1990). It is now well recognised that some survivors will encounter problems at school, and may then be discovered to have learning difficulties. Support for the idea that these NICU graduates may initially appear normal but in fact do have clear deficits in the field of fine motor control and cognition at school age is provided by a number of papers (for example,

Abel-Smith and Knight-Jones, 1990; Stewart *et al.*, 1989; Levene, 1992; Levene *et al.*, 1992). Such children may have been discharged from paediatric follow-up as healthy.

There seem to be at least four possible explanations for the previously widely held view that most pretermers had a good developmental and cognitive outcome. The first is that the distribution of their scores was seen to match the normal curve but, as Lukeman and Melvin (1993) have pointed out, controlled studies have shown that although the scores may fall within the normal range, pretermers' scores are actually lower than those of matched controls. Second, tests carried out early may fail to predict difficulties which will occur at a later stage of development. Third, a number of factors may influence the child's developmental progress, and again early assessment may not predict outcome. Finally, it is important to recognise that studies of children born two decades ago will reflect the medical expertise and technology of the time, and will have used cruder outcome measures

Early studies, such as that of Drillien *et al.* (1980), which did identify problems at school for VLBW infants found associations with a large number of factors, which included social class, evidence of early intrauterine insult, postnatal complications, early developmental and neurological status and gender. Levene (1992) has reviewed more recent research on the impact of intensive care on the frequency of handicap and has drawn attention to studies which have identified neurobiological predictors of adverse outcome. Seven factors have been noted to account for almost all the variance, and these are: pH, ventilation, seizures, intraventricular haemorrhage, periventricular leukomalacia and hypoglycaemia. These factors then seem to have a predictive value in relation to subsequent major disability. The story relating to more subtle impairment appears to be rather more complicated.

The separation out of children who have serious disabilities from more healthy survivors has probably resulted in a shake out of most of the factors which Drillien and her colleagues, among others, identified as being associated with school difficulties. A number of studies are now identifying social factors to be of prime importance. These studies come from both sides of the Atlantic.

A multicentre study in the US evaluated the mental development of 454 neonatal intensive care survivors over the first four to five years of their lives (Resnick *et al.*, 1990). In keeping with other studies, only infants with birth weights of less than 1000 grams had *significantly* lower scores than those in other groups. Sociodemographic factors were found to have a greater impact on developmental outcome overall. Apart from gender, these factors all had well-recognised associations with prematurity. The conclusion that 'mental deficiencies acquired in NICU babies over the first four to five years of life appear to be related primarily to sociodemographic factors' (Resnick *et al.*, 1990: 377) suggests that babies at risk of being born prematurely are also more at risk of the sequelae of prematurity.

A subsequent paper by Resnick *et al.* (1992) examined the educational outcome of this large group three years later, and again concluded that sociodemographic factors had the strongest influence on outcome, with the exception of a small group of children with clearly identified physical or sensory impairments. A large Swiss study has also reached similar conclusions (Largo *et al.*, 1989). Socioeconomic status was found to be strongly related to language and intellectual development at five to seven years.

In the UK, an association between outcome and social characteristics has also been identified. Marlow, reviewing this research, has stated that 'These characteristics were better predictors of performance than birthweight' (Marlow, 1991: 848). He has highlighted the fact that studies to date have not satisfactorily addressed the relative influence of biological and environmental factors.

Behaviour and relationships

Parent–infant interaction in the postnatal period, and following discharge has been noted to be related to the parents' perception of how sick their infant is, as well as to actual morbidity, and duration of illness (Minde *et al.*, 1983). Later relationships have been studied less. A few papers, however, have tried to examine the quality of relationships either with, or around, these children as they grow and develop, and attempted to link the findings with their developmental and psychiatric outcome.

Minde and his colleagues (1989) reviewed the development of sixty-four Canadian VLBW infants at the age of four years. In an earlier study they had reported that the distribution of attachment patterns in this group was not significantly different from that of a group of term infants. This study revealed that 43 per cent were rated as having behaviour disturbances by their mothers, and 24 per cent by their teachers. The behavioural profile of these children often included overactivity, poor concentration and restlessness. This is in keeping with the findings of other studies on premature infants.

The presence of behaviour difficulties was not significantly related to neonatal illness score, intellectual assessment, gender or attachment rating at one year, nor to socioeconomic status, mother's age or mother's mental health. These children had been identified as having difficult temperaments, but this was reported to have changed over time, with most being seen as easier temperamentally at four years. There was a significant correlation between behaviour difficulties and family functioning, particularly marital discord, lack of external support and mother's dissatisfaction with her own role. Psychiatric diagnoses were made in 11 per cent and these included reactive attachment disorder, attention deficit disorder, oppositional disorder and adjustment disorder, all of which were of moderate or marked severity.

The authors concluded that the long-term behaviour of these children was dependent more on the nurturing the child received than on the number and severity of neonatal complications. This was despite the fact that attachment ratings at one year did not initially predict outcome; reviewing these ratings, they questioned this finding as five out of the seven disordered children did have insecure or disorganised attachment patterns. These seven children also had a slightly higher neonatal illness score, and the authors suggest that this might feed into psychosocial variables, such as family functioning, and through them to psychiatric disturbance.

Conflicting findings have been presented by Szatmari *et al.* (1990), who found an increased incidence in attention deficit disorder with hyperactivity (ADDH) in five year olds who weighed less than 1000 grams at birth. This group found that neurodevelopmental status correlated most closely with outcome; when it was controlled for, the difference in rate of psychiatric disorder between this group and the control group was eliminated. It is nonetheless important to note that this study identified 25 per cent of this group as psychiatrically disordered, compared with 16 per cent of controls; the increase was accounted for solely by the higher incidence of ADDH. In contrast to Minde's study, there were no significant differences between the groups in measures of marital discord, maternal mood or family dysfunction.

Leonard *et al.* (1990) found that 15 per cent of 129 VLBW infants followed up were referred to Social Services for abuse or neglect. Interestingly, these researchers chose to see abuse as a risk factor for later developmental delay, rather than something which was a consequence of prematurity or developmental problems. The results showed a clear association between parenting risk and outcome at four and a half years; a higher incidence of neurological and cognitive abnormalities was found in this group than in association with intracranial haemorrhage or severe chronic lung disease.

The specific conclusion of two of these studies is that the quality of parenting or family relationships can make a difference to both developmental and psychiatric outcome. Coupled with the findings about sociodemographic factors, the implication is that difficulties for particular families might be anticipated. Early interventions aimed at helping 'at-risk parents' to care for their children might result in a different outcome. However, these findings might also be seen to place a burden on already stressed families struggling in difficult circumstances, especially if there is a lack of resources to meet their needs (Lukeman and Melvin, 1993).

In their report of a study of parental attitudes to prematurity, Stern and Karraker (1990) have drawn attention to what they call 'prematurity stereotyping'. In a laboratory situation, these authors found that a group of parents were more aroused by a baby's crying but less likely to respond if they thought the infant was premature. This finding, coupled with evidence from studies of term babies identifying links between early mother–child interaction and later competence in the child, suggests that, hypothetically, mothers might prejudice their preterm infants by their style of interaction. How generalisable this is to actual parents of premature infants is questionable and still to be researched.

However, it is clear from the studies which have been carried out that developing relationships *are* influenced by parental perceptions of their child's capabilities. Prematurity stereotyping may represent one aspect of a complex mix of factors which contribute to a less than optimal relationship, with consequent developmental and psychological sequelae for the child.

Confirmation that some parents do think that their relationship with their child has been affected by the experience of special care comes from another Canadian study (Kratochvil *et al.*, 1991). A large sample of parents of intensive care survivors ($n = 597$), both disabled and non-disabled, were asked eight years on whether they felt that the experience had had an influence on parent–child relationships. Forty per cent of the overall group, with an average birth weight of about 2 kilograms and gestational age of thirty-five weeks, felt that the relationship had been affected, with 22 per cent saying it was more distant, 12 per cent saying it was closer, and 6 per cent simply saying that it was different. Thirty-six per cent of parents of VLBW infants felt that the relationship had been affected. These parental impressions were associated with their infant having had an increased oxygen requirement, but other medical variables were not related to this finding. Fathers in this group were of a higher social class, and mothers were better educated than those in the 'no effect' group.

Full-term neonates

Factors associated with the developmental progress in the first year of full-term neonates requiring intensive care have been discussed by Ludman *et al.* (1989). Reports about this group of infants are rare. The researchers here examined the relative influence of a number of factors on developmental outcome, and included mother's mental health, length of stay in hospital, repeated admissions to hospital and postnatal complications. Thirty of the forty-three infants under study required surgery, the majority having serious congenital malformations. Fourteen required ventilation. The results indicated that this group's development was comparable to controls at six months, but that by one year was significantly behind that of a control group. Psychiatric morbidity in mothers of these children was higher, and was associated with the developmental status of their child. The three variables – length of stay, repeated admissions and postnatal complications – were strongly intercorrelated, and were also related to developmental outcome. Early developmental status (six months) was most strongly associated with maternal psychiatric morbidity, whereas later outcome was most strongly associated with length of time in hospital and the severity of the infant's condition in the neonatal period. The developmental progress of control infants was not related to maternal mental health.

These findings, while interesting, do not lead to a sense of the processes involved. The authors speculated that the stress of having a sick child combined with other factors to precipitate depression in some mothers. There is a link between developmental outcome and maternal depression but the mechanism of the connection here is unclear. The authors reported that the mother–child relationships in this group were generally as secure as in the control group, which is interesting considering that maternal depression has in other studies been associated with relationship difficulties (Murray, 1992), as well as developmental delay and cognitive difficulties (Cogill *et al.*, 1986).

This study and others (for example, Douglas, 1975; Quinton and Rutter, 1976) draw attention to the potential stress of prolonged and repeated hospitalisations, which may be a factor which will influence the quality of the child's later relationships.

Neligan *et al.* (1976), reporting the outcome for infants who were born 'too small' or born 'too soon', concluded that *within certain parameters*, the small-for-dates baby was at much greater risk of behavioural and intellectual problems than the premature baby. Children born between thirty-six and forty-four weeks who suffered from intrauterine growth retardation, and whose weight was below the fifth centile were studied at age five to seven years. Adverse social and environmental factors were correlated with a poor outcome. In a subsequent study, one of the original authors, Kolvin, has revisited this topic (Hawdon *et al.*, 1990). A group of boys born later, whose weight was below the second centile, were followed up at age ten to eleven years, and compared with closely matched controls. This matching included social class. They had a much better outcome than the children in the previous study; in particular, there were no differences in intelligence and school achievement. However, there was a significant association 'with a pattern of abnormal features representative of the attention deficit disorder, i.e. distractibility, poor attention and high activity' (Hawdon *et al.*, 1990: 950). The generally improved outcome seems likely to be attributable to earlier detection of intrauterine growth retardation, and good neonatal care which included attention to hypoglycaemia. However, the authors also speculated that early impairments might have resolved with age, or that better controlling for social class might have led to more representational results.

Whatever the reason for the improved outcome, these children would have had a different experience of neonatal intensive care than those born thirteen years earlier.

MULTIPLE BIRTHS

Multiple birth is a risk factor for prematurity and a significant number of these babies will begin their lives in a special care baby unit. The most common multiple birth will be a twin birth, and it is often the case that multiple conception leads to a variable outcome for each infant. In some cases, one will die *in utero*, and in others, the perinatal period will be more hazardous for one or more of the infants. In many instances, the parents will not take their babies home at the same time. Each of these scenarios has potential implications for each of the infants involved.

Intrauterine or neonatal death in this situation is rarely mourned in the way that a singleton miscarriage or stillbirth is. There is often little opportunity for grief when a live baby or babies are either struggling for survival or are fit enough to enter into a relationship with their parents. But their death is not forgotten, and the loss will often be felt later on. The survivor will often be treated as a very special and precious child, and may be overprotected. Bender (1990) has presented a poignant case history of a twin survivor who presented with behaviour difficulties at the age of seven. In this family, the parents had never really mourned the early loss of this boy's brother, and he, as if on their behalf, became preoccupied with his dead twin. In some families the fact that one child has survived is often a cause for celebration, particularly if there have been previous miscarriages. In this situation, it is often difficult for the family to allow themselves to be sad, but again, brothers and sisters may not be able to bury the loss in their unconscious as easily as their parents appear to have. As in other situations of this kind, the parents will often be trying to protect their children from distress, and likewise the children will try to protect them, with the result that unexpressed emotions often manifest themselves through conflict in other areas. Magical thinking by the surviving twin, other siblings and even grown-ups in the family may prevail. There may be a belief that talking about what happened may place the other twin's life in jeopardy too.

A recent television programme shown in the UK told the story of Siamese twins who were surgically separated some years after birth. One died. The consequences for the family, and the other twin in particular, are probably not yet fully known. The surviving twin had effectively lost a part of herself, and this is likely to have been especially hard to mourn. The more usual situation is less dramatic than this, but twin loss even at an early age may indeed be like losing a part of oneself and, as such, the psychological processes surrounding this event may be far more complex than those surrounding other losses.

When one twin goes home from hospital before the other, parents may be torn about which one to attend to. If the second child is particularly unwell, the parents may unconsciously choose to invest emotionally in the fitter child. It may be very hard subsequently to make up for this early bias in relationships, and 'left behind' twins may always be more distant from their mothers, in particular. Of course, the reverse could be true – with the healthy twin being more neglected as parent or parents spend long hours in hospital. My impression is that the former pattern is the commoner.

I have been involved clinically with two families of triplets. In both cases, one baby had died, one came home early and one was left in hospital. In the first case, Esther remained in hospital for well over a year, and her grandmother appeared to become her main attachment figure. Potentially, this could have been a reasonably satisfactory solution to an insoluble dilemma, but the actual situation was less than satisfactory because of the relationship difficulties between the grandmother and her daughter, which led to a rivalrous and competitive relationship with Esther.

In the second family, the consequence of Emma's longer stay in hospital was that mother and daughter were always distant. The father's role here could have been to offer a closer relationship, but he was a businessman with heavy work commitments outside the home. Real difficulties in family relationships emerged as Emma entered adolescence, and tried to go her own way, rebelling against the family rules. Unlike her triplet sister, she seemed unable to talk with her mother about her personal emotional turmoil, and her mother, who had always labelled her as a defiant and difficult girl, was unable to reach her emotionally. Interestingly, Emma's obstinancy and defiance had until this point been seen as the positive features of her personality which had contributed to her tenacious grip on life early on.

In both of these cases, the early relationship with the sicker survivor was made more difficult by the previous loss of one of the babies. It seemed to be the case that these parents found it even harder to get to know a child who might also have been facing death.

Twin births offer positive opportunities for fathers too, who often feel that it is hard to find a role, and for older siblings, who may also feel left out.

There has been little systematic research into the consequences of multiple births, except perhaps in genetic studies where the aetiology of specific disorders has been examined. Once again, Minde and his colleagues (1990) have examined the topic of developing relationships, in this case in relation to twin births. They studied twenty-four pairs of twins over four years. Their results have indicated that many mothers develop a preference for one twin within a few weeks of the birth, and maintain this preference thereafter. They found that preferred twins had fewer behaviour problems later on. This group of researchers' experience was that mothers showed a preference for the stronger and fitter twin; however, they have pointed out that this is in contrast to a 1971 study, where mothers were found to have developed a stronger relationship with the weaker of the pair. The small number of women (five) in their study who showed no preference showed less overall interaction with their babies, and at the age of one year most of these infants did not have a secure attachment using Ainsworth's classification.

A number of mechanisms were postulated to account for these findings. Not surprisingly, these included the view that a mother might hold back from making a relationship with a sick child for fear of loss. However, characteristics of the infant also seemed to be important, and early on, personality attributes were ascribed to these babies, which seemed then to make them more or less favoured. The authors hypothesised that the infant's behaviour may have triggered specific maternal mental representations early on, and thus operated via Bowlby's proposed inner working model to influence the relationship. The behavioural outcome for each child may then be mediated via the relationship. Thus, mothers in this study were noted to respond to the preferred infant more sensitively, allowing the baby to direct the interaction, whereas they initiated interaction with the other twin and did not seem to respond so easily to behavioural cues.

No matter how many genes are shared, individual children in one family, or even one monozygous twinship, turn out differently (Dunn and Plomin, 1991). Minde *et al.*'s paper begins to shed some light on these processes by specifically examining the developing relationships of twins. The view that children in one family experience a non-shared environment is tentatively confirmed by this study. However, multiple births are likely to present some specific relationship issues, which are different from those in non-twin relationships. They seem then to offer some insight into this area, but they do also merit particular attention in their own right from both a research and a therapeutic perspective.

THE OUTCOME FOR THE FAMILY

As already stated in Chapter 2, families face a crisis when an infant is admitted to special care. When the child makes a good recovery after a period of uncertainty, the family may have to deadapt and get back to as normal a life as possible. Sometimes this is difficult; the family may have been thrown off balance in a way that is difficult to recover from. Relationships in the family may remain skewed in a variety of ways; for example, the mother and child may remain 'overclose', while the marital relationship is distant. In other families, the crisis will have had a positive effect on family functioning. The parents may have been brought closer or roles may have been shared among family members more appropriately, with resulting benefits for each person in the family. In this situation, the special care infant will be allowed to develop age-appropriate autonomy in the context of a secure parent–child relationship.

When the child is left chronically disabled, through physical illness or learning disability, the family will be required to adapt to having a sick member. Again, this may be done in different ways with different consequences.

Recent research has led to the recognition that there may be yet another possible course of events. The child's discharge as healthy may not be the end of the story. The identification of minor disability in children of school age suggests that the first group of families may have to cope with yet another crisis later on. The long-term effects of this on both the individual's and the family's functioning have yet to be addressed.

Research to date on family functioning in relation to a child's illness has primarily focused on the effects of disability and chronic illness. However, as Tunali and Power (1993) have pointed out, the research on adjustment in families of developmentally handicapped children has presented contradictory findings. Likewise, research into adjustment to chronic illness has been inconclusive. In both examples, studies can be found both to support an association with marital discord and psychological distress in parents and siblings, *and* to refute such associations. It is also important to note that associations which have been found have been interpreted in various ways, so that, for example, marital discord may be seen as contributing to a maladaptive response or may be viewed as a consequence of the stress on the family.

This lack of a clear message from the literature is not surprising, as each child's illness will follow a variable course, with consequent modifying circumstances 'bumping' the system at every stage. Some children will require repeated and prolonged hospital admissions, for example. Most research studies have focused on a particular disability, but unfortunately a controlled course of illness does not necessarily ensue from controlling for the type of illness or disability. As in the case of follow-up studies of special care infants, it is difficult to know what to present from the vast amount of literature in this area.

Siblings

Siblings are generally neglected, both as participants in the special care unit, and in research. They have similarly been neglected in this account, partly because so little has been written about them. However, two papers published over a decade ago are worthy of mention.

Breslau *et al.* (1981) studied siblings of children suffering from a range of disabilities from birth, including cerebral palsy and multiple handicaps, in 239 families. These children did not score as more disturbed overall than controls but did have significantly higher scores for interpersonal aggression with peers. Type and severity of their sibling's illness, and age and sex were not related to psychological functioning, but there was a statistically significant interactive effect of birth order, gender and psychological functioning, with older female siblings and younger male siblings showing deleterious effects. These findings contradict that of a similar study by Lavigne and Ryan (1979) who examined siblings of children with acquired and congenital chronic illness, and did find a higher level of disturbance, which manifested itself as irritability and social withdrawal. Their findings also differed in respect of the association with birth order and gender. The population studied by Breslau and colleagues is, however, likely to be closest in character to that of siblings of special care infants. Although some of this group may have acute-on-chronic illnesses, they are not likely to be in the same situation as, say, siblings of paediatric haematology patients, one of the populations included in Lavigne and Ryan's study.

Breslau's study sought to examine assumptions made about sibling neglect in families with a disabled child leading to attention seeking through aggressive and antisocial behaviour. However, even though sibling aggression was noted, there was little evidence of parental inattention. There were no clear pointers to explanations for the outcomes, and the authors offered a number of explanations, which included the possibility that the effects had been mediated through the mothers' physical and emotional health.

Even though this study, like others, failed to find a significant overall difference in siblings of children with disability, these young people were still recognised to be at risk. The complex interaction of factors which determine outcome has been well recognised, and research is now beginning to address the finer details of the process whereby some siblings are affected and others are not.

My personal conclusions about the impact of acute or chronic disability are naturally influenced by my own clinical experience, so that I am aware of families where things have not gone smoothly because they have been referred to me. Evidence from research studies does not prevent me from citing examples of siblings of disabled children, for example, who have appeared to react to the situation they find themselves in.

Andrew was one. He was ten years old and the middle of three children. His brother, John, was fifteen and had a mild learning disability. John was subject to outbursts of temper when he did not get his own way. As he had got bigger, this had led to increased tension within the family. Fights with his brothers became a cause for concern for his mother who feared that he would injure someone. Andrew had recently overtaken his brother in ability in a number of areas of functioning; he was afforded more independence, and in addition began to have John entrusted to his care when they were out playing. This new relationship with his brother had been accompanied by headaches. Physical investigations had been unrevealing. Andrew, John and the rest of the family did not seem to have noticed that Andrew's headaches often prevented him from being able to take John out with him to play with his friends. Exploration of relationships outside the family revealed that Andrew had a number of close friends; John, who had no friends of his own outside of school, had recently come to regard his brother's friends as his, much to Andrew's dismay. The consequence of Andrew's headaches, however, was that he had not only relieved himself of the responsibility of looking after John and stopped his brother crashing in on his social life, but he had also managed to isolate himself.

Jane was also ten. She too had an older brother with a learning disability, in this case accompanied by severe epilepsy. She was generally quite a happy-go-lucky child, who had lots of friends and got on well at school. She was referred when her parents noticed that she had become much less happy. She had started to have huge rows with her mother, in particular, and seemed to have become quite preoccupied with how much money was spent on her brother. Her parents' account was that they were very fair and in fact had tried to bend over backwards to be even-handed. They said that they often talked with Jane about her brother's special needs. Recently, however, he had been much more ill and had definitely required more care and attention than usual. It transpired that somehow Jane had not noticed this, and had not heard their explanations about why things were a bit different from usual. Her focus on the money seemed in fact to represent her need for attention, which she had unconsciously not even noticed was missing.

The influence of past events

Both of these examples illustrate how powerful here-and-now factors are in relation to a sibling's adjustment. The mental health of individuals, and the family's way of functioning, may also be affected by past events or beliefs. In Chapters 1 and 2, I discussed how factors related to pregnancy, delivery and special care might influence early relationships. The effects of these can also be more far-reaching.

In Janet's case, her presentation to an adolescent psychiatric service at the age of twelve with a history of bullying and poor peer relationships was accompanied by a story about anxiety, particularly on her mother's part, that she was suffering from a serious physical illness. Following her difficult beginning, she had repeatedly been referred to paediatricians from an early age. Janet was also described as a wilful child who often got her own way at home. The therapist helped the family to draw a geneogram, and discovered that Janet was the second child to survive out of six pregnancies. Her mother gave a heart-rending account of how she felt that she had failed as a woman because of her inability to produce live children. Janet was a precious child, who was anxiously attached to her mother. Her behaviour difficulties and inability to form peer relationships seemed to be related to her enmeshed relationship with her mother, who had suffered from chronic depression related to unresolved grief and feelings of failure.

Stephen's long history of restlessness and poor attention, which had been accompanied by an increasingly severe conduct disorder following school entry, seemed to be related to his biological vulnerability (he was born at thirty weeks gestation) and his insecure attachment. As he grew up, he spent increasing lengths of time in care, and was repeatedly 'rejected' by his parents, who had gone on to have four more children. At the age of sixteen, his emotional immaturity and lack of conscience were striking, and his academic attainments were minimal. He had become more delinquent and faced a lonely future on the fringes of criminality.

David was born with cerebral palsy, and at the age of only three days old developed meningitis and had to be admitted to intensive care. In his early years his mother worked hard to promote his physical development, and proved the specialists, who'd predicted severe physical impairment, wrong. However, when I met them when David was thirteen, neither parent remembered being told that he would have a learning disability. He had failed badly at primary school, both scholastically and behaviourally. Professionals had advised early on that he should have special schooling, but his parents resisted this. After a year in secondary school, he had not only failed to make any educational progress, but had also been excluded on several occasions for disruptive behaviour. His peer relationships were poor, he was bullied and sought to create a role for himself by acting as daredevil and class clown. He was bullied even more, and became increasingly unhappy and defiant at home too. His parents finally accepted that he had a significant learning disability, and needed more specialist educational resources to help him to achieve scholastically, and to promote and support his social and emotional development.

The process of developing relationships

Factors at different levels combine to create a potentially infinite number of complex influences on the special care baby's developing relationships. I have suggested that three broad categories might encompass the tasks which face these children and their families as they grow and develop. First, after a hazardous beginning, the child has a good neurodevelopmental outcome, and the family have to get on with their lives and 'allow' the child to do so too. Second, the child and family have to adjust to the child's chronic disability. Third, after a poor start and a good recovery, they have to cope with hidden disability which presents later on.

Outcome in each category may reflect the influence of social context, high order beliefs, past events or experience around the time of the birth, as well as biological vulnerability. The ability to reflect on these possible influences on coping, and make sense of the experience seems important so that youngsters may be more vulnerable in families where, for example, past loss has not been resolved or disability has not been accepted and mourned. The quality of other relationships involving the mother, in particular, may either facilitate or inhibit her ability to form a strong bond with her child. Multiple births present particular difficulties.

The child's peer relationships in the early school years may not only be affected by the security of the primary relationship but, importantly, may be influenced by the presence of hidden disability. Difficulties at school for this group of children may be misconstrued. Subtle cognitive or motor disabilities may contribute to poor concentration in class, and diversion into deviant behaviour. Some may suffer from restlessness and overactivity, which may be helped or hindered by the classroom regime. Teachers and peers may decide that the child is naughty or badly behaved, and the failure to recognise and attend to the learning problem may result in the child being trapped in a cycle of scholastic failure, behaviour problems and increasing isolation. Relationships at home often then start to break down too, as parents join forces with teachers to discipline the child in question.

Crucial interactions take place at different stages in each child's life. As in any family, developmental tasks have to be negotiated not only by the child but by other family members too. At any one point in time, there is the potential for things to go wrong. In some families, a crisis will have deleterious knock-on effects, and as such will never really be recovered from. In others, each hurdle will present a positive opportunity for the strengthening of bonds and the development of new strategies with a positive outcome for both child and family.

SUMMARY

The outcome for special care infants is affected by a number of factors ranging from biological to social. Numerous follow-up studies have reported on outcome in terms of physical and cognitive functioning, while a few have also addressed behaviour and relationships. Methodological difficulties and the heterogeneity of the populations studied make it difficult to compare or generalise from these findings. Despite this, a common finding is that sociodemographic factors are the best predictors of outcome. The management of special care infants has changed dramatically in the last ten years, but an early finding that most of these youngsters were unscathed has recently been questioned as an increasing number of studies report that children who have been discharged have had later educational difficulties. These seem to contribute to behaviour problems and poor relationships, particularly if unrecognised initially.

The emotional consequences of prematurity, disability or multiple birth are related to the family's coping mechanisms. Unresolved grief, for example, may continue to affect family relationships for many years.

Chapter 9

Therapeutic interventions

Interventions which have the potential to alter the outcome for each special care infant may be made at different levels in the system, and at different points in time. They may be informed by different theoretical viewpoints which should not be seen as mutually exclusive. Books could easily be devoted to particular intervention strategies, such is the wealth of literature on this topic. Two books, in particular, have already made suggestions about policies and practices aimed at reducing the stress for infants, their families and staff (Brimblecombe *et al.*, 1978; Davis *et al.*, 1983).

The aim of this chapter is not to replicate these accounts but rather to place them in context and present an overview of treatment approaches.

The developmental support of the preterm infant

Wolke (1991) has ably reviewed this topic and highlighted the principles of intervention as well as areas of concern. Neonatal intensive care itself is, of course, the main intervention to be considered. High-tech procedures are primarily aimed at saving life and promoting a good quality of life. For premature babies, adequate circulatory, respiratory and nutritional support are essential if the neurodevelopmental consequences of their early birth are to be minimised. Close monitoring of the infant's physiological state is a *sine qua non* of an active approach to intervention. This monitoring will comprise both invasive and non-invasive techniques. Likewise, supported ventilation and intravenous lines will not be optional if a commitment has been made to support the life of a very low birth weight baby.

There is increasing recognition that in this context, particular strategies might lead to a better experience for the infant at the time, and possibly an improved outcome in the longer term. Wolke has referred to intervention programmes which 'aim to counteract neonatal sensory deprivation or overload' (1991: 728). However, before programmes are evolved to test out particular hypotheses about what is important, there is a need to recognise the everyday stresses for an infant in such a situation. I believe that changes can be made even before an intervention programme is 'invented'. Attention to the messages that infants give about what is happening to them, and a sensitive response, could reduce their experience of discomfort, pain or distress. As Gorski (1983) has indicated, the way that these messages are transmitted is not always obvious, but the infant's behaviour may provide enough of a clue so that, if an infant winces when a light is put on or a baby's monitor shows an increased heart rate in relation to sequential and closely spaced procedures, it may be that the child is giving a message about how that experience has been perceived or what it has *felt* like.

Nurses working in SCBUs do not have the time to observe and empathise with these babies in the way that child psychotherapists or researchers do, but that is not to say that they don't notice these things. They do. However, they may not have the time to reflect on what they notice or their feelings about that. In this situation, I believe that specific interventions aimed at directly reducing the infant's stress are less likely to work than if they are carried out in the context of some sort of emotional support for staff. I will return to this topic later.

Are special care infants deprived or overstimulated? This question in itself represents a gross oversimplification of the process of physical, cognitive and emotional development. If it is to be asked at all, it must be asked in relation to each infant, and those supporting or developing a relationship with that child. The question must also be placed in a temporal and developmental context. There is no place for generalisation of policies and practice without the simultaneous acknowledgement that each infant is an individual with unique strengths and vulnerabilities, and a personality of its own right from the beginning. Each family is also unique, and must be treated as such.

Having said all that, some very important research has been carried out on interventions aimed at improving the neonate's experience of special care. Tiffany Field has both carried out and reviewed such research (1990a and b). Using physiological measures such as oxygen tension, cortisol and growth hormone levels as indicators of the infant's stress, clear relationships have been demonstrated between the infant's state and the number and frequency of interventions. Reduction in the amount of handling of VLBW infants and the number of invasive interventions, as well as attention to the timing of these, has been shown to reduce the number of episodes of hypoxaemia and result in improved growth rate. By implication, it can be concluded that a more stable physiological state may help the infant to feel more emotionally contained. The introduction of simple measures to soothe infants, such as gentle stroking and the use of pacifiers (dummies) to permit non-nutritive sucking, while stressful procedures are carried out has also been demonstrated to reduce physiological indices of stress, and result in an improved physical outcome.

The implications of the above findings for the infant's developing relationships are at least twofold. First, some mothers may be right when they intuitively resist encouragement to handle their preterm babies. Second, if babies are subject to repeated physiological imbalance in relation to handling, they may be sensitised in some way, and feel stressed even when this handling does not result in pain or discomfort. This may result in infants trying to withdraw from contact in order to somehow hold themselves together, both physiologically and emotionally. Helping a mother to get to know her infant may involve a difficult balancing act; on the one hand there will be positive effects of close physical contact in both the short and long term for both participants, and on the other, if the infant feels too stressed by this contact there may be enduring effects on what sort of intimacy he or she is able to manage, and on the relationship.

Klaus and Kennell (1983) have supported this idea, and have discussed the implications for the developing mother–infant relationship in the context of research on both full-term and premature infants. Mothers and infants seem to do best when the mother allows her baby to dictate the terms of the interaction so that, during the course of any one period of interaction, a percentage of the time will be spent directly interacting, while the rest will be spent 'just' being together. An increase in her 'attention-getting' behaviour will often result in a decrease in the amount of time the infant spends gazing at her. Drawing on the work of Winnicott, Trevarthen and Field, these authors have concluded that an infant's responsiveness may be gradually increased by sensitive tuning in to the infant's movements and state, and imitation, or mirroring, by the mother or the nurse. Thus:

> Once a person has a well-integrated self, any imitation is an invasion of that individual's integrity. However, during the early months when the infant's self is incompletely formed, imitation of the infant's gestures and facial expressions appears to be a help in the process of self-discovery. All these observations suggest that we should be careful about recommending increased stimulation for the premature infant. Instead, it would appear to be more appropriate to suggest that the mother attempt to find her infant and move at the infant's pace.
> (Klaus and Kennell, 1983: 89)

With this in mind, it is clear that moves to counteract developmental delay by introducing infant stimulation in special care nurseries must always be made in the context of developing relationships. Research findings need to reviewed critically before any apparent messages are acted upon, and, most importantly, each infant's condition and responsiveness need to be taken account of.

Sensory stimulation includes visual, auditory, vestibular, tactile, olfactory and gustatory interventions (Chaze and Ludington-Hoe, 1984). This approach requires much more rigorous evaluation before any conclusions can be drawn. Studies that have examined the outcome of infant stimulation programmes alone have so far not demonstrated any lasting effects on either the infant's cognitive functioning or relationships (Patteson and Barnard, 1990). However, as Chaze and Ludington-Hoe (1984) have noted, these programmes do encompass attention to already present inappropriate stimulation as well as the active introduction of new stimuli. Thus, the first step, which makes sense to all participants, is to attend to the many sudden attacks, such as loud noises, heel stabs or the switching on of bright lights, for which the infant is unprepared. Approaches to infants as real people, who feel pain and are startled by sudden events, will help them to build on their fragile and early sense of integration rather than to disintegrate both physiologically and emotionally.

Promoting the parent–child relationship

The parent–child, and especially the mother–child, relationship may be influenced by an enormous number of factors, which include events around the time of conception and birth, as well as the history of individual family members and the sense they make of their experiences, past and present.

Parenting intervention studies have been thoroughly reviewed by Patteson and Barnard (1990) who included a range of treatment programmes in their account. These included approaches at the more educative end of the spectrum through to more broadly supportive interventions such as parent support groups. Some involved training parents to assess or stimulate their infants, while others provided specific opportunities for more intimate early contact. Most were only offered while the infant was in hospital, while some followed hospital intervention up with home visiting. Only one study under review concerned clinic-based intervention alone. The most immediate effect of hospital interventions appeared to be on maternal visiting which was generally increased. Interestingly, the majority of the studies that included both hospital and home contacts reported an improved outcome, regardless of which theoretical framework they were based upon. As these authors have pointed out, it often seemed that, inadvertently, a combination of approaches had been used, and the commonality in positive outcome was associated with the occurrence of many parental contacts with the same professional over a period of at least a year. Successful interventions had also involved the parents as active participants. However, 'the content of the intervention seemed less important than the interaction involved and the development of a relationship between parents and the intervener' (Patteson and Barnard, 1990: 52). Parents of low birth weight infants, those with more perinatal complications and those from a poor socioeconomic situation have been found to benefit most from such programmes.

Affleck *et al.* (1991) have questioned the value of supportive intervention programmes. In their own research into parents' adaptation to the crisis of intensive care, they offered 'a transitional consultation program' to half of the mothers in their study.

> This service was based on a consultation model of helping, as opposed to a parent-training or infant-curriculum model. The defining feature of this model is allowing mothers to dictate the specific topics for discussion within the broad guidelines of the consultant's view of the child's and family's best long-term interests.
>
> (Affleck *et al.*, 1991: 139)

Their finding that this benefited only those mothers who themselves desired a high level of support, and seemed to threaten rather than improve the adaptation of less needy mothers, raises questions about the indiscriminate use of intervention. They concluded that it would be more appropriate for mothers to determine what level of support they should have, the availability of support if required being seen as a valued resource in itself.

Psychoanalytically informed, and more broadly psychotherapeutic interventions have been evaluated less thoroughly than more didactic or behaviourist approaches. In particular, controlled studies seem to have only been done in this area in relation to parent support groups. This seems strange given the conclusions offered by Patteson and Barnard. Nonetheless, I want to go on and discuss what mental health professionals, in particular child psychiatrists and psychotherapists, can offer to babies, their families and the staff caring for them in the special care setting.

Holding the child in mind

Child psychotherapists working in special care baby units (for example, Szur (1981) and Earnshaw (1981)) have drawn attention to the value of observation of babies and their context. Infant observation can be considered to be both an informer of intervention, and an intervention in itself. As Bender has pointed out, psychoanalysts have emphasised the value of attentive observation and reflection as a healing process in itself (1983: 166). At its simplest, an active interest in the baby, no matter how premature, fragile or disabled, provides a model for both parents and staff. The curiosity aroused in those observing the observer often seems to act as a powerful catalyst for a new kind of way of looking at the infant, and consequently a new kind of interaction. The idea that spending time tuning into what these babies might be feeling might be mad may be dispelled as rich rewards, particularly for parents, are experienced at an emotional level. Parents can then begin to do the job, which they do naturally with older and fitter infants, of acting as an emotional container for their baby. They can allow themselves to bear to receive the baby's projections, and help to process and make sense of the experience; that is, they can begin to help the infant to grow emotionally. Parents can be supported in this task, which is of course often a painful one when the child is in a life-threatening situation, by sensitive staff. If they are able to feel emotionally contained by the unit or by one or two people working in the unit, they will be able to respond far more sensitively to their child.

A professional who is able to spend time observing babies in the unit may also be able to help both parents and nursing staff to give meaning to what they see, hear and feel. Thus, a psychotherapist can not only help parents to process their own and their babies' feelings, she or he can also 'educate', that is, lead them gently towards some ways of making sense of things.

I believe that therapists who work in this way, that is through the baby and with the baby's subjective experience always in mind, are in a much stronger position to help parents and other professionals to cope with what has happened than those who do not have the same focus on the infant. Parents of children with life-threatening illness often interpret offers of psychological support as a sign that they have failed or are not managing well enough or, even more worryingly, as an indication that they are mad. They frequently feel that the support will be too painful to bear, and see the shutting out of emotions and those who seem to threaten their defences as the only way to survive intact. Consequently offers of help are often rejected.

By focusing on a system which includes the infant, therapists are less likely to be seen as pathologising, and thus are less likely to be rejected. Their motives will seem clearer, and they will somehow have more credibility in the parents' eyes.

Similarly, staff working every day in a special care baby unit are less likely to feel persecuted by someone who is interested in emotions and feelings if the focus is on the infant. Staff support groups in these settings are famously difficult to run. Staff's commitment is found to vary enormously, and it is not uncommon to find that when things are particularly stressful in the unit, when a number of babies have died or staff sickness rates are high, for example, no one turns up for 'staff support'. Like parents, staff are often concerned that they will be seen as sick or inadequate. Staff support which is clearly set up with the babies in mind is likely to be a freer and less persecuting experience. Staff may be able to talk about their innermost feelings and phantasies without fear that they will be turned into the patient. Relationships between different staff members or parents and staff will often mirror the infant's own internal experience and primary relationship. Thus, insight into the way in which the infant's internal world is split may facilitate understanding of the rivalries between those around the infant. Of course, sometimes these rivalries are confronted head on, and in this situation again, acknowledgement of the infant's inner world and the parents' feelings of fragility and disintegration may help staff to begin to look inside themselves and give meaning to their own confusion.

Bender and Swan-Parente (1983), in their account of their experience of supporting staff and parents, identified themes common to both groups. They included: rivalry, identification with the baby, attachment and separation, mourning and guilt. Similarly they identified shared defence mechanisms such as denial and avoidance, displacement, projection and splitting, manic reparation and magical thinking. Classically, it seems that parents are usually recognised as potential benefiters of support, while staff are seen as carers and givers. Given that there are so many shared experiences, it seems likely that staff will not be best placed to help parents in their emotional task unless they have gained some insight into the mental mechanisms which underpin their own coping strategies. Coming full circle, once staff are clearer about their own internal processes, they will be able to bear to observe and to make relationships with the infants themselves, and will be able to support parents to do this too.

The value of storying

Following on from the other major theme of this book, narrative, I want to emphasise the importance of this in the process of healing and relationship-making.

Presenting parents, and particularly mothers, with the opportunity to recount their own stories, about pregnancy, labour, their own childhood, their current situation, their baby or whatever can be seen as offering them an opportunity to make sense of things. Elkan has emphasised 'the urgent desire demonstrated by mothers to recount the birth experience' (1981: 144) in an attempt to gain recognition and acknowledgement of their emotions. Others, carrying out parent–infant psychotherapy as a treatment for all manner of problems presented in infancy, have also emphasised the importance of letting parents tell their own story. The rationale for this, in Daws' words, is that 'as they tell their story, unconscious threads draw together and connections emerge' (1989: 22).

Affleck *et al.* have reported that 'parents who are able to restore a sense of meaning and mastery in the face of the profound challenges to their "assumptive world"' (1991: 129) are more likely to do well than those who cannot. The perceived benefits of this way of coping were felt by parents themselves who were ultimately less emotionally distressed, and were evidenced by the developmental outcome of their infants. The opportunity to talk about their experience with family members, friends or, in their absence, professionals was seen as an important part of the process of meaning-making for these parents. As such, storying can be seen as contributing to a positive adaptation to having a very sick infant

These findings are in keeping with the philosophy underpinning the use of narrative as a tool in family therapy. The use of narrative here is implicitly linked with the recognition of the importance of past experience and high order beliefs. Successful outcome is not only associated with the ability to make sense of what has happened, but also the ability to use the process of narrative in a generative way; that is, to use it in the service of mastery or the development of agency. As illustrated earlier in the book, simply having a story which makes sense of the situation may not necessarily help parents to call their child into life or into a relationship with them so that, while emotionally a parent may be protected from feelings of guilt or blame or a clinical depression by virtue of a fatalistic belief system, that parent might also be quite unavailable emotionally to the infant. The value of narrative as a way of promoting the infant's early relationships depends strongly on the potential to see each story as one of a number of possible stories. Therapeutic storying is possible when parents are helped to identify 'those aspects of lived experience that fall outside of the dominant story' which 'provide a rich and fertile source for the generation, or re-generation, of alternative stories' (White and Epston, 1990: 15). In relation to powerful high order beliefs of an incapacitating nature, therapeutic success depends on reflexivity; that is, although religious beliefs, for example, may be perceived as being at a different and 'higher' level than current experience in a hierarchy of meaning, they can still be redefined in the context of current experience.

A more specific use of storying as a therapeutic tool is exemplified in John Byng-Hall's description of rescripting (Byng-Hall, 1988). His specific reference to alternative *parenting* scripts provides a way of conceptualising the dilemmas for mothers such as Ms A and Ms B. In cases like these, the therapist, by supporting the telling of the story and helping the parent to gain insight into unconscious processes, can facilitate the emergence of emotional connections which empower the parent to do things differently. This, I think, is of crucial importance for many special care infants. Within this population, as I have noted earlier, are a significant number of young emotionally deprived women whose own experience of being mothered is recalled with despair and anger. For these women, whose motives for conception have often been fuelled by their need to have someone of their own to love, it is vital that their developing relationship with their infant is supported in a way that enables them to break free from this cycle of deprivation. The intergenerational transmission of attachment disorders and its association with child abuse is well recognised (Minde and Benoit, 1991); therapeutic rescripting offers the potential to interrupt this process in families of special care infants.

Infant–parent psychotherapy

This style of therapeutic work, described originally by Fraiberg (1980) in relation to the treatment of children in the first year of life, has more recently been described and illustrated by a number of British child psychotherapists (Daws, 1989; Hopkins, 1993; Miller, 1993). In many respects this intervention can be seen as one which effectively combines the use of observation and narrative.

Hopkins has summarised the features of this approach and the rationale for adopting it:

> Infant–parent psychotherapy relies on the assumption that there is no such thing as individual psychopathology in infancy. This does not mean that babies do not contribute individual differences from their side of the relationship. It does mean that symptoms in the infant can best be treated by treating the infant–parent relationship, rather than by treating either infant or parent separately. Like all short-term therapies, infant–parent psychotherapy is focused, and the focus is on the development of the infant who is always present in the sessions. The infant's presence ensures that parental feelings towards him are readily available in the here-and-now for exploration and interpretation. Interpretation, as practised by Selma Fraiberg, utilised a combination of object-relations and attachment theory to understand the ways in which the parental past interfered with relating to the baby in the present. The symptomatic infant was found to be the victim of negative transference, haunted by 'ghosts in the nursery'. The primary focus of the work was on understanding the parents' transference to their baby, rather than on understanding their transference to the therapist.
>
> (Hopkins, 1993: 5)

There is also an assumption with this approach that the infant, present in the session, will help both parents and therapists to make sense of things. Thus, this intervention, while supporting the parents emotionally, also aims 'to demonstrate their [the parents'] own unique importance to their child and to help them to observe and think about the reasons for their child's behaviour' (Hopkins, 1993: 6).

The aim of infant–parent psychotherapy is to help children and parents who are having relationship problems which may manifest themselves in a number of ways. Emde and Sameroff's understanding of early relationship problems (1989) focuses on the contrast between perturbation, disturbance and disorder.

The concept of perturbation is implicit in development. Development advances through the meeting of challenges and the overcoming of problems. . . .

For most children these perturbations are soon resolved as competence is reached in a new area. For others, however, a failure to attain a given developmental milestone becomes a disturbance if it interferes with other areas of adaptation and a disorder if it persists far beyond normative bounds.

(Emde and Sameroff, 1989: 9)

They considered that relationships could not be evaluated out of their developmental context. Their ideas about degrees of relationship problem can usefully be applied to the special care infant's relationships. In many cases, the experience of admission to special care will only perturb the developing relationship which will get back on course fairly quickly once the crisis is over. In this case, active psychotherapeutic intervention may not be deemed necessary, but may be a valuable preventative piece of work. Early help to identify the potential influences on the quality of the relationship may help parents to recognise or anticipate later difficulties.

Disturbance or disorder may be apparent while the infant is still in the unit or may manifest itself later. In both cases, infant–parent psychotherapy may facilitate a resolution over a fairly short time period. Like infants themselves, who may appear to be critically ill one minute and in good health the next, infants' behaviour problems seem to have a remarkable capacity to recover with prompt and effective intervention. As Miller (1993) has pointed out, there is often an urgency about problems involving infants or small children. Anxiety is frequently experienced as overwhelming and has a contagious quality to it, often affecting both close and more distant family members. The capacity of therapists to be prompt and flexible in their response will allow this anxiety to be harnessed in the service of change.

Practice and policy

Finally, I want to consider some aspects of the care of special care infants which can only loosely be described as therapeutic intervention. I want to consider the context of intervention; that is, the policies of special care and neonatal intensive care units, and policies which affect such children as they grow and develop. Many of these have been referred to in other publications, which can also be seen to have influenced particularly the emotional care given to such children and their parents.

Partnership with parents

Parent involvement in the provision of health care for their child has been advocated for many years but even now is probably not given the place that it deserves. This should span the life of the child from the period of perinatal care through education to adulthood.

In the special care unit, parents need to be supported to make decisions about their infants' care, and to provide for their infant as best they can in the circumstances. Particular attention still needs to be paid to the individuality of each family's response to the situation, so that those who are more distant and tentative initially will not then feel shut out by the professionals. Similarly, as the child's later health and educational needs are considered, parents must be helped to make an informed choice about the provision of services for their child.

Special care units

Recognition of the potentially damaging effects of admission to special care units has contributed to a reappraisal of admission criteria (National Children's Bureau, 1987) and widespread acceptance of open access for parents. However, the move to create regional centres of excellence has been associated with families often having to travel long distances to visit. Few hospitals have sufficient facilities for parents to stay overnight, and many units are still intolerant of the presence of siblings on the ward.

Parents try to get to know their babies in a busy and crowded environment which affords no room for intimacy. Parents often feel that they are on display, and are being judged on their performance, and this tends to constrain their abilities rather than promote them. Those who lack confidence or are particularly unsure how to be a parent anyway often find it difficult to know what to do, and others, whose parenting skills seem to be suspended in the context of a very fragile infant, similarly feel unsupported and persecuted by feelings of exposure. Some attention to ways of giving families a degree of privacy while still ensuring that the infant is closely monitored is merited.

Communication is also worthy of attention. Clear and prompt communication with parents about their infant's condition and prognosis is essential if unnecessary and debilitating anxiety is to be avoided. Similarly clear interprofessional communication is essential both in relation to specific infants and as a general rule within the unit. Staff who feel uncertain about how government policy and management decisions are going to affect their future will not be in a position to offer psychological containment to parents. Their own anxieties about such matters as well as the ethical dilemmas inherent in their task need to be addressed if they are to function efficiently in both practical and emotional terms.

Continuity of care is important for all children but particularly for those who are of low birth weight. As described earlier, the full extent of any disability consequent on their precarious beginning is often unknown. The recognition that these children often suffer from 'hidden' or undetected disabilities which may lead to school failure and relationship difficulties suggests that their early discharge from medical follow-up is inappropriate. Community paediatricians are probably best placed to carry out regular surveillance of these children, but need to be alerted to the potential problems that each child may develop in order to intervene appropriately.

The wider context

The 1987 National Children's Bureau review *Child Health Ten Years after the Court Report* drew attention to the 'clear-cut link between [such] deprivation and many of the health problems from which children suffer' (p. 11). The association between social factors and later morbidity has been clearly evidenced by a number of follow-up studies of special care infants. Health professionals cannot alleviate poverty or poor housing yet there is no doubt that the consequence of social deprivation is to increase the amount and the cost of care needed by these children as they go through their lives. This connection cannot and should not be overlooked if a preventative approach to health is to be adopted.

SUMMARY

Therapeutic interventions for special care infants can be made at different levels in the system and at different points in time. They range from the general to the particular, the former embracing national, hospital and unit policy relevant for each child, and the latter perhaps being reserved for families in most obvious difficulty. The value of keeping the child in mind is emphasised. Helping staff and parents to focus on the infants in their care will not only contribute to a better relationship with the child but may also permit these grown-ups to accept support themselves. Offering parents an opportunity to tell their story may also offer an opportunity for the development of agency, which is likely to have a beneficial effect on their relationship with their child.

Concluding comments

Special care infants are a heterogeneous population who share a difficult beginning. In terms of mortality, their outcome has improved enormously. However, a large number of children are left with minor disabilities which may have an effect on their later relationships with peers and family members. In most cases, their early relationships will have developed in what can only be described as a stressful context.

In the wake of the impressive advances in the technological aspects of the care of these infants has come increasing concern about the enduring emotional effects of what is often a hazardous start to life. The treatment of special care infants now embraces consideration of their psychological and social development as well as their neurobiological functioning.

The impact of disturbances in early relationships on later emotional health, and the effects of relationships on relationships are now being researched in a more rigorous way than ever before. Theories previously held dear by psychoanalysts are being supported to some extent by research in the fields of developmental psychology and psychiatry. A new wave of studies into the intergenerational transmission of attachment disorders also support the idea that the quality of the early parent–infant relationship may be predictive of an individual's later relationships, mental health, and capacity to parent.

In this book, I have tried to draw attention to the complex interaction of possible mediating factors which operate both pre- and postnatally to influence the special care baby's developing relationships. The early parent–infant relationship seems to be extremely sensitive to its context, which includes psychological and institutional processes operating within both the family and the hospital. In an attempt to understand this complex intertwining of potential influences, I have offered the notion of a hierarchy of meaning. My main contention has been that each participant's perceived experience has equal validity, and offers the potential for further understanding of the processes involved in the development of each infant's relationships.

The period of time which the infant spends in the special care unit presents both obstacles and opportunities to parents and professionals, and to the infants themselves. Recognition of the powerful effects of past experience, beliefs and social context is essential if parents and infants are to be adequately emotionally contained by the hospital. Interventions of both a medical and psychological nature must be made with both the infant and the wider context in mind if families are to be helped to cope well enough with the crisis of intensive care and with the rest of their lives.

Further reading

Those who are unfamiliar with the literature referred to in this book may be interested in some of the following texts.

About psychoanalysis:

Mitchell, J. (1986) *The Selected Melanie Klein*, Harmondsworth: Penguin.
Stafford-Clark, D. (1967) *What Freud Really Said*, Harmondsworth: Penguin.

About attachment:

Bowlby, J. (1953) *Child Care and the Growth of Love*, Harmondsworth: Penguin.
Rutter, M. (1972) *Maternal Deprivation Reassessed*, Harmondsworth: Penguin.

About early parent–infant relationships:

Brazelton, T. B. & Cramer, G. (1991) *The Earliest Relationship. Parents, Infants, and the Drama of Early Attachment*, London: Karnac Books.
Stern, D. (1977) *The First Relationship. Mother and Infant*, Cambridge, Mass.: Harvard University Press.
Stern, D. (1990) *Diary of a Baby*, New York: Basic Books.
Winnicott, D. W. (1964) *The Child, the Family, and the Outside World*, Harmondsworth: Penguin.
Winnicott, D. W. (1988) *Babies and Their Mothers*, London: Free Association Books.

About child development in a social context:

Richards, M. P. M. (ed.) (1974) *The Integration of a Child into a Social World*, London: Cambridge University Press.
Richards, M. and Light, P. (eds) (1986) *Children of Social Worlds: Development in a Social Context*, Cambridge, Mass.: Harvard University Press.
Rutter, M. & Rutter, M. (1992) *Developing Minds. Challenge and Continuity across the Life Span*, Harmondsworth: Penguin.

About special care babies:

Affleck, G., Tennen, H. & Rowe, J. (1990) 'Mothers, fathers, and the crisis of newborn intensive care', *Infant Mental Health Journal*, *11*, 12–25.

Davis, J. A., Richards, M. P. M. & Roberton, N. R. C. (eds) (1983) *Parent–Baby Attachment in Premature Infants*, London: Croom Helm.

Goldberg, S. & DiVitto, B. (1983) *Born Too Soon: Preterm Birth and Early Development*, San Francisco: Freeman.

Hudson, G. B. (1985) *You and Your Premature Baby*, London: Sheldon Press.

Szur, R., Freud, W.E., Elkan, J., Earnshaw, A., & Bender, H. (1981) 'Hospital care of the newborn: some aspects of personal stress', *Journal of Child Psychotherapy*, *7*, 137–159. (This is a series of papers by child psychotherapists working in special care baby units.)

References

Abel-Smith, A. E. & Knight-Jones, E. B. (1990) 'The abilities of very low birthweight children and their classroom controls', *Developmental Medicine and Child Neurology*, *32*, 590–601.

Affleck, G., Tennen, H. & Rowe, J. (1990) 'Mothers, fathers, and the crisis of newborn intensive care', *Infant Mental Health Journal*, *11*, 12–25.

Affleck, G., Tennen, H. & Rowe, J. (1991) *Infants in Crisis: How Parents Cope With Newborn Intensive Care and its Aftermath*, New York: Springer-Verlag.

Ainsworth, M. D. S. (1967) 'Patterns of infant attachment to mother', in Y. Brackbill & G. Thompson (eds) *Behaviour in Infancy and Early Childhood*, New York: Free Press.

Ainsworth, M. D. S. (1977) 'Social development in the first year of life: maternal influences on infant–mother attachment', in J. M. Tanner (ed.) *Developments in Psychiatric Research*, Sevenoaks: Hodder & Stoughton.

Alvarez, A. (1992) *Live Company: Psychoanalytic Psychotherapy with Autistic, Borderline, Deprived and Abused Children*, London: Tavistock/Routledge.

Anderson, H. & Goolishian, H. A. (1988) 'Human systems as linguistic systems: preliminary and evolving ideas about the implications for clinical theory', *Family Process*, *27*, 371–393.

Audit Commission (1993) *Children First: A Study of Hospital Services*, National Health Service Report No. 7, London: HMSO.

Auerswald, E. H. (1987) 'Epistemological confusion in family therapy and research', *Family Process*, *26*, 317–330.

Bateson, G. (1972) *Steps to an Ecology of Mind*, New York: Ballantine.

Bateson, G. (1979) *Mind and Nature*, New York: Dutton.

Bedrick, A. D. (1989) 'Neonatal intensive care: at what price?', *American Journal of Diseases in Children*, *143*, 451–452.

Belsky, J. & Isabella, R. (1988) 'Maternal, infant, and social contextual determinants of attachment security', in J. Belsky & T. Nezworski (eds) *Clinical Implications of Attachment*, Hove and London: Lawrence Erlbaum Associates.

Bender, H. (1981) 'Experiences in running a staff group', *Journal of Child Psychotherapy*, *7*, 152–159.

Bender, H. (1990) 'On the outside looking in: sibling perceptions, dreams and fantasies of the premature infant', *International Journal of Prenatal and Perinatal Studies*, 133–143.

Bender, H. & Swan-Parente, A. (1983) 'Psychological and psychotherapeutic support of staff and parents in an intensive care baby unit', in J. A. Davis, M. P. M. Richards & N. R. C. Roberton (eds) *Parent–Baby Attachment in Premature Infants*, London: Croom Helm.

Bentovim, A. (1979) 'Child development research findings and psychoanalytic theory – an integrative critique', in D. Shaffer & J. Dunn (eds) *The First Year of Life: Psychological and Medical Implications of Early Experience*, Chichester: John Wiley.

Bick, E. (1964) 'Notes on infant observation in psychoanalytic training', in M. Harris Williams (ed.) *Collected Papers of Martha Harris and Esther Bick*, Perthshire: Clunie Press.

Bion, W. R. (1967) *Second Thoughts: Selected Papers in Psychoanalysis*, New York: Aronson.

Birch, J. (1991) 'Reinventing the already punctured wheel: reflections on a seminar with Humberto Maturana', *Journal of Family Therapy*, *13*, 349–373.

Blackman, J. A. (1991) 'Neonatal intensive care: is it worth it? Developmental sequelae of very low birth weight', *Pediatric Clinics of North America*, *38*, 1497–1511.

Bowlby, J. (1946) *Forty-four Juvenile Thieves: Their Characters and Their Home Life*, London: Bailliere, Tindall & Cox.

Bowlby, J. (1951) *Maternal Care and Mental Health*, Geneva: World Health Organization.

Bowlby, J. (1953) *Child Care and the Growth of Love*, Harmondsworth: Penguin.

Bowlby, J. (1969) *Attachment and Loss: Volume 1: Attachment*, Harmondsworth: Penguin.

Bowlby, J. (1973) *Attachment and Loss: Volume 2: Separation*, Harmondsworth: Penguin.

Bowlby, J. (1980) *Attachment and Loss: Volume 3: Loss*, Harmondsworth: Penguin.

Bowlby, J. (1988a) 'Changing theories of childhood since Freud', in E. Timms & N. Segal (eds) *Freud in Exile*, New Haven, Conn.: York University Press.

Bowlby, J. (1988b) 'Developmental psychiatry comes of age', *American Journal of Psychiatry*, *145*, 1–10.

Brazelton, T. B. & Cramer, G. (1991) *The Earliest Relationship: Parents, Infants, and the Drama of Early Attachment*, London: Karnac Books.

Brazelton, T. B., Koslowski, B. & Main, M. (1974) 'The origins of reciprocity: the early mother–infant interaction', in M. Lewis & L. A. Rosenblum (eds) *The Effect of the Infant on Its Caregiver*, New York: John Wiley.

Brazelton, T. B., Tronick, E., Adamson, L., Als, H. & Wise, S. (1975) 'Early mother–infant reciprocity', in *Parent–Infant Interaction*, Ciba Foundation Symposium 33, Amsterdam: Elsevier Publishing Co.

Breen, D. (1975) *The Birth of a First Child*, London: Tavistock.

Breslau, N., Weitzman, M. & Messenger, K. (1981) 'Psychologic functioning of siblings of disabled children', *Pediatrics*, *67*, 344–353.

Bretherton, I. (1985) 'Attachment theory: retrospect and prospect', in I. Bretherton & E. Waters (eds) *Growing Points in Attachment Theory and Research*, Monographs of the Society for Research in Child Development, *50* (1–2 Serial No. 209).

Brimblecombe, F. S. W., Richards, M. P. M. & Roberton, N. R. C. (1978) *Separation and Special-care Baby Units*, Clinics in Developmental Medicine No. 68, London: Heinemann Medical Books.

Britton, R. (1986) 'The infant in the adult', *Psychoanalytic Psychotherapy*, *2*, 31–44.

Bruner, J. (1990) *Acts of Meaning*, London: Harvard University Press.

Byng-Hall, J. (1973) 'Family myths used as a defence in conjoint family therapy', *British Journal of Medical Psychology*, *46*, 239–249.

Byng-Hall, J. (1988) 'Scripts and legends in families and family therapy', *Family Process*, *27*, 167–179.

Campbell, D. M., Gandy, G. M. & Roberton, N. R. C. (1983) 'Which babies need admission to special care baby units?', in J. A. Davis, M. P. M. Richards & N. R. C. Roberton (eds) *Parent–Baby Attachment in Premature Infants*, London: Croom Helm.

Carter, E. & McGoldrick, M. (1989) *The Changing Family Life Cycle: A Framework for Family Therapy*, London: Allyon & Bacon.

Casaer, P. (1993) 'Old and new facts about perinatal brain development', *Journal of Child Psychology and Psychiatry*, *34*, 101–109.

Cecchin, G. (1987) 'Hypothesising, circularity and neutrality revisited: an invitation to curiosity', *Family Process, 26*, 405–413.

Chaze B. & Ludington-Hoe, S. M. (1984) 'Sensory stimulation in the NICU', *American Journal of Nursing, 84*, 68–71.

Cogill, S. R., Caplan, H. L., Alexandra, H., Robson, K. M. & Kumar, R. (1986) 'Impact of maternal postnatal depression on cognitive development in young children', *British Medical Journal, 292*, 1165–1167.

Cronen, V. E. & Pearce, W. B. (1985) 'Towards an explanation of how the Milan method works: an invitation to a systemic epistemology and the evolution of family systems', in D. Campbell & R. Draper (eds) *Applications of Systemic Family Therapy: The Milan Approach*, London: Grune & Stratton.

Cronen, V. E., Johnson, K. M. & Lannaman, J. W. (1982) 'Paradoxes, double binds, and reflexive loops: an alternative theoretical perspective', *Family Process, 21*, 91–112.

Cronen, V. E., Pearce, W. B. & Tomm, K. (1985) 'A dialectic view of personal change', in K. E. Davis & K. J. Gergen (eds) *The Social Construction of the Person*, New York: Springer-Verlag.

Crown, S. (1968) 'Psychoanalysis and problems of scientific method', in J. D. Sutherland (ed.) *The Psychoanalytic Approach*, London: Bailliere, Tindall & Cassell.

Culp, R. E. & Osofsky, H. J. (1989) 'Effects of caesarian delivery on parental depression, marital adjustment, and mother–infant interaction', *Birth, 16*, 53–57.

Dare, C. (1979) 'Psychoanalysis and systems in family therapy', *Journal of Family Therapy, 1*, 137–151.

Davis, J. A. (1989) 'More on the follow-up of low birth-weight infants', *Developmental Medicine and Child Neurology, 31*, 143–144.

Davis, J. A., Richards, M. P. M. & Roberton, N. R. C. (eds) (1983) *Parent–Baby Attachment in Premature Infants*, London: Croom Helm.

Daws, D. (1989) *Through the Night: Helping Parents and Sleepless Infants*, London: Free Association Books.

Dell, P. F. (1985) 'Understanding Bateson and Maturana: toward a biological foundation for the social sciences', *Journal of Marital and Family Therapy, 11*, 1–20.

Delucca, A., Messini, S., Moroder, W., Bortolotti, D. P. & Cavosi, M. T. (1989) 'Hospitalisation for preterm labour: implications in the bonding process, a pilot study', *International Journal of Prenatal and Perinatal Studies*, 67–74.

Donley, M. G. (1993) 'Attachment and the emotional unit', *Family Process, 32*, 3–20.

Douglas, J. W. B. (1975) 'Early hospital admission and later disturbance of behaviour and learning', *Developmental Medicine and Child Neurology, 17*, 456–480.

Drillien, C. M., Thomson, A. J. M. & Burgoyne, K. (1980) 'Low-birthweight children at early school age: a longitudinal study', *Developmental Medicine and Child Neurology, 22*, 26–47.

Dunn, J. B. & Plomin, R. (1991) 'Why are siblings so different? The significance of differences in sibling experiences within the family', *Family Process, 30*, 271–283.

Dunn, J. B. & Richards, M. P. M. (1977) 'Observations on the developing relationship between mother and baby in the neonatal period', in H. R. Schaffer (ed.) *Studies in Mother–Infant Interaction*, London: Academic Press.

Earnshaw, A. (1981) 'Action consultancy', *Journal of Child Psychotherapy, 7*, 149–152.

Eichenbaum, L. & Orbach, S. (1983) *What Do Women Want?*, Glasgow: Fontana.

Elkan, J. (1981) 'Talking about the birth', *Journal of Child Psychotherapy, 7*, 144–148.

Emde, R. N. & Buchsbaum, H. K. (1989) 'Toward a psychoanalytic theory of affect: II. Emotional development and signaling in infancy', in S. I. Greenspan & G. H. Pollock (eds) *The Course of Life, Vol. 1: Infancy*, Madison: International University Press.

Emde, R. N. & Sameroff, A. J. (1989) 'Understanding early relationship disturbances', in A. J. Sameroff & R. N. Emde (eds) *Relationship Disturbances in Early Childhood*, New York: Basic Books.

Ferholt, J. B., Hoffnig, R. J., Hunter, E. E. K. & Leventhal, J. M. (1986) 'Clinical investigators under stress: a critique of Garmezy's commentary', *Journal of the American Academy of Child Psychiatry*, 25, 724–727.

Field, T. M. (1990a) 'Neonatal stress and coping in intensive care', *Infant Mental Health Journal*, 11, 57–65.

Field, T. M. (1990b) 'Alleviating stress in newborn infants in the intensive care unit', *Clinics in Perinatology*, 17, 1–9.

Fivaz-Depeursinge, E. (1991) 'Documenting a time-bound, circular view of hierarchies: a microanalysis of parent–infant interaction', *Family Process*, 30, 101–120.

Fraiberg, S. H. (1980) *Clinical Studies in Infant Mental Health: The First Year of Life*, London: Tavistock.

Freud, W. E. (1981) 'To be in touch', *Journal of Child Psychotherapy*, 7, 141–143.

Freud, W. E. (1989a) 'Prenatal attachment and bonding', in S. I. Greenspan & G. H. Pollock (eds) *The Course of Life, Vol. 1: Infancy*, Madison: International University Press.

Freud, W. E. (1989b) 'Notes on some psychological aspects of neonatal intensive care', in S. I. Greenspan & G. H. Pollock (eds) *The Course of Life, Vol. 1: Infancy*, Madison: International University Press.

Frodi, A., Bridges, L. & Shonk, S. (1989) 'Maternal correlates of infant temperament ratings and of infant–mother attachment: a longitudinal study', *Infant Mental Health Journal*, 10, 273–281.

Garmezy, N. (1986) 'Children under severe stress: critique and commentary', *Journal of the American Academy of Child Psychiatry*, 25, 384–392.

Gilligan, C. (1982) *In A Different Voice*, Cambridge, Mass.: Harvard University Press.

Goffman, E. (1961) *Asylums*, Harmondsworth: Penguin.

Goldberg, D. & David, A. S. (1991) 'Family therapy and the glamour of science', *Journal of Family Therapy*, 13, 17–30.

Goldberg, S. & DiVitto, B. (1983) *Born Too Soon: Preterm Birth and Early Development*, San Francisco: Freeman.

Gorell-Barnes, G. (1985) 'Systems theory and family therapy', in M. Rutter & L. Hersov (eds) *Child and Adolescent Psychiatry: Modern Approaches*, Oxford: Blackwell Scientific Publications.

Gorell-Barnes, G. (1990) 'Making family therapy work: research findings and family therapy practice', *Journal of Family Therapy*, 12, 17–29.

Goren, C., Sarty, M. & Wu, P. (1975) 'Visual following and pattern discrimination of face-like stimuli by newborn infants', *Pediatrics*, 56, 544–549.

Gorski, P. A. (1983) 'Premature infant behavioral and physiological response to caregiving interventions in the intensive care nursery', in J. D. Call, E. Galenson & R. L. Tyson (eds) *Frontiers of Infant Psychiatry: Volume 1*, New York: Basic Books.

Gosling, R. (1968) 'What is transference?', in J. D. Sutherland (ed.) *The Psychoanalytic Approach*, London: Bailliere, Tindall & Cassell.

Graves, P. L. (1989) 'The functional fetus', in S. I. Greenspan & G. H. Pollock (eds) *The Course of Life, Vol. 1: Infancy*, Madison: International University Press.

Greenspan, S. I. & Lieberman, A. F. (1989) 'Infants, mothers, and their interaction: a quantitative clinical approach to developmental assessment', in S. I. Greenspan & G. H. Pollock (eds) *The Course of Life, Vol. 1: Infancy*, Madison: International University Press.

Grossmann, K., Grossmann, K. E., Spangler, G. Suess, G. & Unzer, L. (1985) 'Maternal sensitivity and newborn's orientation responses as related to the quality of attachment in Northern Germany', in I. Bretherton & E. Waters (eds) *Growing Points of Attachment Theory and Research*, Monographs of the Society for Research in Child Development, 50 (1–2 Serial No. 209).

Haley, J. (1976) *Problem-Solving Therapy*, San Francisco: Jossey-Bass.

Hawdon, J. M., Hey, E., Kolvin, I. & Fundudis, T. (1990) 'Born too small: is outcome still affected?', *Developmental Medicine and Child Neurology*, 32, 943–953.

Hinde, R. A. & Stevenson-Hinde, J. (eds) (1988) *Relationships within Families: Mutual Influences*, Oxford: Clarendon Press.
Hoffman, L. (1988) 'A constructivist position for family therapy', *Irish Journal of Psychology*, *9*, 110–129.
Hoffman, L. (1990) 'Constructing realities: an art of lenses', *Family Process*, *29*, 1–12.
Hopkins, J. (1993) 'Infant–parent psychotherapy', *Journal of Child Psychotherapy*, *19*, 5–17.
Hudson, G. B. (1985) *You and Your Premature Baby*, London: Sheldon Press.
Ingleby, D. (1986) 'Development in social context', in M. Richards & P. Light (eds) *Children of Social Worlds: Development in a Social Context*, Cambridge, Mass.: Harvard University Press.
Irvine, A. H. (ed.) (1956) *Collins New English Dictionary*, London: Collins.
Jellinek, M. S., Catlin, E. A., Todres, I. D. & Cassem, E. H. (1992) 'Facing tragic decisions with parents in the neonatal intensive care unit: clinical perspectives', *Pediatrics*, *89*, 119–122.
Jones, C. L. (1982) 'Environmental analysis of neonatal intensive care', *Journal of Nervous and Mental Disease*, *170*, 130–142.
Kaye, K. (1982) *The Mental and Social Life of Babies*, London: Methuen.
Keeney, B. P. & Sprenkle, D. H. (1982) 'Ecosystemic epistemology: critical implications for the aesthetics and pragmatics of family therapy', *Family Process*, *21*, 1–19.
Kitzinger, S. (1984) *The Experience of Childbirth*, Harmondsworth: Penguin.
Klaus, M. & Kennell, J. (1983) 'Care for the family of an infant with a congenital malformation', in J. A. Davis, M. P. M. Richards & N. R. C. Roberton (eds) *Parent–Baby Attachment in Premature Infants*, London: Croom Helm.
Klaus, M. H., Jerauld, R., Kreger, N. C., McAlpine, W., Steffa, M. & Kennell, J. H. (1972) 'Maternal attachment: importance of the first post-partum days', *New England Journal of Medicine*, *286*, 460–463.
Kohon, G. (1986) 'Introduction', in G. Kohon (ed.) *The British School of Psychoanalysis: The Independent Tradition*, London: Free Association Books.
Kraemer, S. (1987) 'The process of child psychiatry', unpublished paper.
Kratochvil, M. S., Robertson, C. M. T. & Kyle, J. M. (1991) 'Parents' view of parent–child relationship eight years after neonatal intensive care', *Social Work in Health Care*, *16*, 95–118.
La Fontaine, J. (1986) 'An anthropological perspective on children in social worlds', in M. Richards & P. Light (eds) *Children of Social Worlds: Development in a Social Context*, Cambridge, Mass.: Harvard University Press.
Largo, R. H., Pfister, D., Molinari, L., Kundu, S., Lipp, A. & Duc, G. (1989) 'Significance of prenatal, perinatal and postnatal factors in the development of AGA preterm infants at five to seven years', *Developmental Medicine and Child Neurology*, *31*, 440–456.
Lavigne, J. V. & Ryan, M. (1979) 'Psychologic adjustment of siblings of children with chronic illness', *Pediatrics*, *63*, 616–627.
Lee, S. K., Penner, P. L. & Cox, M. (1991) 'Comparison of the attitudes of health care professionals and parents toward active treatment of very low birth weight babies', *Pediatrics*, *88*, 110–114.
Leonard, C. H., Clyman, R. I., Piecuch, R. E., Juster, R. P., Ballard, R. A. & Behle, M. B. (1990) 'Effect of medical and social risk factors on outcome of prematurity and very low birth weight', *Pediatrics*, *116*, 620–626.
Levene, M. I. (1992) 'The impact of intensive care on the frequency of mental and motor handicap', *Current Opinion in Neurology and Neurosurgery*, *5*, 333–338.
Levene, M. I., Dowling, S., Graham, M., Fogelman, K., Galton, M. & Phillips, M. (1992) 'Impaired motor function (clumsiness) in five year old children: correlation with neonatal ultrasound scans', *Archives of Disease in Childhood*, *67*, 687–690.

Lissenden, J. V. & Ryan, M. M. (1982) 'Parents' view of newborn intensive care', *Australian Nurses Journal*, *11*, 34–36.

Ludman, L., Landsdown, R. & Spitz, L. (1989) 'Factors associated with developmental progress of full term neonates who required intensive care', *Archives of Disease in Childhood*, *64*, 333–337.

Lukeman, D. & Melvin, D. (1993) 'The preterm infant: psychological issues in childhood', *Journal of Child Psychology and Psychiatry*, *34*, 837–849.

Luthar, S. S. (1993) 'Methodological and conceptual issues in research on childhood resilience', *Journal of Child Psychology and Psychiatry*, *34*, 441–453.

Lynch, M. A. (1975) 'Ill-health and child abuse', *Lancet*, *2*, 317–319.

Macdonald, A. M. (ed.) (1972) *Chambers Twentieth Century Dictionary*, Edinburgh: W. & R. Chambers.

MacFarlane, A. (1977) *The Psychology of Childbirth*, London: Fontana/Open Books.

Main, M. & Goldwyn, R. (1984) 'Predicting rejection of her infant from mother's representations of her own experience: implications for the abused–abusing intergenerational cycle', *Child Abuse and Neglect*, *8*, 203–207.

Main, M., Kaplan, N. & Cassidy, J. (1985) 'Security in infancy, childhood and adulthood: a move to the level of representation', in I. Bretherton & E. Waters (eds) *Growing Points of Attachment Theory and Research*, Monographs of the Society for Research in Child Development, *50* (1–2 Serial No. 209), 66–104.

Marlow, N. (1991) 'Very low birthweight children at school', *Hospital Update*, *17*, 847–848.

Marshall, R. E. (1989) 'Neonatal pain associated with caregiving procedures', *Pediatric Clinics of North America*, *36*, 885–903.

Maturana, H. R. & Varela, F. J. (1988) *The Tree of Knowledge. The Biological Roots of Human Understanding*, Boston: Shambhala Publications.

Mead, M. (1975) *Growing Up in New Guinea*, Harmondsworth: Penguin.

Meltzer, D. (1978) *The Kleinian Development Part III: The Clinical Significance of the Work of Bion*, Perthshire: Clunie Press.

Mendez, C. L., Coddou, F. & Maturana, H. R. (1988) 'The bringing forth of pathology', *Irish Journal of Psychology*, *9*, 144–172.

Menzies-Lyth, I. (1959) 'The functioning of social systems as a defence against anxiety', in I. Menzies-Lyth (1988) *Containing Anxiety in Institutions*, London: Free Association Books.

Miller, L. (1989) 'Introduction', in L. Miller, M. Rustin, M. Rustin & J. Shuttleworth (eds) *Closely Observed Infants*, London: Duckworth.

Miller, L. (1993) 'The relation of infant observation to clinical practice in an under fives counselling service', *Journal of Child Psychotherapy*, *19*, 19–33.

Minde, K. & Benoit, D. (1991) 'Infant psychiatry: its relevance for the general psychiatrist', *British Journal of Psychiatry*, *159*, 173–184.

Minde, K., Corter, C., Goldberg, S. & Jeffers, D. (1990) 'Maternal preference between premature twins up to age four', *Journal of the American Academy of Child and Adolescent Psychiatry*, *29*, 367–374.

Minde, K., Goldberg, S., Perrotta, M., Washington, J., Lojkasek, M., Carter, C. & Parker, K. (1989) 'Continuities and discontinuities in the development of 64 very small premature infants to 4 years of age', *Journal of Child Psychology and Psychiatry*, *30*, 391–404.

Minde, K., Whitelaw, A., Brown, J. & Fitzhardinge, P. (1983) 'Effect of neonatal complications in premature infants on early parent–infant interactions', *Developmental Medicine and Child Neurology*, *25*, 763–777.

Minuchin, P. (1988) 'Relationships within the family: a systems perspective on development', in R. A. Hinde & J. Stevenson-Hinde (eds) *Relationships within Families: Mutual Influences*, Oxford: Clarendon Press.

Minuchin, S. (1974) *Families and Family Therapy*, London: Tavistock Publications.

Mitchell, J. (1986) *The Selected Melanie Klein*, Harmondsworth: Penguin.

Murray, L. (1991) 'The impact of postnatal depression on infant development', paper given at 9th Congress of the European Society of Child and Adolescent Psychiatry, London.

Murray, L. (1992) 'The impact of postnatal depression on infant development', *Journal of Child Psychology and Psychiatry, 33*, 543–561.

Murray, L., Kempton, C., Woolgar, M. & Hooper, R. (1993) 'Depressed mothers' speech to their infants and its relation to infant gender and cognitive development', *Journal of Child Psychology and Psychiatry, 34*, 1083–1101.

National Children's Bureau (1987) *Investing in the Future: Child Health Ten Years after the Court Report*, London: NCB.

Neligan, G. A., Kolvin, I., Scott, D. M. & Garside, R. F. (1976) *Born Too Soon or Born Too Small*, Clinics in Developmental Medicine No. 61, London: Heinemann Medical Books.

Newman, L. F. (1981) 'Social and sensory environment of low birth weight infants in a special care nursery. An anthropological investigation', *Journal of Nervous and Mental Disease, 169*, 448–455.

Newson, J. & Newson, E. (1974) 'Cultural aspects of childrearing in the English-speaking world', in M. Richards (ed.) *The Integration of a Child into a Social World*, Cambridge: Cambridge University Press.

Nordio, S. & de Vonderweid, U. (1990) 'The parents of premature babies: epistemology of perinatology', *International Journal of Prenatal and Perinatal Studies*, 101–113.

Oehler, J. M., Davidson, M. G., Starr, L. E. & Lee, D. A. (1991) 'Burnout, job stress, anxiety, and perceived social support in neonatal nurses', *Heart and Lung, 20*, 500–505.

Packer, M. & Rosenblatt, D. (1979) 'Issues in the study of social behaviour in the first week of life', in D. Shaffer & J. Dunn (eds) *The First Year of Life: Psychological and Medical Implications of Early Experience*, Chichester: John Wiley.

Patteson, D. M. & Barnard, K. E. (1990) 'Parenting of low birth weight infants: a review of issues and interventions', *Infant Mental Health Journal, 11*, 37–56.

Pharoah, P. O. D. (1986) 'Perspectives and patterns', *British Medical Journal, 42*, 119–126.

Plomin, R. (1990) 'The role of inheritance in behaviour', *Science, 248*, 183–188.

Quinton, D. & Rutter, M. (1976) 'Early hospital admissions and later disturbances of behaviour: an attempted replication of Douglas' findings', *Developmental Medicine and Child Neurology, 18*, 447–459.

Reiss, D. (1989) 'The represented and practicing family: contrasting visions of family continuity', in A. J. Sameroff & R. N. Emde (eds) *Relationship Disturbances in Early Childhood*, New York: Basic Books.

Relier, J. P. (1990) 'Dilemmas in neonatal intensive care', Proceedings of the International Congress on *Development, Handicap, Rehabilitation: Practice and Theory*, 49–55.

Resnick, M. B., Stralka, K., Carter, R. L., Ariet, M., Bucciarelli, R. L., Furlough, R. B., Evans, J. H., Cuman, J. S. & Ausbon, W. W. (1990) 'Effects of birth weight and sociodemographic variables on mental development of neonatal intensive care survivors', *American Journal of Obstetrics and Gynecology, 162*, 374–378.

Resnick, M. B., Roth, J., Ariet, M., Carter, R. L., Emerson, J. C., Hendrickson, J. M., Packer, A. B., Larsen, J. J., Wolking, W. D., Lucas, H., Schenek, B. J., Fearnside, B. & Bucciarelli, R. L. (1992) 'Educational outcome of neonatal intensive care graduates', *Pediatrics, 89*, 373–378.

Richards, M. P. M. (1974a) 'Introduction', in M. P. M. Richards (ed.) *The Integration of a Child into a Social World*, London: Cambridge University Press.

Richards, M. P. M. (1974b) 'First steps in becoming social', in M. P. M. Richards (ed.) *The Integration of a Child into a Social World*, London: Cambridge University Press.

Richards, M. P. M. (ed.) (1974c) *The Integration of a Child into a Social World*, London: Cambridge University Press.

Richards, M. P. M. (1978) 'Possible effects of early separation on later development of children – a review', in F. S. W. Brimblecombe, M. P. M. Richards & N. R. C. Roberton (eds) *Separation and Special-care Baby Units*, Clinics in Developmental Medicine No. 68, London: Heinemann Medical Books.

Richards, M. P. M. (1979) 'Effects on development of medical interventions and the separation of newborns from their parents', in D. Shaffer & J. Dunn (eds) *The First Year of Life: Psychological and Medical Implications of Early Experience*, Chichester: John Wiley.

Richards, M. P. M. (1983) 'Parent–child relationships: some general considerations', in J. A. Davis, M. P. M. Richards & N. R. C. Roberton (eds) *Parent–Baby Attachment in Premature Infants*, London: Croom Helm.

Richards, M. (1986) 'Introduction', in M. Richards & P. Light (eds) *Children of Social Worlds: Development in a Social Context*, Cambridge, Mass.: Harvard University Press.

Rolland, J. S. (1987) 'Chronic illness and the life cycle: a conceptual framework', *Family Process*, *26*, 203–221.

Rosenblatt D. B. & Redshaw M. E. (1984) 'Factors influencing the psychological adjustment of mothers to the birth of a preterm infant', in J. D. Call, E. Galenson & R. L. Tyson (eds) *Frontiers of Infant Psychiatry: Volume 2*, New York: Basic Books.

Rustin, M. (1989) 'Observing infants: reflections on methods', in L. Miller, M. Rustin, M. Rustin & J. Shuttleworth (eds) *Closely Observed Infants*, London: Duckworth.

Rustin, M. (1989) 'Encountering primitive anxieties', in L. Miller, M. Rustin, M. Rustin & J. Shuttleworth (eds) *Closely Observed Infants*, London: Duckworth.

Rutter, M. (1972) *Maternal Deprivation Reassessed*, Harmondsworth: Penguin.

Rutter, M. (1987) 'Psychosocial resilience and protective mechanisms', in S. Rolf, D. Cicchetti, K. Muechterlein & S. Weintraub (eds) *Risk and Protective Factors in the Development of Psychopathology*, New York: Cambridge University Press.

Rutter, M. (1988) 'Functions and consequences of relationships: some psychopathological considerations', in R. A. Hinde & J. Stevenson-Hinde (eds) *Relationships within Families: Mutual Influences*, Oxford: Clarendon Press.

Rutter, M. & Rutter, M. (1992) *Developing Minds: Challenge and Continuity Across the Life Span*, Harmondsworth: Penguin.

Sameroff, A. J. (1989) 'Principles of development and psychopathology', in A. J. Sameroff & R. N. Emde (eds) *Relationship Disturbances in Early Childhood*, New York: Basic Books.

Schaffer, H. R. (1977) 'Early interactive development', in H. R. Schaffer (ed.) *Studies in Mother–Infant Interaction*, London: Academic Press.

Segal, H. (1982) *Introduction to the Work of Melanie Klein*, London: The Hogarth Press.

Selvini-Palazzoli, M., Boscolo, L., Cecchin, G. & Prata, G. (1978) *Paradox and Counterparadox: A New Model in the Therapy of the Family in Schizophrenic Transaction*, New York: Aronson.

Selvini-Palazzoli, M., Boscolo, L., Cecchin, G. & Prata, G. (1980) 'Hypothesising-circularity-neutrality: three guidelines for the conductor of the session', *Family Process*, *19*, 3–12.

Shearer, E. L. (1989) 'Commentary: Does caesarian delivery affect the parents?', *Birth*, *16*, 57–58.

Sherman, M. H. (1990) 'Family narratives: internal representations of family relationships and affective themes', *Infant Mental Health Journal*, *11*, 253–258.

Shuttleworth, J. (1989) 'Psychoanalytic theory and infant development', in L. Miller, M. Rustin, M. Rustin & J. Shuttleworth (eds) *Closely Observed Infants*, London: Duckworth.

Sluckin, W., Herbert, M. & Sluckin, A. (1983) *Maternal Bonding*, Oxford: Basil Blackwell.

Sluzki, C. E. (1992) 'Transformations: a blueprint for narrative changes in therapy', *Family Process*, *31*, 217–230.

Speed, B. (1991) 'Reality exists O. K.? An argument against constructivism and social constructionism', *Journal of Family Therapy*, *13*, 395–409.

Sroufe, L. A. (1988) 'The role of infant–caregiver attachment in development', in J. Belsky & T. Nezworski (eds) *Clinical Implications of Attachment*, Hove and London: Lawrence Erlbaum Associates.

Stafford-Clark, D. (1967) *What Freud Really Said*, Harmondsworth: Penguin.

Stern, D. (1974) 'Mother and infant at play: the dyadic interaction involving facial, vocal, and gaze behaviours', in M. Lewis & L. A. Rosenblum (eds) *The Effect of the Infant on Its Caregiver*, New York: John Wiley.

Stern, D. (1977) *The First Relationship: Mother and Infant*, Cambridge, Mass.: Harvard University Press.

Stern, D. (1985) *The Interpersonal World of the Infant*, New York: Basic Books.

Stern, D. (1990) *Diary of a Baby*, New York: Basic Books.

Stern, M. & Karraker, K. H. (1990) 'The prematurity stereotype: empirical evidence and implications for practice', *Infant Mental Health Journal*, *11*, 3–11.

Stewart, A. (1989) 'Having a baby on a neonatal unit: what do parents feel? How can health visitors help?', *Health Visitor*, *62*, 374–377.

Stewart, A. L., Costello, A. M. deL., Hamilton, P. A., Baudin, J., Townsend, J., Bradford, B. C. & Reynolds, E. O. R. (1989) 'Relationship between neurodevelopmental status of very preterm infants at one and four years', *Developmental Medicine and Child Neurology*, *31*, 756–765.

Symington, N. (1986) *The Analytic Experience: Lectures from the Tavistock*, London: Free Association Books.

Szatmari, P., Saigal, S., Rosenbaum, P., Campbell, D. & King, S. (1990) 'Psychological disorders at 5 years among children with birthweights less than 1000 grams: a regional perspective', *Developmental Medicine and Child Neurology*, *32*, 954–962.

Szur, R. (1981) 'Infants in hospital (Hospital care of the newborn: some aspects of personal stress)', *Journal of Child Psychotherapy*, *7*, 137–140.

Taggart, M. (1985) 'The feminist critique in epistemological perspective: questions of context in family therapy', *Journal of Marital and Family Therapy*, *11*, 113–126.

Thomas, A., Chess, S. & Birch, H. (1968) *Temperament and Behavioral Disorders in Childhood*, New York: New York University Press.

Tomm, K. (1985) 'Circular interviewing', in D. Campbell & R. Draper (eds) *Applications of Systemic Family Therapy: The Milan Approach*, London: Grune & Stratton.

Trevarthen, C. (1974) 'Conversations with a two-month old', *New Scientist*, *62*, 230–233.

Trevarthen, C. (1977) 'Descriptive analyses of infant communicative behaviour', in H. R. Schaffer (ed.) *Studies in Mother–Infant Interaction*, London: Academic Press.

Trowell, J. (1982) 'Possible effects of emergency caesarian section on the mother–child relationship', *Early Human Development*, *7*, 41–51.

Tunali, B. & Power, T. G. (1993) 'Creating satisfaction: a psychological perspective on stress and coping in families of handicapped children', *Journal of Child Psychology and Psychiatry*, *34*, 945–957.

Urwin, C. (1986) 'Developmental psychology and psychoanalysis: splitting the difference', in M. Richards & P. Light (eds) *Children of Social Worlds: Development in a Social Context*, Cambridge, Mass.: Harvard University Press.

Waddell, M. (1988) 'Infantile development: Kleinian and post-Kleinian theory, infant observational practice', *British Journal of Psychotherapy*, *4*, 313–329.

White M. (1988) 'The process of questioning: a therapy of literary merit?', *Dulwich Centre Newsletter*, *Winter*, 8–14.

White, M. & Epston, D. (1990) *Narrative Means to Therapeutic Ends*, New York: W. W. Norton.

Winnicott, D. W. (1958) 'The capacity to be alone', in D. W. Winnicott (1990) *The Maturational Processes and the Facilitating Environment*, London: Karnac Books.

Winnicott, D. W. (1960) 'The theory of the parent–infant relationship', in D. W. Winnicott

(1990) *The Maturational Processes and the Facilitating Environment*, London: Karnac Books.

Winnicott, D. W. (1964) *The Child, the Family, and the Outside World*, Harmondsworth: Penguin.

Winnicott, D. W. (1966a) 'The beginning of the individual', in D. W. Winnicott (1988) *Babies and Their Mothers*, London: Free Association Books.

Winnicott, D. W. (1966b) 'The ordinary devoted mother', in D. W. Winnicott (1988) *Babies and Their Mothers*, London: Free Association Books.

Winnicott, D. W. (1968) 'Communication between infant and mother, and mother and infant, compared and contrasted', in W. G. Joffe (ed.) *What is Psychoanalysis?*, London: Bailliere, Tindall & Cassell.

Wolke, D. (1991) 'Supporting the development of low birthweight infants', *Journal of Child Psychology and Psychiatry*, 32, 723–741.

Yelloly, M. A. (1980) *Social Work Theory and Psychoanalysis*, London: Van Nostrand Reinhold.

Yogman, M. W. & Brazelton, T. B. (1986) 'Introduction: the family, stressed yet protected', in M. W. Yogman & T. B. Brazelton (eds) *In Support of Families*, Cambridge, Mass.: Harvard University Press.

Zuravin, S. J. & DiBlasio, F. A. (1992) 'Child-neglecting adolescent mothers: how do they differ from their non-maltreating counterparts', *Journal of Interpersonal Violence*, 7, 471–489.

Name index

Subject index

abuse: attachment disorder and 167; constructivism and 65–66; effect on social relationships 25; infant ill health, early separation and 54; intergenerational 26; social construction theory and 65–66
adjustment disorder 149
adultomorphisisation 36, 45
agency: ascription of 77, 83; denial of 62
attachment disorders 23, 149, 167, 171
attachment theory 20–26; attachment system 21, 23; Bowlby and 20–23, 146; childbirth, attitude to 25; criticisms of 22; ethology and 20; intergenerational continuity of attachment 23–24; internal working models 21–22, 146; maternal deprivation 23; measurement of attachment behaviour 21; object relations theory and 20; parental factors 24–26; pre-attachment behaviour 21, 23; pregnancy, attitude to 24–25; prehistory of attachment 24; principal propositions of 20–21; Strange Situations test 21
attention deficit disorder 149, 152; with hyperactivity (ADDH) 150

behavioural problems in later life 4, 145; adjustment disorder 149; in adolescence 42, 145; attachment disorders 149, 167; attention deficit disorder 149, 152; attention deficit disorder with hyperactivity (ADDH) 150; family relationships 150; oppositional disorder 149; parent–child relationships and 149–151; quality of parenting 150; reactive attachment disorder 149; small-for-dates babies 152; sociodemographic factors 150; VLBW

babies 149–151
bonding 19, 48

caesarian section, delivery by 25, 130, 136
calling: into life 83, 136; 'claiming' 83
child abuse see abuse
childbirth: caesarian section, delivery by 25, 130, 136; experience of 25, 52, 130, 137, 165; length of labour 25; mothers' attitude to 25; narcotic analgesia 25; as near death experience 122, 128
choice: parents and 46, 53; premature babies and 43–44
chronic illness, adjustment to 155
co-constructivism 65–66; see also constructivism
communication: complementarity of beliefs and 128; early 26; language see language; maternal depression and 26; 'motherese' 26, 32, 83; narrative see narrative; projective identification 101; questions see questions; in SCBUs 169; staff and parents 117; synchrony 78
communication theorists 62
congenital malformation 2, 42, 53; parents' reaction to 48, 54–55
constructivism 63–65; abusive relationships 65–66; co-constructivism 65–66; feminist criticism of 66; see also social construction theory
containment: of baby 4, 18–19, 127, 128, 164; Bion on 18–19; by mother 4, 18–19, 127, 128, 164; of mother 19, 83, 127; of parents 93, 169, 172; of staff 4, 19; see also holding
context 61, 63; coordinated management of meaning see coordinated management of meaning; defining 65; levels of 67, 107; of narrative 61,